PEAKS, POLITICS & PASSION

GRAND TETON NATIONAL PARK COMES OF AGE

By Robert W. Righter

All photographs courtesy of the National Park Service and Grand Teton Association unless noted beside image.

ISBN 0-978-0-931895-95-1

For information on reprinting and purchase, contact:
Grand Teton Association
PO Box 170
Moose, WY 83012
www.grandtetonpark.org

Design: Carole Thickstun, Ormsby & Thickstun
Project Coordinator: Jan Lynch, Executive Director, Grand Teton Association
Editor: Mary Anne Maier, Mary Anne Maier Editorial Services
Indexer: Bookmark: Editing & Indexing

Printed in the USA on recycled paper by Paragon Press, Salt Lake City, Utah

Cover and back cover photographs by Thomas D. Mangelsen. Historical photo on back cover from the collections of Jackson Hole Historical Society & Museum.
Endpaper photo by Sandra Nykerk.

Many of the photographs in this book are courtesy of Thomas D. Mangelsen.
Visit his online gallery at www.mangelsen.com.

For Sherry

Contents

Photo by Bonnie Sanders

PEAKS, POLITICS, AND PASSION: GRAND TETON NATIONAL PARK COMES OF AGE

An ideal is something
toward which to work;
it should not be something
that prohibits us from working.

—Arno Cammerer, National Park Service

Foreword

I FINISHED READING HISTORIAN BOB RIGHTER'S first book regarding Grand Teton, *Crucible of Conservation,* in March 2004 shortly after being announced as the superintendent of Grand Teton National Park. As I read the last page, I knew there was a need for the author to record the next chapters of this dramatic story, documenting what has happened since passage of the 1950 legislation that expanded this iconic national park to its current boundaries. Though I had researched and identified many of the contemporary issues facing Grand Teton in preparation for my new National Park System (NPS) posting (the only commercial airport in a national park, large tracts of land owned by the state of

Wyoming, expanding grizzly bear habitat, the pressures to complete the park's first visitor center in 50 years, and the pending gift of the most valuable land the park and Service had likely ever seen) it was only after reading *Crucible* that I could fully comprehend and put into perspective the depth and intensity of the opposition that had faced the park from the late 19th century through 1950.

The drama and struggle surrounding the establishment of Grand Teton National Park is legendary in the chronicles of National Park Service history. Unlike the effort to create Yellowstone National Park—which lasted only two years culminating in 2.2 million acres being set aside by an act of Congress—the struggle to create and expand Grand Teton continued for decades. The 1950 law that established the park is primarily about the compromises that were necessary to finally resolve the decades-long controversy about how the lands of Jackson Hole should be managed. Although the law included virtually no mention of the superlative scenery, wildlife, and other values that Congress presumably found compelling enough to warrant the area being set aside as a national park, it devoted whole sections to describing a controlled elk reduction program, the continuation of cattle grazing, and the prohibition against the creation of any new national monuments in the state of Wyoming. In short, the 1950 Act revealed and addressed those issues that were at the heart of the dispute over expanding the park, and the role of the federal government in managing those park lands in Wyoming.

Although the 1950 legislation established the park in its current form, it did not entirely put to rest the issues over which park proponents and those who opposed its expansion struggled with for so long. Although grazing has greatly diminished over the years, and many of the private lands have been acquired from willing sellers, enormous challenges continue to confront park managers today. The tension between preserving the national resource and scenic benefits of the southernmost part of the Greater Yellowstone Ecosystem, against those of state, local and private interests, has been a consistent theme throughout the park's history. As this tension plays out in the pages to come, some issues have been resolved, such as that of snow planes. However, divergent opinions as to the adequate level of resource preservation as well as what constitutes compatible enjoyment of those resources—consistent with the sole National Park Service mission of conserving park resources and values for now and future generations—seems to have escalated through the second half of the 20th century and are most certainly continuing into the 21st. And with each passing decade, individual issues erupt, die down, resolve, or lay dormant until another opportunity arises for spirited debate.

In this volume, Bob Righter helps the reader navigate through the myriad of post 1950s issues, whether they be the future of a growing regional airport, the frequently contentious federal land acquisition involving longtime settlers, the use of snowmobiles, livestock grazing, and the appropriate use of the park for a wide variety of new or expanded recreational activities. Overlaying all of these challenges is the sea change that occurred in 1980, with the Service's issuance of its first single set of policies that directed consistent management of all national park areas, and the evolution of historic preservation in what was once considered simply a 'natural' park, and all of the other challenges that were and are Grand Teton. And in doing so, the author—a longtime friend of the Grand Teton National Park, and occasional critic— continues his documentation of how the park evolved, the influences of individual interests, as well as the focus of various park superintendents and those of the agency over time. It is important to note that this is not a dry NPS administrative history; it is the author's own perspective as a recognized environmental historian and a long time Jackson Hole resident.

In my experience of serving over 34 years throughout the National Park System, each national park has its own story of how it was set aside, and is the products of the individuals that fought over time for its creation. And having spent nearly one-third of my National Park Service career as superintendent of Grand Teton, this national park's personality is charged with high energy, with controversy and strongly held opinions, and with an ongoing complex debate about what it is and should become.

What ties all national parks together into a National Park System is the fact that they reflect all Americans' desire to protect special places, places that collectively comprise America's own legacy. Without that connection across the System, parks like Grand Teton could be considered no more than a state or county park.

As I first set eyes on this mountain range and its incredible wildlife, I knew it is one of the world's most iconic national parks, and is worthy of significant and deep debate. That we all must continue to work towards the intentional preservation of such a special place as Grand Teton National Park is both our individual and collective responsibility as Americans.

Mary Gibson Scott
Grand Teton National Park Superintendent
May 2004–January 2014

PEAKS, POLITICS, AND PASSION: GRAND TETON NATIONAL PARK COMES OF AGE

Introduction

HOW MANY PHOTOGRAPHS have been taken of the Tetons? From park roads visitors are constantly lining up their spouses, children, relatives, or friends with the perfect mountain backdrop image to show back home. Driving the Jackson Hole Highway east of the Snake River on a brilliant summer day, one cannot pass the Glacier Turnout, the Teton View Turnout, or the Snake River Overlook without noting people snapping pictures of beaming individuals or families, occasionally whole bus loads posing and offering the obligatory smile. From all over the park, from a thousand different angles, the cameras are clicking. Occasionally I meet people who say they have never seen Jackson Hole or the mountains.

My response has been: yes you have, you just didn't realize it. The mountains are often the subject of polished professional photographs, but just as often employed as a setting for advertisements. They have a way of enhancing pedestrian products. Interestingly, even adjoining states such as Montana or Colorado travel bureaus have poached Wyoming's Tetons to boost the beauties of their own states. In short, millions of American and foreigners have "seen" the Tetons before they ever visit. Once they do visit, they rarely leave disappointed. They are majestic mountains. It does not take Ansel Adams' iconic photo of the range from the Snake River Overlook to confirm that conclusion.

What makes them so special? There are higher mountains, there are much more extended ranges, and even more jagged peaks. What makes the Tetons so special is one of the quirks of geology. In the process of forming, foothills were forgotten. They never materialized. A favorite phrase in Jackson is "in shadow of the Tetons." In the late afternoon, or evening, the shadows creep across the valley in a natural show not found elsewhere, as the peaks become mirrored in the crystalline lakes at their base. No intervening hills obstruct the craggy mountains from bottom to top. Only a few mountain ranges evoke such strong emotions. The Tetons are one. Once seen, they are seldom forgotten.

It seems near impossible to imagine that this sublime patch of the earth could be "managed" by any land agency other than the National Park Service

(NPS). Preservation of these majestic peaks, wild canyons, glacial lakes, forests and sagebrush, bisected by the Snake River are surely what the federal government had in mind when it established the Park Service in 1916. Yet in the early 20th century people disputed the proper management of these mountains and broad level vistas of Jackson Hole with a ferocity unmatched in national park history. For over 35 years Americans with contesting views of this land's use fought over its fate. Rugged individualists, cattleman, Easterners, "New Dealers," "states righters," state of Wyoming officials, Forest Service personnel, and Park Service leaders all wanted hegemony over this magical land. The way they cajoled, fought, and sued each other and ultimately resolved the issue represents a classic case in the difficulty of "park making." When John D. Rockefeller, Jr. and the Snake River Land Company first purchased and then turned over 33,562 acres of Jackson Hole property to the federal government in 1949, Congress finally enacted legislation the following year that created the current Grand Teton National Park configuration. This accomplishment represented one of the most notable conservation victories of the 20th Century.

After the protracted and difficult birth of Grand Teton National Park, controversies did not end. Disputes continued and various issues led to sleepless nights for Park Service administrators over the following sixty years. This book is about those "sleepless nights." It is about the paths, or policies, that the park followed as it emerged from its long gestation period.

For many the direction seemed quite clear: buy up private land, get rid of old buildings, encourage a natural park and the wildlife within it, stop wildfires, build a competent ranger team, encourage tourism through good roads, construct visitor centers, allow an airport, and leave entertainment to the town of Jackson. Above all, mend fences and make friends in the community as well as ameliorate politicians. There were times when park administrators lost their way. There were times when they realized they had followed a mistaken policy, and needed realignment. These were the trials and tribulations of a youth growing up, evolving to maturity. The park, now over 60 years old, has ironed out many of the wrinkles of trial and error, to become a seasoned park. However, a park in its prime does not suggest stagnation. Grand Teton Park is ever changing in response to the needs of people as well as the flora and fauna who call the park home. It can be no other way.

One reality that has changed little is the physical size of the Grand Teton National Park. Although we seldom think of Grand Teton park in terms of size, it is actually one of the smaller major scenic parks in the nation, consisting of only 310,000 acres. It boils down to a question of wise use of a small area. Rockefeller and the park founders did the best they could to create an expansive park, but they did not succeed in acquiring enough land to accommodate all natural and human uses, from grizzlies to airplanes. If they had, many—but not all—of park management issues could be resolved. Consequently, the park, crowded with humans and teeming with wildlife, will always face controversies exacerbated by a diversity of interests and stakeholders.

Human use and rights are the primary considerations for many politicians who, of course, represent their constituents. Their role is quite clear: Optimize recreational and economic opportunities for park users. Grand Teton administrators' role, however, is more multifaceted. They do respect that the parks are for people, but it is more than that. They must base decisions on long-standing management policies.[1] Often the Grand Teton park superintendent and his/her staff must adhere to park principles over political expediency. This may cause a problem. Michael Frome, who served in the Park Service for many years, points out that "park superintendents walk on eggs. Each one knows that a congressman with clout, even a little, can bring him down."[2] So it is inevitable: parks are political. Respected superintendents are those who can negotiate with city, county and state officials, and yet not compromise park values. Preserving the natural and cultural resources, and yet making them available to the public, is the goal.

In the end, the park is much more than a political or economic commodity. People often forget that park administrators are guardians committed to the idea that people must enjoy and learn from the park, but not at the expense of nature. The plants and animals have rights, and above all, it is the priority and purpose of the Park Service to guarantee those rights.

A philosopher once said that decision-making on the big issues was easy. His criteria: What is best for the children? But at Grand Teton the superintendent must add another element: What is best for nature? What is in the best interests of the park? These questions would seem to cover the need to manage for the needs of people and yet prevent deterioration of nature's resources now and in the future. But the pressure from people who do not share these goals complicates the situation. Much of the story to follow seeks to explain, if not always resolve, the interplay of forces that has resulted in a great national park, still evolving but certainly in the appropriate direction.

This positive path has been assisted by many park friends. During the long struggle for creation, influential individuals such as Struthers Burt, Olaus and Mardy Murie, Henry Stewart of the JY Ranch, and Coulter Huyler of the Bear Paw Ranch defended the preservation idea. Federal agencies were also instrumental. The National Elk Refuge worked closely with the park from the beginning. The U.S. Forest Service, while initially opposed to the loss of thousands of acres of land to the Park Service in the 1940s, eventually accepted the park, and now coordinates closely on fire and wildlife issues. With 97 percent of Teton County land, controlled by these three federal agencies, cooperation is imperative.

Environmental organizations were slow to come to Wyoming. To favor resource restraint was not popular, and to safeguard the park could court political ruin. While the Sierra Club's David Brower was laboring to save Dinosaur National Monument and Grand Canyon National Park from possible dam projects, conservationists were not yet aware of Grand Teton. Only Teno Roncalio, Wyoming's sole member in the U. S. House of Representatives (1965–1967, 1971-1978), had a positive attitude toward the park and wilderness issues. When the Sierra Club wished to honor him for his work, Roncalio was pleased to accept the award, but stipulated that the honor *not* be made public. More than one Wyoming politician echoed Roncalio's reluctance to be associated with conservation issues or as park advocates.

It was not until 1979–1980 that local conservationists organized the Jackson Hole (JH) Conservation Alliance and the Jackson Hole Land Trust to take political positions supporting (usually) that of Grand Teton National Park, the Land Trust to preserve land from development outside the park. Since the early 1980s local environmental and interest groups have played an important part in developing park policy. At times they have been a thorn to administrators, but sometimes their objections have validity. The JH Conservation Alliance has sued the park more than once. In the majority of situations, however, the Conservation Alliance or such environmental groups as the Greater Yellowstone Coalition and the National Parks and Conservation Association, have agreed with park policies, acting as a foil in their support of park positions.

More and more local people love the park, sharing their political and environmental opinions. Rarely does a week go by that *The Jackson Hole News and Guide* does not contain an opinion piece or a letter that agrees or disagrees with the park's decision or position. If the writer castigates administrators, however, it is often a manifestation of concern. However, it would be a mistake to assume Grand Teton National Park does not have enemies, and a few individuals who feed on a steady diet of bile toward the park. Their extreme dislike may arise from the difficulties and occasional past injustices in the fight to establish and enlarge the park. Some are inherently opposed to federal ownership of land, especially the most spectacular landscapes. However, the majority of naysayers focus on issues of wildlife and their management. In the 19th century the American military was often charged with the difficult task of keeping settlers and Indians at arms length. Today the park staff often must keep tourists and animals at arms length. Neither situation was easy. The wildlife, of course, are forgiving while humans are often not.

In short, people care about Grand Teton National Park. Nowhere in the country does a national park have a nearby neighbor which is so educated, so supportive, and yet so critical. People feel compelled to agree or disagree with policy with equal passion. For park administrators, it is a challenging job, yet many have told me that they would want it no other way. At Grand Teton an administrator is always in the vortex of both local and national environmental issues.

This volume, titled *Peaks, Politics, and Passion: Grand Teton National Park Comes of Age,* chronicles the events of the past 60 years. This book focuses on some of those ongoing issues, both local and national, which have challenged the park in the past and will continue to do so in the future. However, to understand this more contemporary period, the earlier fight to establish Grand Teton is crucial. I have briefly recounted highlights of the earlier history and park fight in this volume, but if the reader desires more detail he/she should consult my *Crucible For Conservation: The Struggle for Grand Teton National Park* or NPS historian John Daugherty's *A Place Called Jackson Hole.*

In closing, the objective of this book is to offer an interpretation of Grand Teton National Park over time. As the aesthetics and values of society change, so too must park policies, reflecting the nation's attitudes as well as local considerations. A park born in controversy remains embroiled in controversy, at least periodically. Such disagreement can be expected in a democracy, but perhaps intensified in Jackson Hole and the Tetons, where the spectacular scenery inspires deep feelings and connections. The stakes are so high! The Organic Act of 1916, creating the National Park Service, mandates that a superintendent will manage the natural and historic resources of the park for the satisfaction of the people, but in such a way that "will leave them unimpaired for the enjoyment of future generations." Of course the act has been construed in various ways, but the federal courts have consistently interpreted the act in favor of resource protection, declaring "that when there is a conflict between conserving resources and values and providing for enjoyment of them, conservation is to be predominant."[3] Thus the park resource is foremost, the pleasure of the people second. As an example, when in recent years the Grand Teton superintendent has closed the Moose-Wilson Road for the benefit of feeding grizzly bears, the travelling public has been inconvenienced and denied the delight of seeing a bear in the wild. Yet this is the application of the preeminence of conservation and the future, and a basic creed of the park. Certainly Superintendent Mary Gibson Scott would say that the superintendent has some leeway in decision-making, sometimes based on new scientific knowledge and "best" knowledge, but yet is guided by NPS policy and laws.

There are so many issues that park administrators must address over the years. What of the invasion of exotic weeds? What of the Snake River fishery and the effort to bring back the native cutthroat trout? What of the park's effort to address climate change? These are just a few of many issues this book does not address. Obviously they are important, but I have tried to speak to the most significant subjects over time: issues which have been of concern to both the public and the park's administrators. Clearly, the choice of topics is a subjective one, but also a result of a desire to created a manageable book which represents key issues over the past sixty years.

Most of the millions of tourists who are clicking those thousands upon thousands of photographs of the Tetons are unconcerned with such policy issues.

They enjoy the park and are inspired by the mountain pageant, and like Fritiof Fryxell suggested, "likely to gaze silently upon them, conscious of the futility of speech."[4] Yet beyond such revelries, we know that policy decisions affect what visitors see, how they see it, and what they do not see. What the visitors learns in the visitor centers, from wayside signs, in evening campground presentations and the mountain "viewscapes" offered throughout the park, are the product of park interpreter's often vigorous debate. What are the messages that the Park Service wishes to convey? How have these "messages" changed over time? The park today is so different than in 1950. That should not be surprising, for the park itself is a living entity, reflecting changing attitudes and times even as the majestic mountains themselves remain immutable.

---

[1] Most people are unaware that Park Service administrators are guided in policy decisions by a 168-page book called *Management Policies*, 2006 (Washington D.C.: National Park Service, 2006).

[2] Michael Frome, *Regreening of the National Parks* (Tucson: The University of Arizona Press, 1992), 108.

[3] "Management Policies," National Park Service, 2006.

[4] Fritiof Fryxell, *The Tetons: Interpretations of a Mountain Landscape* (Moose: The Grand Teton Association, 1995, 1st printing, 1938), 12. Fryxell short work represents the finest description of the Teton mountains yet written.

PEAKS, POLITICS, AND PASSION: GRAND TETON NATIONAL PARK COMES OF AGE

Chapter 1

The 1950 Act to Establish Grand Teton National Park

THE MAJESTIC QUALITY OF THE TETONS gives viewers a powerful sense of confronting the primeval and eternal. The peaks inspire as they stand above all they survey. It is easy to forget that the National Park Service could not protect these splendid vistas and spacious surroundings until only after World War II. Protection would seem automatic, but it was not until the 1950 Act, establishing the boundaries of Grand Teton National Park, that federal guardianship was assured. When this great national park came into being, so too did compromises that affect the park to this day.

The nature of these compromises can be found in the provisions of the Act. Equally significant is the context in which the administrators and legislators carved out their rapprochement.[1] Behind the written words rest attitudes and convictions born of decades of contentious debate. This chapter reviews the specifics of the 1950 Act and contextualizes it. In the end—although it signaled the beginning of a new era—the law represented the protracted fight for hegemony in the valley called Jackson Hole.

Background

It is fair to say the 1950 Act represented a minor miracle. Not only did Grand Teton have many enemies, but even "friends" had doubts about the park's scenic integrity. Robert Sterling Yard of the National Parks Association, for example, opposed inclusion of thousands of acres of commonplace sagebrush in the expanded park. He also loathed the incorporation of the Jackson Lake Dam, the presence of which violated his concept of a primitive park and resurrected the bitter memory of the Hetch Hetchy Valley fight, in which Congress allowed a spectacular Yosemite National Park glacial carved valley to be dammed and inundated with two hundred feet of water.[2]

Others wondered, if created, what kind of park would emerge? Would it feature Rockefeller's interest in an "old West" theme? National Park Service (NPS) Director Newton Drury as well as Yard pre-ferred the "primitive park" scenario, with a minimum of services and conveniences.

Local issues also undermined the supposed cohesion of the pro-park forces. Laurance Rockefeller and his Jackson Hole Preserve, Inc. managers foolishly insisted on suing the popular dude ranch owner and loyal friend to the park, Coulter Huyler. The issue was over road access on Huyler's Bear Paw Ranch, adjacent to the Rockefeller-owned JY Ranch. To the community it seemed a case of eastern wealth beating up on the local guy. More important events were taking place in 1943, and Huyler wisely suggested that he and Laurance Rockefeller could "agree to disagree" until after the war. Laurance refused the suggestion. Influential environmentalist Olaus Murie strenuously objected to the suit, questioning the political acumen of Rockefeller and his advisors.[3] Laurance persisted, losing his case in court and gaining nothing but bad publicity.

A more serious miscalculation occurred, in Murie's view, when Laurance Rockefeller teamed up with Henry Fairfield Osborn of the New York Zoological Society to establish a wildlife park at the Oxbow Bend of the Snake River. The plan called for displaying wild animals under fence, a program that many wildlife experts found objectionable in a national park. Yet Rockefeller persisted, and Olaus Murie consequently resigned from the Jackson Hole Preserve.[4] Happily, however, these rifts within the conservation community did not permanently detour the path to a larger

Grand Teton National Park. They were cracks, but not insurmountable chasms.

Of course, the most sustained opposition to the 1950 Act came from local residents who had long despised both the Park Service and the Rockefeller involvement in Jackson Hole. There were many reasons for such determined opposition. It was in the Wyoming tradition for residents to distrust the federal government, owner of almost one-half of the state. Combine the federal bureaucracy and the eastern wealth of the Rockefeller family, and you have a volatile mixture that smacked of colonialism. Locals had opposed the ambitions of the National Park Service since 1916. When Congress authorized the first Grand Teton National Park in 1929, it included only the mountains and a few glacial lakes. Essentially, this action represented a transfer of U.S. Forest Service land to the National Park Service. The 1950 situation, however, was different. Now 221,610 acres of valley land and lakes would be incorporated into an enlarged park. Some of this more level land had been privately owned and remained so until Rockefeller purchased it. The Forest Service managed the lion's share of the 221,000 acres and most local people were happy with the agency's multiple-use management. The Wyoming congressional delegation agreed with the Forest Service, and had for a decade (1933-1943) vehemently opposed accepting the Rockefeller gift for park land. Finally, Rockefeller and Park Service leadership turned to President Franklin Delano Roosevelt, who proclaimed Jackson Hole National Monument in 1943. This bypass of congressional and state authority proved one of the most controversial federal actions in Wyoming history. The Wyoming Congressional Delegation fought the monument in the courts (*State of Wyoming v. Franke*), in the halls of Congress, and through the "power of the purse" by cutting off three years of appropriations for the new monument. Wyoming congressman Frank Barrett opposed every effort to transfer the property to the park. He continued his opposition as governor (1951–53) and as United States senator (1953–59). Wyoming senator Edward Robinson and prominent local politicians, such as rancher Cliff Hansen and banker Felix Buchenroth, followed Congressman Barrett's lead.

However, two events served to undercut the congressman's tough stance: the end of World War II and a changing economic climate. With the close of the war thousands of Americans and their families had money and gasoline, combined with a pent-up desire to travel. They descended on Jackson Hole. If it was not clear before, this influx of visitors now demonstrated that long-term prosperity lay with tourism, not cattle. Shop owners prospered. Sales tax revenues doubled between 1943 and 1946. Real estate values skyrocketed. Up and down the economic charts, every indication showed that the town and the county were experiencing economic prosperity, due in large part to the Tetons. In this atmosphere a number of locals, though still not a majority, saw the pres-

ence of the National Park Service and the Jackson Hole National Monument as an asset, not a liability.[5]

Political alliances also changed. The Forest Service, so enraged by the Park Service's appropriation of their land earlier in the century and even into the 1940s, began to mellow and reassess. They concluded that their true adversaries were not the Park Service officials but rather Wyoming Senator Edward Robinson and Congressman Frank Barrett. These two legislators led the effort to transfer millions of acres of federal land to the respective states, with the expectation that the states would either lease or sell this surplus land to livestock ranchers at bargain rates. Barrett sponsored a number of public hearings in the West to further the cattlemen's interest. Conservationist Bernard DeVoto labeled these hearings "Barrett's Wild West Show," with Barrett harassing the Bureau of Land Management and intimidating the Forest Service, then "bleed[ing the Forest Service] to death by cutting down its appropriation."[6] Against the backdrop of these developments on the national stage, the Forest Service rethought its position on Jackson Hole. Barrett was unsuccessful in his "land grab," but he was inadvertently successful in unraveling the alliance between the cattlemen and the Forest Service. No longer were the cattle interests and those of the Forest Service in harmony. As the various interests worked toward a resolution of the Grand Teton park fight, the Forest Service sat on the sidelines, content to let others do battle.

Although the Forest Service stayed out of the picture, its conservation philosophy of wise use of Jackson Hole land remained in play. Local ranchers, marginal farmers, loggers, and those who grew forage for cattle all wanted to use and profit from the land, not simply preserve it. They loved the scenic splendor of the valley, but to survive in Jackson Hole they had to develop the land resources. They had to make a living. The Park Service, it seemed to them, privileged the needs of the leisure class (tourists), who visited but made their money elsewhere. Locals who depended on the valley's resources to exist understood that the Park Service would put up barriers to such activities. Whose interests would prevail—those of wealthy tourists or hardworking Wyomingites?

So if northern Jackson Hole was destined to become a park, local opponents hoped at least to limit Park Service jurisdiction. They did not relish the prospect of a 20th bureaucracy with all its rules and regulations. Residents liked to compare Yellowstone's rules impeding individual freedom with the laissez-faire attitude in Jackson Hole. Most locals wished to continue harvesting the raw materials of the valley at the base of the Tetons, whether this meant entitlement for damming a river, owning a home in the park, running cattle, cutting trees, or taking an elk. Historian Richard White's essay "Are You an Environmentalist or Do You Work for a Living?" underscores the distinction between those making a living from the land and those who do not.

The two groups considered nature differently. Tourists would support the goal of scenic protection advocated by the Park Service, while locals would resent the lock-up of resources.[7] The park in 1950, then, faced animosity, for locals saw the expanded Park Service power as placing the interests of the leisure tourist class ahead of their own.[8] Had a local poll been taken regarding jurisdiction, the majority of Jackson Hole residents would have preferred the much more resource-development-oriented U.S. Forest Service than the preservation-oriented National Park Service.

Although all parties agreed that land west of the Snake River would go to the Park Service, argument focused on the east side. Many residents believed that the Antelope Flats area should be turned over to the State of Wyoming. Others contended that the landlord should be the U.S. Fish and Wildlife Service, which already administered the adjacent National Elk Refuge. A few favored management by the Forest Service. All these opinions regarding land options, however, were mere speculation, for they did not take into account the views of John D. Rockefeller, Jr., who still owned 33,562 acres within the boundaries of the monument.

THE ROCKEFELLER PLEDGE

John D. Rockefeller, Jr. first came to Yellowstone in 1924 and then returned with his wife and boys in 1926. During that second trip Horace Albright, then superintendent of Yellowstone National Park, shepherded the family south to Jackson Hole. With Albright's assistance and that of dude ranchers Struthers Burt and Henry Stewart, Rockefeller realized that with a modest investment, he could make a remarkable difference in preserving the dramatic Jackson Hole landscape. If he was willing to chance an amount of $1.5 million as a future donation to the nation, he could acquire sufficient land to guarantee a striking expansion of the paltry little Grand Teton National Park established in 1929. He took up the challenge, and with the encouragement of the Park Service, he and his Snake River Land Company acquired more than 30,000 acres of land in the valley by 1932.

Having succeeded in his first objective, Rockefeller now waited on the federal government to accept his gift. In 1932 there was every reason to expect that a grateful government would receive this generous donation. But as often happens in a democracy, powerful local interest groups protested, and by the fol-

JOHN D. ROCKEFELLER, JR. HIS RESOURCES, DETERMINATION, AND FORESIGHT CREATED GRAND TETON NATIONAL PARK AS WE KNOW IT TODAY.

lowing year they weighed in to defeat the bill to enlarge the park. These same Wyoming interests continued to stymie the effort to enlarge Grand Teton National Park throughout the 1930s. Finally, in 1942 the Park Service urged a change in strategy: bypassing Congress altogether and using a presidential decree to declare a national monument. John D. Rockefeller, Jr. listened and concurred. In 1943 President Roosevelt proclaimed Jackson Hole National Monument.

Most proclamations call for celebration. This one called for denigration. The people of Wyoming did not cheer. Senator Edward Robertson declared it "a foul, sneaking Pearl Harbor blow." In the midst of war, there could be no stronger epithet. Congressman Frank Barrett agitated to repeal the proclamation and would have succeeded, except for President Roosevelt's pocket veto of Barrett's bill to abolish the monument. Barrett and Wyoming leaders tried various legislative moves and then turned to the judicial branch with the expectation that the hated monument would be struck down in court. *State of Wyoming v. Franke* sought to invalidate the monument on the basis that it had no significant historic or scientific interest. Wyoming lost its case in 1945 when the court ruled that the state could only seek redress through Congress. The monument survived the courts and the withering fire of the Wyoming congressional delegation. In the meantime, the people of Jackson Hole found that the world had not come to an end and that perhaps the congressional delegation had not considered all aspects of the monument. As the war concluded, tourists arrived, and the town began to prosper. Perhaps they could learn to live with this intrusion. In the meantime, John D. Rockefeller, Jr. waited patiently to see his wish fulfilled.

Meanwhile the bitterness persisted. The animosity became apparent to NPS Director Conrad Wirth as he prepared to attend a hearing in Jackson Hole, organized by a joint meeting of the House and Senate committees. Wirth arranged for a caravan of cars to drive participants from Yellowstone to the valley. The committee chairpersons wanted each car to contain advocates for and against the park, along with one committee member. As the meeting date approached, Wirth telephoned Frank Barrett to finalize the arrangement. The fiery congressman, however, had a different idea. Barrett informed Wirth "in no uncertain terms that [he] shouldn't go, that people were so angry out there that somebody was liable to be crazy enough to shoot me." Wirth, however, was not intimidated. Nor was he shot, but he did experience a nasty encounter: "As we came out of Old Faithful Inn to set out for the Grand Tetons, a car drove up, jammed to a halt, and out came Frank Barrett and another opponent, Felix Buchenroth. Barrett rushed up to me and shook his fist in my face, accusing me of trying to run the State of Wyoming. The discussion got a little loud and almost to a pushing stage." They were beginning to attract tourist attention when Congressman Pete of Florida broke it up and ushered the two men to their respective cars.[9] Wirth and the whole party went on to Jackson Hole, where they witnessed a very loud and boisterous hearing dominated by anti-monument people.

Thus, although many believed the time for compromise had come, emotions still ran high, and as

Wirth recalled, it "was a real hornet's nest." While locals expressed their opposition to national park status for the monument, Rockefeller remained unmoved. For many years, he had considered only one outcome. As the two sides moved toward the give and take of the bargaining table, the pendulum swung toward the feisty, determined National Park Service and its insistence on a national park for the valley and for all Americans.

HAMMERING OUT THE 1950 ACT

In January 1949 Harry Miner, president of the Izaak Walton League chapter in Wyoming, sent out an invitation to all interested parties to meet in Washington. The object of the conference would be to hammer out a bill to resolve the park controversy. In April 1949, 22 people gathered, representing the congressional delegation (Senators Joseph O'Mahoney and Lester Hunt and Congressman Barrett), Secretary of the Interior Oscar Chapman, NPS Acting Director Arthur Demaray, Leslie Miller and Harold Fabian representing the Jackson Hole Preserve, Lester Bagley of the Wyoming Game and Fish Commission, and Felix Buchenroth and Clifford Hansen from Jackson Hole.[10]

Cliff Hansen, then a Teton County commissioner, opened the first session on a positive note. As Conrad Wirth noted, Hansen was "the opposition's most articulate leader."[11] Furthermore, he was emotionally mature and able to move the group toward solutions.

Hansen informed the gathering that the people of Teton County wanted three problems resolved before they could support park expansion: the elk herd, grazing rights in the proposed park, and resolution of the property tax problem. When all the bluster and posturing was done, it really seemed quite simple. As often is the case, the devil was in the details. For the next two days a working committee of six explored solutions. The tax problem was very understandable to Teton County representatives. The removal of 33,562 acres from a total of 114,491 acres on the tax rolls represented a funding calamity that even the federal Bureau of the Budget could understand. Although reluctant to compensate the county for its tax loss in perpetuity, the bureau finally agreed to reimburse the county the total tax for four years, and then for the next 20 years the amount would decrease at a rate of five percent per year. This was a victory for the county, and had such a financial arrangement been agreed to by the Bureau of the Budget in 1933, the debate could have been resolved at that time.

The Jackson Hole elk herd proved the knottiest problem to unravel or unwind. Outside of the park boundaries, elk were the property of the State of Wyoming. However, within Grand Teton the herd belonged to the park. Further complicating jurisdiction, most of the Jackson Hole elk population wintered on the National Elk Refuge, managed by the U.S. Fish and Wildlife Service. Thus, the management and "ownership" of an elk depended on where the

IN 1943, CLIFF HANSEN, LEFT, AND ACTOR WALLACE BEERY, CENTER, LED A CATTLE DRIVE ACROSS THE NEWLY-CREATED JACKSON HOLE NATIONAL MONUMENT.

animal chose to subsist during which part of the year, as it migrated from one jurisdiction to another. Lester Bagley, director of the Wyoming Game and Fish Commission, feared the state would lose control of what it considered its property. Determined to see that the state's "property rights" were respected, Bagley argued for state hunting jurisdiction within the park. NPS representatives found hunting antithetical to their concept of a national park. The discussion was long and loud, and the two sides remained at loggerheads. Perhaps the solution should be turned over to a board? Reluctantly, the sides agreed to form the

Jackson Hole Elk Herd Advisory Committee, composed of representatives from the State of Wyoming and Grand Teton National Park. When the director of the Wyoming Game and Fish Commission and the superintendent of Grand Teton National Park agreed that hunting was necessary within the park (and they always did, with one exception when the herd was too small), hunters would be licensed by the state and deputized by the NPS as temporary rangers to carry out the harvest. Compromises are never fully satisfactory, and for more than 60 years this one has been notorious for its capacity to stir up emotions. It is significant that the elk issue takes up more space in the 1950 park enabling act than does any other subject.[12]

While the Jackson Hole elk herd dispute was contentious, resolving cattle grazing in the new park went smoothly. Park Service representatives knew there was no hotter issue, and they therefore quickly conceded the right of ranchers to continue their grazing privileges as originally granted by the U. S. Forest Service and continued under the provisions of the 1943 Jackson Hole National Monument. To resist would have endangered the whole compromise process. Thus under the 1950 Act, each rancher with

CLIFF HANSEN

a grazing permit was guaranteed a 25-year lease and "thereafter during the lifetime of his heirs, successors, or assigns, but only if they were members of the immediate family on such date, as determined by the Secretary of the Interior."[13] Grazing leases of ranches *within* the park, such as the Pinto Ranch and the Moosehead Ranch, were guaranteed grazing rights in perpetuity. In short, ranchers and their children could count on grazing rights for many years to come.

There are special moments when adversaries are able to come together and address, if not completely resolve, their differences. The Washington conference was one of those meetings where cooperation prevailed. John D. Rockefeller Jr. was so encouraged that in December 1949, he deeded over his 33,562 acres of Jackson Hole land to the federal government. However, in a cautionary move he stipulated that should the land not be used for park purposes, nearly half the acreage would revert to the Jackson Hole Preserve. With barriers breaking down, Wyoming Senator Joseph O'Mahoney drafted Senate Bill 3409, abolishing the monument and incorporating that land into an enlarged Grand Teton National Park. With all the hard-fought compromises in place, the bill sailed through Congress and received President Harry Truman's signature on September 14, 1950.

Significance

To some, the concessions made to create Grand Teton National Park seemed overwhelming. However, pure parks, defined as free of human development, were a thing of the past. All the newly established NPS units represented a basketful of compromises. Congress accepted Mesa Verde, Denali, and Grand Canyon National Parks with mining privileges for those already operating there. Although they entered the system much earlier than Grand Teton, enabling legislation for Glacier and Lassen National Parks accepted summer homes, which became permanent inholdings. Mount Rainier National Park and Glacier granted electric railway privileges, and in some cases rights for tramways. The objective of the superintendents of such parks consisted of accepting the imperfect park. Hopefully then, park leaders could work diligently to free the parks of such intrusions, or at least minimize their effects. Back in the 1930s Director Arno Cammerer, in a mild critique of the "purist" faction, put it well when he asserted that "an ideal is something toward which to work; it should not be something which prohibits us from working."[14]

When one looks at the 1950 Act, however, there is little of the "ideal." It is a hard-nosed document of compromise, and underneath the legal language there is even a hint of animosity and skepticism that this park would ever work. Twenty-five years of controversy could not be wiped away in a two-day conference.

Guidelines for Grand Teton, 1962

In the early years of this new, expanded Grand Teton National Park there seemed to be little attention directed to laying out the fundamental mission of the park. It was a time for healing with the Jackson Hole community and maintaining specific principles while keeping a low profile. However, by 1962—a dozen years after the achievement of park expansion—Superintendent Harthon Bill and his staff finally crafted 35 guidelines for the park. Their Master Plan for the Preservation and Use of Grand Teton National Park was a remarkably comprehensive yet succinct document.[15] The plan identified nearly all the issues that have dominated Grand Teton management ever since. One could be critical of the brief, general nature of the 35 objectives and policies, but they nevertheless provide a valuable template. The document offers a glimpse into the areas where the superintendent and his staff directed their energies in 1962. It also provides an opportunity to compare the past with the present, noting the evolution and change of these issues over time.

In 1962, acquiring inholdings was of paramount importance, and the plan recommended purchase "as rapidly as availability of funds and willingness of owners to sell will permit." Priority would be given to the "scenic centers" of the park and places where purchases would "forestall future subdivision, commercial or specula-

WITH CONSTRUCTION OF THE MOOSE VISITOR CENTER IN 1960, PARK HEADQUARTERS MOVED FROM BEAVER CREEK TO MOOSE.

tive ventures." As Chapter 2 indicates, administrators carried out this objective vigorously. The park personnel acknowledged that some property owners would not sell without a lifetime lease, and the staff thus fully cooperated in such arrangements. For inholders who would not budge, the park kept on good terms with them by continuing "to maintain access roads and to plow snow from such roads used by winter residents."[16] Time changes situations, and patience might be rewarded.

Regarding the park boundary, the plan suggested adjustments when feasible. Without ever mentioning the problem of private land and houses in Kelly, it advised the staff to "study the possibilities of excluding developed areas and subdivisions just inside the present park boundaries." However, to give up public land would set an unwanted precedent. Whether the

staff explored the feasibility of turning Kelly free of park jurisdiction is unknown. In retrospect, it might have resolved some problems, but it surely would have created new ones.[17]

The staff did not seem intent on capital improvements. Visitor centers were well underway or had been completed under "Mission 66" at Moose and Colter Bay, and the 1962 master plan recommended that additional visitor facilities be added "with restraint" and shifted "more toward the eastern portion of the Jackson Hole area." Ever since the 1930s, but with little success, park planners had stressed the need to minimize future development near the foothills and mountains. Visitors continued to flock to Jenny Lake. The plan also suggested increasing the length of the visitor season, but without any ideas of how to accomplish that objective.

The 1962 policy regarding concession development was to "evaluate all expansion proposals with a view to allowing only those which are unquestionably essential to properly serve the visitors." Development should remain at the present size and location, with the exception of Moose, which should have a "cafeteria and store." This particular recommendation raises questions about the commercial complex known as Dornans. The new 1956 bridge across the Snake River cut off direct access to Jack Dornan's cabins, restaurant, and store. There was no love lost between the NPS and Jack Dornan. The question is, did park planners believe that the new bridge location and the new Moose Visitor Center would wipe out Dornan's business? There is no paper trail, and we may never know, but the proposal for food facilities and a store at Moose suggests that the park possibly hoped to buy out Jack Dornan, ending an ongoing feud.

With 97 percent of Teton County managed by the federal government, it is not surprising that the plan emphasized strong cooperation with the Wyoming Game and Fish Department, the U. S. Fish and Wildlife Service, and the U. S. Forest Service. The need to cooperate both inside and outside the park was evident, particularly since emotional fences still had to be mended with both the state and the Forest Service. It may indeed be fortunate that "institutional memory" seems to be short. During the first 35 years of the agency's existence, the NPS was an aggressive and confident bureau. It incurred the displeasure of other agencies, particularly the Forest Service, which suffered land loss to the NPS. But by 1962, the park no longer had major land enhancement aspirations and could focus instead on being a good neighbor.

Superintendent Harthon Bill and his staff made special efforts to uphold the 1950 agreement on elk management. The park would fully participate in the elk reduction program, but the activity was to be "confined to the smallest area consistent with effective elk control." Also, as a member of the group of "Cooperative Elk Study agencies," the park would participate in research on and management of the herd.

By 1962 backcountry visits were rapidly increasing, with increasing use by climbers, day hikers, backpackers, and horseback riders. According to one of the objectives, the park encouraged hiking and horseback riding, as well as safe rock climbing. The park would also "study the alpine areas to obtain the information to properly manage the use" of such country, but the managers made no mention of designated camping areas or camping permits. The park did not address the subject of wilderness, and the neglect of any mention of wilderness perhaps indicates ambivalence or political timidity, for in Washington, D.C., the topic was being widely discussed by Congress, the upshot being passage of the Wilderness Act of 1964. Grand Teton National Park took no position, at least not in the 1962 Master Plan. On the national level, the NPS was lukewarm at best regarding the new act, feeling that it was well qualified and committed to managing its wilderness and backcountry.[18]

Cattle grazing presented a different picture. The 1962 Master Plan supported the 1950 agreement, but without enthusiasm. The policy stressed grazing on lands east of Pacific Creek and east of the Snake River on pasture land (as opposed to the dry "Potholes" region land) "until it can be eliminated entirely." In its irrigated fields approach, the park hoped "to reduce the land area devoted to grazing."[19] The long-term goal was clear: eventual elimination.

The completed Jackson Hole Highway, the current Highway 89, would continue to be the main access road to and within the park. There was no concern that visitors who used only the highway would not be subject to an entrance fee. Although no figures were given, the assumption was that most visitors would continue to Yellowstone and would pay the entrance fee at Moran, rather than exit the park via Togwotee Pass. Regarding traffic, the new popularity of four-wheel-drive trucks raised new concerns. The plan called for "rigidly" controlling "valley areas against casual and promiscuous off-road vehicle use"

WHAT WAS MISSING

From a contemporary perspective, what was absent from the 1962 policies and objectives is also significant. What was missing provides a glimpse into the evolving concerns at Grand Teton National Park.

The policy makers, for example, appeared unconcerned with the qualities of silence and of solitude. Excessive noise in the park was apparently not an issue. In fact, among winter activities that the park encouraged was the use of snowplanes. This may have been a concession to a small group of local enthusiasts, but snowplanes do create outrageously high decibel levels in the quiet winter environment. There is no mention of snowmobiles. The year 1962

was still early for the appearance of snowmobiles, but the initial policy regarding snowplanes suggests they would have welcomed snowmobiles too. In fairness, however, the document could not completely anticipate future problems.

The Jackson Hole Airport failed to make the list of concerns. This intrusion on the serenity of the park, or its economic impact on growth, warranted no attention. Not until another decade passed would the airport become the most disputed park subject in the valley, drawing attention on a national level. In 1962, the little airport out in the sagebrush coasted through the last of its halcyon days, its users unaware of the storm that was to come.

Activities on the Snake River also did not seem to appear on the radar screen of policy topics. While there was support for climbing in the mountains and concern over people's safety, that concern did not seem to carry over to the river, even though the popularity of rafting, both commercial and private, was on the upswing, as was guided trout fishing.

Finally, aside from rock climbing, there is no mention of danger in the park. Of course the National Park Service did not want to stress perils in the park, with the exception of wild animals. An in-house document with no mention of law enforcement or search and rescue seems to suggest that the park was a safe, trouble-free environment with neither park personnel nor the public concerned about crime or risk. As with the airport, however, the park's focus on law enforcement would later take on greater importance as conditions, as well as the world, changed.

One last observation on this revealing set of 1962 objectives and policies: there is little evidence of partnering with private interests or fund-raising groups affiliated with the park to support its mission. True enough, the Grand Teton Association traced its roots to 1936 when the park superintendent and some prominent local citizens met to discuss park objectives. They decided to provide written information for tourists and establish the Jackson Hole Museum and Historical Association.[20] This was the beginning of collaboration with the local community as well as other federal agencies. Notwithstanding such cooperation, the plan said little about how its "partners" might contribute to the education of the public or their enjoyment of the park. In that respect the Grand Teton National Park of 1962 seems an impoverished place indeed. It appears to have had few friends, perhaps a result of its contentious birth. In 1962, the park still suffered from its difficult birth pangs, struggling to win the support of the community and surviving on limited federal funds supplemented by the significant philanthropy of the Jackson Hole Preserve, Inc.[21]

Surely one of the reasons the 1962 Plan did not address some of the future aspirations and problems was the need to address immediate, basic issues. Americans' pent-up urge to travel was unleashed with the end of World War II. Could Grand Teton park meet the needs of the upsurge in public visitation? Of course Jackson Hole had an infrastructure before the Park Service ever arrived. It started in 1884 when John Carnes and his Indian wife, Millie, came down the Gros Ventre River to become the first permanent settlers in the valley. It increased as pioneer farmers braved the trails and the weather to scrape out primitive roads, build cabins, clear meadows, and plant simple crops. But ranch cabins and barns and two-track roads, which the park eventually acquired by 1950, could not be modified to meet tourists' needs. In the main, they were unusable. The park and/or the Jackson Hole Preserve burned or removed as much as 70 percent of that early infrastructure.[22] (See chapter 6) In 1950, visitors could either camp or find overnight lodging in the town of Jackson. Good roads and visitor services were minimal, or nonexistent. To make the park functional, the Park Service had to think about a massive building program.

BUILDING THE PARK THROUGH MISSION 66

Across America, as well as at Grand Teton, the national parks were neglected during World War II. So inconsequential were the parks, that the National Park Service, along with other Department of the Interior agencies, were kicked out of Washington, D.C., banned to Chicago for the duration of the war, not to return until 1947.[23] During the war effort and without available gasoline, the parks were without visitors. Instead they were used by lumber companies to cut down trees or for livestock operators to fatten their cattle. The Navy was more creative, occupying Yosemite's

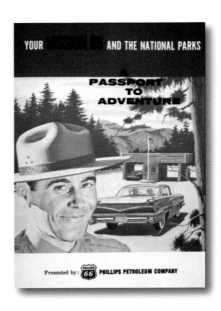

Ahwahnee Hotel as a hospital for shell-shocked veterans. The parks lost their mission during the war— and almost lost their identity.

Grand Teton National Park's experience, however, was somewhat different. At first Jackson Hole focused on the war effort. But on March 15, 1943, Roosevelt dropped his bolt from the blue, establishing Jackson Hole National Monument. We need not review the fight except to note that Congress put the new monument on a starvation diet by denying it any budget appropriation for the first three years of its existence. Not only were no new cabins or buildings constructed, but those that existed were denied maintenance.

Park administrators simply had no funds. Grand Teton was almost a charity case. Elsewhere the situation was not much better. Director Conrad Wirth compared the postwar condition of the National Park Service to "a big bear coming out of hibernation. We had a lot of aches and pains and we were hungry."[24] *Starving* would be a more appropriate word choice. Superintendents allocated whatever monies were available to salaries, basic needs, and a largely neglected infrastructure.

Unbelievable as it seems, in 1945 Congress appropriated less than $5 million to manage 180 parks.[25] Such miserly support could not go on, and the well-known historian and journalist Bernard DeVoto said so in a provocative 1953 article that suggested closing the national parks.[26] He noted that in spite of much increased visitation, park staffs had not increased since before the war, and they lived in "antiques or shacks," grouped together like slums. Infrastructure was crumbling away. If Congress could do no better, suggested DeVoto, they ought to shut down the parks. Meanwhile, Congress paid no attention to the parks, consumed with the "cold war" and national security issues. When Stewart Udall became Secretary of the Interior in 1961 he questioned the

nate construction.[28] So in talks with his branch heads, he developed the concept of a 10-year scheme for the National Park Service, as well. The year was 1956, with the golden anniversary of the Park Service coming up in 1966. The project needed a name. What better than Mission 66? It was the perfect designation to catch the eye of congressmen. The need was undeniable and the extensive projects would aid almost every state in the union.

Earlier in national park history, the Civilian Conservation Corps had contributed immeasurably to the national parks infrastructure. Now it was time for Mission 66 to attack the post-war inadequacy of the parks in order to serve the needs of the American public. Each park submitted an expansion wish list. Congress granted most of their requests. Park personnel rolled up their sleeves and became developers. Some of the most remarkable achievements were outlined by Director Wirth, as evidenced by the following statistics:

1. Trails—total of 936 miles of new or reconstructed trails.

2. Campgrounds—increased campsites by 17, 782 to a total of 29,782.

direction of a society that "achieved so much in the way of material progress, but at the same time allowed many of its basic values to fall by the wayside."[27] Both Udall and DeVoto viewed the NPS as an "impoverished stepchild."

Of course DeVoto's motivation was to loosen the governmental purse strings, not abandon the parks. When at last NPS Director Conrad Wirth saw the tide turning after the war toward moderate funding, he began to think creatively. He noted in his autobiography how the Bureau of Reclamation and the Army Corps of Engineers received lavish appropriations from Congress because they had big ongoing plans. Once a dam project was underway, for instance, it would be difficult for Congress to cut funds and termi-

3. Park roads—1,197 miles of new roads, 1,570 of reconstructed roads, for a total of 2,767.

4. Administrative and service buildings—164 new buildings.

5. Visitor centers—114.

6. Utilities—new or additional systems: 836 water systems, 744 sewer systems, and 397 power systems.

7. Historic buildings—458 reconstructed or rehabilitated.

8. Employee residences, dorms, etc.—1,239 constructed.

Other construction projects included picnic areas, campfire circles, comfort stations, marina improvements, entrance stations, and sewage disposal stations. Perhaps the most interesting and controversial Mission 66 project provided funding for 30 miles of airport runways, all outside the parks.[29]

In Grand Teton, the park staff created a 48-page *Mission 66 Prospectus*, outlining the multiple tasks to be accomplished. The prospectus included a "Statement of Significance," which provided the park's direction in 1956:

Grand Teton National Park contains the Teton Range and Jackson Hole, which together form a mountain and valley landscape of grandeur and majesty unlike any other in America. The fauna and flora are famous for unique components which must be protected to survive. It is rich in associations with the historic pageant of the exploration and settlement of the West. The fame of the area is worldwide and it should be protected and administered as a national treasure.[30]

TO SUPERINTENDENT FRANK OBERHANSLEY'S CREDIT, the prospectus emphasized visitor needs. The recently constructed Jackson Lake Lodge and the Colter Bay Cabins accommodated 689 visitors, while under the Mission 66 program the Colter Bay campground would be expanded by 200 new campsites, including those for recreational vehicles. Day use picnic areas more than doubled. There would be three

IN MANY WAYS THE MISSION 66 PROGRAM IMPROVED THE PARK FACILITIES, MAKING IT MORE "VISITOR FRIENDLY."

visitor centers. The Jenny Lake Visitor Center continued in use, but two new centers greatly increased the park's interpretive facilities. Workers built the Colter Bay Visitor Center in 1956, and it soon featured programs in the auditorium and also campfire talks, where audiences of 1,500 could be accommodated. Colter Bay also boasted the above-mentioned enlarged campground, a result of a partnership with John D. Rockefeller, Jr.

The Moose Visitor Center and park headquarters was dedicated on July 17, 1960. It would be the primary center, dispensing information and permits, selling books, and featuring a display about the fur trade and the old West. Additionally, a gallery of donated artwork from primarily local artists was displayed on the walls of the visitor center lobby.[31]

At that time, interpretive rangers expanded their use of audiovisual media (photo slides, 16 mm films, record players, tape recorders), developing new methods to reach the public. The new equipment, however, was not provided by Mission 66 monies, but rather through the Jackson Hole Museum sales publication program. In the field of natural history, the prospectus acknowledged that in the areas of plant ecology, birds, and mammals, the park needed to develop complete checklists. In the field of history and cultural resources, the Mission 66 prospectus suggested that local people from the town of Jackson might donate materials of historic interest, although recognizing that it would "probably be difficult to persuade residents of the county to donate materials in their possession to the National Park Service."

The report acknowledged that the protective division of the park "must be amplified." Existing staff could not protect the natural features or physical improvements, nor could they safeguard park visitors. In sum, the 1956 staff was "geared to operations of ten years ago" and simply needed to be upgraded. The report anticipated a much enlarged workforce by 1959.[32]

While acknowledging the need for more ranger staff, the real emphasis was on capital improvements, increasing the valley's built landscape. Mission 66 funds provided not only new visitor centers at Moose and Colter Bay, but 44 new housing units at Moose, sewer plants, and utility systems. These construction projects involved a considerable outlay of money. The bulk of the $8,273,786 flowed to roads and highways, primarily the completion of the Jackson Hole Highway, stretching from Jackson along the east side of the Snake River to Moran, with scenic turnouts. Mission 66 monies made possible the funding of this "fast" highway from Moose to the Moran junction, essentially following the Snake River and providing eye-catching turn-outs.

The highway provided an important change in the road infrastructure of Grand Teton, one that has influenced the park and what many visitors see. An undated Mission 66 typescript outlined that the Mission 66 team "proposed moving the traffic east of the Snake River by construction of a new park roadway." This was the fruition of an old idea. A highway had often been proposed in the 1920s and 1930s to replace the old Yellowstone wagon road that meanders above and to the east of the present road. A primary reason for the long desired highway was to ease traffic on the inner road to Jenny Lake. For example, in 1939, the innovative NPS landscape architect Sanford Hill had proposed only stagecoach access to the west side of the Snake River (see chapter 6). His plan was dependent on construction of a highway east of the river. We also know that William and Francis Gordon sold their 245-acre Blacktail Ranch in 1955 because they knew that the new highway would bisect their place (see chapter 2). Completing the new highway centered on funding. Now Mission 66 resolved the problem, and the Park Service constructed the highway as we know it today.[33]

The prospectus concluded with the following summary of a mountain park that had grown in visitation from 41,349 in 1945 to 1,197,200 in 1956:

Public use and enjoyment of Grand Teton National Park and its protection and preservation for future generations will be tremendously improved by the accomplishment of the MISSION 66 program. Improved roads will direct commercial travel from the vacation use areas of the park, will reduce traffic hazards and travel delays, and at the same time provide for leisurely recreational motoring. Eating establishments will be increased in capacity; overnight lodging will be much more plentiful and available; camp-grounds and trailer camps will be expanded to serve more people with greater privacy and convenience; picnic and other day use areas and stopping places will be more numerous and convenient. With all of this development, the paramount values of the park will be better protected than they are today, because of the careful location and design of the new installations. Future generations will have ever improved opportunities for relaxation, inspiration and use of the area than the smaller numbers of visitors now enjoy.[34]

MISSION 66 CHANGED GRAND TETON from a park offering visitors minimal services and interpretive material to one that would soon attract well over two million visitors each year. Grand Teton, once a footnote to Yellowstone, would now take its place among the crown jewels of the National Park System. Visitation to the park soared from the 1956 figure to 2,673,100 in 1966. In 1969, visitation figures topped three million at 3,134,400.[35]

MISSION 66—GOING TOO FAR?

When NPS Director Conrad Wirth formally announced the Mission 66 program at a celebratory banquet on February 8, 1956, one of the sponsors was the American Automobile Association.[36] Given that association's interests, it should not be surprising that criticism would emerge over the Mission 66 park plan, particularly regarding its emphasis on road building and improvements. Wirth attempted to make this program palatable by publishing in 1957 a handsome color brochure titled *The National Park Wilderness*. It identified different types of wilderness, with emphasis on a new type: "accessible wilderness." This new species of wilderness would allow a visitor to take a 10-minute walk from a park road and "see, sense, and react to wilderness, often without leaving the roadside." Essentially, with Mission 66 you could have it all.[37]

HOWARD ZAHNISER, MARDY MURIE, AND OLAUS MURIE. THESE WILDERNESS SOCIETY LEADERS WERE CRITICAL OF ASPECTS OF THE MISSION 66 PROGRAM.

Sierra Club leader David Brower did not agree. Neither did the environmental leaders who lived just one mile from the Moose park headquarters. In their quiet but effective way, Olaus and Adolph Murie and their families, all vigorous defenders of wilderness, made their voices heard. Adolph had fought and defeated a plan to expand the primitive road deep into the heart of Mt. McKinley National Park (now Denali) up to modern highway standards. Olaus was by then co-director of the Wilderness Society with Howard Zahniser, a society focused on the threat of the modern, mechanized world of automobiles and roads and their effects on America's primitive land, as well as on

the character of its people.[38] Olaus, Howard Zahnizer, Aldo Leopold, and many others were already writing, organizing, and lobbying for wilderness. Their efforts paid off with passage of the Wilderness Act of 1964.

But in 1958, they were concentrating on challenging Mission 66. Olaus sent letters to Wirth (with copies to environmental organizations) questioning the road program, stating that he was simply expressing the concern of numerous people around the country. He suggested that many believed the bulldozer was the appropriate symbol for Mission 66, and in time the Park Service would have to establish "'Mission 76' to undo the damage done in Mission 66."[39] The Park Service noted such criticism, but continued with the program, although one suspects that in Grand Teton the park administrators could feel the heat from the Murie family.

Other authorities found aspects of the Mission 66 building program too extensive and too prosaic. In his Yellowstone Mission 66 talk, Wirth emphasized to the assembled superintendents that "we must . . . get full value out of every dollar given us and see that every project is sound, serviceable, and not just fancy."[40] Translated, this meant the Mission 66 building program must be utilitarian, obtaining as many square feet of space per dollar as possible. Perhaps this need for economy explains the undistinguished housing designs reflected in the structures erected at Moose. They represented the functional ranch-style home popular at the time, with no consideration given to local climate. Yet Wirth made no apologies, even featuring a floor plan of the "Three Bedroom Standard" in his autobiography.[41] It was an era when uniformity and economy triumphed over distinctive architecture. Between 1947 and 1951, the 6000-home community of Levittown, Pennsylvania, emerged, featuring mass production and low prices in a modern suburbia. On the West Coast, 11,000 Eichler homes spoke to the advantages of uniform tract homes.

Within the Park Service, Wirth praised "the ladies of the National Park Service…[who] took it upon themselves to study our housing problem." The wives of Grand Teton employees participated. The women produced a fine report that Wirth believed was a tremendous help to the Park Service. The report rejected traditional rustic architecture, with its dark interiors, lack of convenience, and drafty log work. They preferred modern, efficient homes. Thus for more serviceable residences, Grand Teton employees easily abandoned the rustic log cabin architecture produced by the Civilian Conservation Corps as evident at the Beaver Creek housing complex, for the mediocrity of military-type tract housing at Moose. Although the need for better housing cannot be denied, for many years these tract homes diminished the park's natural appearance. Why they were not shielded from the main road by landscaping is a mystery.

Design of the 114 Mission 66 visitor centers nationwide suggests that the plans for the Grand Teton visitor suffered from the same cookie-cutter problem of mass production, although a few were designed by such esteemed architects as Richard Neutra and Frank Lloyd Wright. Certainly the Moose visitor center represented influences of modernism rather than the romanticism of rustic architecture. Reactions to the old Moose Visitor Center differed, but the building seemed to express the lightness of a beach park rather than the massive stone/log grandeur of the mountains. Lightness is reflected in the construction as well as the architecture. Wirth's reminder to make every dollar count resulted in using modern building materials, but cutting corners with hollow doors, cheap fixtures, a weak roof, and a location which failed to feature the mountains. Eventually problems arose. Part of the roof collapsed in the winter of 1985–6 (fortunately after visitor center hours) under a heavy snow load. Today the Colter Bay Visitor Center has been remodeled, while the old Moose Visitor Center has been torn down.

Shortcomings notwithstanding, the Mission 66 program in Grand Teton National Park was considered a great success, especially from the visitor point of view. People continued to come to the park in

ARROWLEAF BALSAMROOT BRIGHTEN SPRINGTIME IN THE PARK.

greater and greater numbers, and the upgrading of numerous facilities surely had something to do with the astounding increase in visitation. Grand Teton would not have to consider Bernard DeVoto's proposal to close the park. The successful Mission 66 program matched by the remarkable popularity of national parks led some rangers to fear Grand Teton National Park was being "loved to death."

Mission 66 swung the funding pendulum toward capital improvements, which surely served visitors interests. Now they could have such luxuries as a roof over their heads, visitor centers, flush toilets, smooth roads, and marked trails. But the park accomplished all this construction of facilities at what price? Did tourists need slick visitor centers at *both* Moose and Colter Bay? Were new campgrounds featuring hookups for recreational vehicles really necessary? Was the park spoon-feeding nature to the tourists, while neglecting nature's representatives or pushing them onto the back burner?

It was time to swing back to a sharper focus on nature. The history of the National Park Service has included a series of such shifts from the "parks are for people" philosophy to the parks are for flora and fauna creed. The first gives priority to humans, the second gives priority to natural resources. In 1963 the NPS Leopold Report urged park leaders to emphasize "an illusion of primitive America," and create a "mood of wild America." The report suggested that the building program had gone far enough, and it was time to emphasize the natural qualities of Grand Teton, as well as all parks. [42]

WILDERNESS

At the same time that Olaus Murie castigated the Mission 66 emphases on development and Conrad Wirth's idea of "accessible wilderness," Murie and his friends in the Wilderness Society fought for a much broader concept. And after an eight-year political battle, the Wilderness Act of 1964 passed Congress and received President Lyndon Johnson's signature.

Along with the Leopold Report of 1963, the new wilderness legislation might have signaled a new direction for Grand Teton National Park. Unfortunately, this was not the NPS's finest hour. The Park Service saw no need for the legislation.

There were certainly reasons for this ambivalence. Who could manage their lands with more sensitivity than the National Park Service? Certainly not Congress! However, it was more than just a matter of "turf." As has been noted, in Grand Teton National Park and elsewhere, there has always been tension between the advocates of natural parks verses those who wanted no "lockup" from the public. Parks were for the people and should be opened to them. This view was legitimized in the Mission 66 projects. Wilderness advocates were elitists, selfish individuals who wanted a disproportionate part of the park for their own use. Historian Richard Sellers caught the mood when he states, "the wilderness bill represented the antithesis of development programs such as Mission 66—and it got a cool reception from Park Service leadership."[43] Besides, the lofty Teton Mountains were by default wilderness, and any legislation would be redundant and change nothing.

For a half dozen years, Grand Teton ignored the Wilderness Act. But by 1970, the pressure from environmental groups, both national and local, was such that the staff studied the situation and then recommended 115,807 acres be placed in wilderness designation. This would include the heart of the range from south of Granite Canyon to north of Webb Canyon. On March 10, 1972, the Hearing Officer, John M. Davis, opened a public meeting in the Pink Garter Theater in Jackson. About 175 people showed up and fourteen people presented oral statements.[44] It was, perhaps, the least contentious of any Jackson Hole public lands gathering. Hearing Officer Davis opened the meeting at 2:00 p. m. and closed it at 3:47 p. m., which is surely some sort of record. Written responses reflected the sentiment for wilderness designation. Of 641 responses, only 24 organizations or individuals supported the NPS proposal to designate 115,807 acres as wilderness. The sentiment was for an increase, with 554 responses favoring more wilderness up to 200,000 acres. Twenty-four people and organizations wanted no wilderness.[45] The great number of wilderness advocates wanted such areas as Two Ocean Lake and Emma Matilda, Signal Mountain, as well as the Potholes region all designated as wilderness. Many thousands of acres of valley sagebrush land were unavailable, for they were subject to existing grazing rights. Of course, as noted in Chapter 3, cattle leases had now been practically ended. Still that land was questionable for wilderness designation.

ALTHOUGH OPPOSITION TO WILDERNESS DESIGNATION was minimal in 1972, the Wyoming congressional delegation did not introduce a bill. In 1978, the Teton Range, plus about 6,000 acres in the Two Ocean Lake area, were included in a general wilderness bill that failed passage. In 1984, however, the Wyoming Wilderness Act passed and was signed into law. The new wilderness areas were all within Forest Service lands. Since that decade there has been no official action, and no support for any action from Wyoming's two senators and one representative. Grand Teton now has 122,604 recommended wilderness lands, and 20,850 potential wilderness lands.[46] Paradoxically, Grand Teton National Park has no officially designated wilderness areas, although NPS policy requires that the park manage the potential wilderness lands as if they were officially designated as such.

Why not have the Teton Range designated as wilderness? As a historian friend often stated, "it's complicated." From a management viewpoint the designation really makes little difference. But it would be entirely sensible for the Teton Range to be included in the Nation's wilderness system.

REVIEWING THESE EARLY, post-war years, local and national leaders made a herculean effort to overcome their differences and create something new. No national park started its life with more enemies and fewer friends. The Park Service labored to mend the fences of discord by working with the 1950 Act compromises. Of course, the growing popularity of the park, as well as congressional support of the Mission 66, assured that Grand Teton would begin its ascent as one of the nation's premier national parks. By 1962, the park had defined its objectives and policies, many of which are still relevant today. The story of how these policies and objectives worked out over the decades since, is a story of Grand Teton's change and its continuing evolution toward a mature, natural park.

1 *An Act to Establish a New Grand Teton National Park in the State of Wyoming, and for Other Purposes,* approved September 14, 1950 (Public Law 81-787, 64 Stat. 849). The law's full text is at *http://research.archives.gov/description/299863*; a less complete but more user friendly version is at *http://www.nps.gov/grte/parkmgmt/upload/Grand-Teton-NP-enabling-legislation_9-14-1950.pdf.*

2 Robert Righter, *The Battle Over Hetch Hetchy: America's Most Controversial Dam and the Birth of Modern Environmentalism* (New York: Oxford University Press, 2005).

3 Coulter Huyler eventually sold the Bear Paw to Rockefeller, so in the long run the case made no difference.

4 These issues are covered in more detail in Robert W. Righter, *Crucible for Conservation: The Struggle for Grand Teton National Park* (Boulder: Colorado University Press, 1982; repr., Moose: Grand Teton Association, 2000), 126-34.

5 Ibid., 134–35.

6 Bernard DeVoto, "Easy Chair," *Harper's Magazine* 194 (January 1948): 31.

7 Richard White, "Are You an Environmentalist or Do You Work for a Living," in *Uncommon Ground: Rethinking the Human Place in Nature,* ed. William Cronin (New York: W. W. Norton, 1995), 171–85.

8 For other examples of class-based divisions between local economic interests and park proponents see Karl Jacoby, *Crimes against Nature: Squatters, Poachers, Thieves and the Hidden History of American Conservation* (Berkeley: University of California Press, 2001).

9 Conrad L. Wirth, *Parks, Politics, and the People* (Norman: University of Oklahoma Press, 1980), 332–33.

10 An account of this meeting can be found in a Memorandum for the Director from Conrad Wirth, April 21, 1949, in Leo H. Dieterich et al., *Jackson Hole National Monument, Wyoming: A Compendium of Important Papers Covering Negotiation in the Establishment and Administration of the National Monument,* 4 vols. (Washington, D.C.: Department of the Interior, 1945–50),

2: 4, Exhibit 56. This collection can be found in the American Heritage Center, University of Wyoming, Laramie.

11 Wirth, *Parks, Politics, and People,* 333.

12 Ibid.

13 *An Act to Establish a New Grand Teton National Park,* Public Law 81-787, 64 Statute 849 (1950).

14 Director Arno Cammerer to Henry Ward, American Association for the Advancement of Science, June 4, 1935; in a letter to William Wharton of the National Parks Association, June 22, 1935, Cammerer outlined the many violations of park principles in the enabling legislation, all in an effort to convince Ward and Wharton that a "pure" park was impossible and their organizations should support park status for Grand Teton. File 501-23, box 1052, Grand Teton, NPS, Record Group 79, National Archives, College Park, Maryland.

15 *Master Plan for the Preservation and Use of Grand Teton National Park: Objectives and Policies,* April 1962, 10–14.

16 Ibid.

17 Ibid., 10.

18 See Sellers, *Preserving Nature in the National Parks,* 191–94.

19 *Master Plan.*

20 Although 1936 was not a cordial year for NPS interest and those of the local community, there was cooperation. The advisory committee included local druggist Bruce Porter, Stephen N. Leek, Harrison Crandall, Fritiof Fryxell, and Olaus Murie.

21 *Master Plan.*

22 The Park has no record of the buildings removed. The 70 percent figure comes from the estimate of Mike Johnson, NPS Cultural Resources specialist in the 1990s.

23 John Ise, *Our National Park Policy: A Critical History* (Baltimore: Johns Hopkins University Press, 1961), 447–49.

24 "Director Wirth's Opening Remarks at 1957 Park Development Conference," in *Report of National Park Service 1957 Park*

Development Conference, Grand Teton and Yellowstone National Parks, September 10–17, 1957, 3. Copy in GTNP, Cultural Resources, Mission 66 files.

25 Conrad L. Wirth, *Parks, Politics, and the People* (Norman: University of Oklahoma Press, 1980), 234.

26 Bernard DeVoto, "Let's Close the National Parks," *Harper's Magazine* 207 (October 1953): 49–52.

27 U.S. Department of the Interior, Annual Report (Washington, D.C.: Government Printing Office, 1961): 6.

28 Wirth, *Parks, Politics and the People*, 239.

29 Statistics from Wirth, *Parks, Politics and the People*, 262.

30 *Mission 66 Prospectus, Grand Teton National Park*, April 20, 1956, 48 pp., copy in possession of the author. Since the Mission 66 program had just begun, the prospectus is written in the future tense. However, with adequate funding the projects were all completed.

31 Ibid.

32 Ibid., 17–18.

33 "Mission 66 at Grand Teton," a two-page typescript which includes photographs of the new road and infrasture (n. d., n. a.).

34 Ibid.

35 For visitation figures see *http://nature.nps.gov/stats/viewReports.cfm*. This internet site provides statistical data for the total NPS system. However, there can be some confusion. Since 1991 Grand Teton National Park compiles two visitation statistics: One for Recreational Visits and one for Total Park Visitation. Recreational visitation statistics are considerably lower than Total Park Visitation statistics. For instance, in 2012 the Park showed 2,659, 037 Recreational Visits versus 3,901,773 Total Park Visitation. My assumption is that the 1956 to 1969 statistics represent Total Park Visitation. Future statistics will all be Total Park Visitation. Statistics provided by Jackie Skaggs, Public Affairs Officer, GTNP. Also see Grand Teton Superintendent's Annual Reports, 2004 – 2012.

36 Richard W. Sellers, *Preserving Nature in the National Parks* (New Haven: Yale University Press, 1997), 183.

37 Ibid., 187–88.

38 See Paul S. Sutter, *Driven Wild: How the Fight against Automobiles Launched the Modern Wilderness Movement* (Seattle: University of Washington Press, 2002).

39 Olaus Murie to Conrad L. Wirth, February 6, 1958; Olaus J. Murie to Conrad L. Wirth, December 10, 1957, NPS-HC, quoted in Sellers, *Preserving Nature*, 188–89, 334.

40 "Director Wirth's Opening Remarks at 1957 Park Development Conference," 3.

41 Wirth, *Parks, Politics and the People*, 248.

42 See http: *www.nps.gov/history/history/online_books/leopold/leopold.htm*; also see Sellers, *Preserving Nature*, 214-6.

43 Sellers, *Preserving Nature*, 191-4.

44 "Wilderness Recommendation," Grand Teton National Park, Wyoming, August, 1972, 15.

45 Ibid., 22.

46 Shan Burson, Bioacoustic Ecologist, GTNP to Bridgette Guild, Museum Curator, GTNP, April 4, 2013. Letter forwarded to author, April 4, 2013. The "potential" wilderness areas have non-conforming uses such as roads, power lines or other human use evidence.

Peaks, Politics, and Passion: Grand Teton National Park Comes of Age

Chapter 2

Rounding Out the Park

WHEN PRESIDENT HARRY TRUMAN SIGNED into law the bill to create Grand Teton National Park on September 14, 1950, his action established the park boundary as we know it today. The park's perimeter has changed little since. But what of its interior boundaries—the private lands within the park that undermined its coherence? Today we seldom reflect on the 13,296 acres of private inholdings within Grand Teton National Park in 1950, because for the last 60 years park administrators have been preoccupied with the mission of seeing that those private lands became federal, whenever possible.[1] To accomplish this task required wresting funds from within the tight NPS land acquisition fund.

Generally the park was reduced to what NPS Director Conrad Wirth called "the beg, borrow, or steal system."[2] Finding funds was not the only problem. After decades of disputes with local people, some steadfast enemies were totally disinterested in cooperating with the Park Service, least of all over land ownership that would expand park power or jurisdiction. Many landowners had already experienced the pressure from land agents such as Dick Winger and Harold Fabian, representing the Snake River Land Company. They would keep ownership of their land holdings during the turbulent period of 1943–50.

For a time it looked as though Grand Teton National Park might replicate the Indiana Dunes National Lakeshore, where even now one-third of the land inside the boundaries remains in private hands.[3] Within Grand Teton National Park boundaries in 1956, 76 individuals owned private land, then totaling only 6,468 acres at an estimated value of $2,631,430. Park administrators had already reduced private land from 13,296 acres in 1950. The remaining land did not seem a problem, for the acreage represents just a touch over two percent of the park land. But there were mitigating factors. Much of the private land was in the southern reaches of the park, susceptible to development. Furthermore, many of the land owners were not passive inholders, but held the very American attitude that the "highest and best use" of land was development. They were not adverse to the profit motive. As the stories of this chapter will show, each land negotiation is different, requiring diverse

and creative ways to acquire property so essential to the operation of the park.

From the Grand Teton administrator's point of view, purchase of the 6,468 acres of private land was crucial "in order to establish control of the park as a unit."[4] They found sufficient justification in the NPS Organic Act of 1916, which charged that the newly-established Park Service should "promote and administer" the parks "by such means and measures as conform to the fundamental purpose" of the parks. What was the purpose? The act states that the purpose "is to conserve the scenery and the natural and historic objects and the wild life therein. . ."[5] Clearly to fulfill that purpose, the Grand Teton administrators must control the land. In a sense, the park acquired private property based on land use zoning to fulfill their mandate. And to accomplish this mandate they generally rejected any leasing arrangement, or purchase of development rights. There was only one way to assure control, and that was through fee-simple ownership. This objective was not easy. This chapter chronicles the park's remarkable success in eliminating most private land and establishing the cohesive unit that is today's park.

PARK EMPLOYEES' PROPERTY

The 1950 legislation allowed private landowners within the boundaries of the new park to retain full title and rights. Most of these landowners were located within the Jackson Hole National Monument property east of the Snake River. With the monument's controversial establishment in 1943, the Park Service quickly made it clear that private property would be respected, but not for park employees. The Park Service notified employees that they must sell their acreage within Grand Teton. In truth, they were given a choice. They could continue to own their land, or they could continue their employment with the NPS. They could not do both.

The issue first arose with the case of Adolph Murie who, with his brother Olaus, held title to an undivided interest in the STS Ranch (today's Murie Ranch),

having bought it in 1945. Adolph had worked for 32 years as a wildlife biologist for the National Park Service in Grand Teton, Mt. McKinley and Yellowstone National Parks. The Muries acknowledged the ownership problem, and quickly resolved it when Adolph deeded over his ranch interest to his brother. Also, the Muries were willing to give the park first option on the place, should they decide to sell.[6] Obviously they did not want to give up living at the STS place, but eventually the Muries' willingly sold the ranch to the National Park Service in 1966, retaining life leases. In 2006 the Murie Ranch became

Photo by Henry Holdsworth

the second of two sites within the park designated as a National Historic Landmark.[7]

Not everyone would be as amenable as the Muries. Making money on land appreciation is practically an American institution, and land values were rapidly accelerating in Jackson Hole. Land located within the spectacular park could not help but rise in value. Given the market, it is not surprising that employees wished to keep their land. Yet is seemed ludicrous for an NPS employee to believe that purchasing and holding land within the park was completely ethical or acceptable. Park Ranger Clyde Kranenberg was one of those who received a memo informing him that it was against park policy for employees to own land within the park. Kranenberg and his wife Genevieve had purchased Lot 4 in the Craighead Subdivision (near the Antelope Flats Road) in 1954. He had started work in 1951 but claimed that "circumstances beyond my control" had prevented him from purchasing the plot until 1954. He said he intended to build an attractive home that would be an asset to the park. He also claimed that Jackson Hole "has been my home for 21 years and my greatest desire is to continue working for the Park while striving to make a better world for generations to come." Park administrators were unimpressed. Acting Superintendent Thomas Miller continued to press the ranger to sell. As of August 29, 1955, Kranenberg maintained, "We are undecided." But the die was cast, at least if he wanted to continue his ranger career. He sold for $2,380, the appraised value.[8]

Another park employee had much less trouble making a decision. As a part-time worker, Robert Perkins hoped for full-time status. He had paid $1,000 for a summer home site and was quite willing to sell for that amount. However, the prominent local realtor, Richard Winger, appraised his two-acre lot for $1,910, and that was what the park paid. No doubt Perkins was pleased with the price, but whether he became a permanent employee is not clear.[9]

BIG LOTS

Of greater concern to the park was the Blacktail Ranch, a 245-acre spread north of Dornan's, incorporating the whole area at Blacktail Pond and the present-day roadway turnout. The owners, William and Francis Gordon, lived in Fayetteville, Arkansas, but spent their summers on the ranch. On the bench above the river they built a modest modern house and a number of outbuildings to support a cattle operation. On a good portion of the acreage they had cleared away the sagebrush and planted pasture grasses to provide for the livestock. Even if it was not a thriving operation, Gordon and his wife enjoyed the summers at what has been termed their "hobby ranch," fronting the Snake River with a backdrop of mountains certainly not seen in Arkansas. After World War II they realized that their hideaway would soon be bisected by the new highway. In 1954, the Gordons responded favorably to park inquiries about purchase. The coming road surely influenced their decision, but they also believed that the property should become part of the park.

With the understanding of a forthcoming sale, park administrators seemed to relax, paying little attention to the Gordons. That changed dramatically when William Gordon wrote to Superintendent Frank Oberhansley that he was displeased with the lack of progress on the sale, and he would "start to sell acreage on my ranch next summer unless some information reaches me before." A rather somnambulant park administration quickly awoke. It was January 1955, and the superintendent was out of the park, so Chief Ranger Joseph Fraser immediately assured Gordon of their interest. He thanked Gordon for his patience and his willingness to negotiate "before you break it into small plots next summer for sale to the public." It was a large and crucial piece of land, and not only were Superintendent Oberhansley and the regional office engaged in negotiations, but Director Conrad Wirth was as well. They discussed a life lease, but Gordon did not relish living near road construction or the highway itself. Eventually the park bought the Blacktail Ranch for $185,000, giving Gordon a five-year lease to remove or sell his personal property, buildings, and farm equipment.[10]

The ranch was an important purchase, but the area was not free of development threats. Just to the east of the Gordons' Blacktail Ranch, south of the Craighead subdivision and north of the Antelope Flats Road, Charles Ridenour owned a five-acre parcel. Superintendent Oberhansley had his eye on that par-cel, but could not make an offer for lack of funds. In July 1959, money became available and he offered to buy the five acres from Ridenour. Oberhansley promised a fair appraisal and "full weight to the scenic and recreational value." He hoped the whole transaction could be concluded within ninety days.

He was too optimistic. Jackson Hole appraiser Richard Winger valued the land at $1,250 an acre, for a total price of $6,250. Park officials accepted that evaluation without protest. However, two parties are necessary to consummate a real estate agreement, and Charles Ridenour was not ready to put his signature to the deed transfer. He informed Oberhansley that given his land's location, the rising market, and the scarcity of private land, he would take no less than $3,500 to $5,000 per acre. Oberhansley did not take well to Ridenour's counter-offer. One can only imagine the superintendent's reaction when he opened the letter. In a stern, if restrained, 1959 memo to the NPS regional director, he wrote that "in view of the exorbitant asking price . . . Mr. Ridenour has placed on these two parcels of land which he is holding purely for speculation purposes and the threat of possible subdivision and development of these isolated plots which are completely surrounded by Park lands, we strongly urge consideration be given to condemnation."

What happened after the recommendation of condemnation is not recorded, but clearly Ridenour and Oberhansley could not do business together. When a new superintendent, Harthon Bill, took over in 1961, the two men resumed negotiation with more success. They seemed congenial, with notes regarding cattle and ski conditions interspersed with property discussions. Ridenour lowered his price to $2,000 an acre. This was still too rich for the NPS, although Richard Winger raised his appraisal to $1,400 an acre, or $7,000 for the property. In a rather inexplicable move, Ridenour accepted an option, receiving $6,750 for his five acres. He never came close to his $2,000 per acre price, but he took the money and bought land in Wilson.[11]

THE CONDEMNATION OPTION

As years passed, and key properties entered the federal fold, superintendents' attentions turned to other issues. Still, the desire to eliminate inholdings remained. In the early 1980s, park administrators moved aggressively to acquire another large parcel of land east of the Antelope Flats Road belonging to the McReynolds/Thompson family. Claude M. Thompson acquired the 160-acre homestead in 1943 which included a cabin built by Albert Schwabacher's chauffeur in 1937.[12] When Claude died, he willed the land to his two children, Mary McReynolds and James Thompson, each receiving 80 acres. Neither heir seemed interested in living on the land, although Mary did purchased the cabin from Claude. The acreage remained vacant and unused. It would have been difficult to eke out a living, and one is reminded of Joe Jones' homestead west of Blacktail Butte. Joe recalled "betting" the U.S. Land Office ("Uncle Sam") that he could live on the land for five years without starving to death.[13] He won his bet, but not without hardship. He soon sold his homestead and moved to town. Perhaps wiser than Joe, Mary and James let their land lie fallow, leasing it for grazing to rancher Clark Moulton. The land also provided a welcome respite for migrating elk and, more recently the bison that frequent the Antelope Flats area. The McReynolds family made little effort to sell the land to the Park Service or anyone else. However by 1977 the McReynolds family was prepared to open negotiation. Lyle McReynolds remembers that the family approached Grand Teton administrators, offering to turn over their land for $10,000 per acre. The NPS did not register interest, at least not at that price. The family was ready to sell, but not desperate to do so. Taxes were low and the land would appreciate— it was a good investment.[14]

On June 19, 1981, Mary McReynolds made application to Teton County for a building permit for a 2,000-square-foot home on a 40-acre parcel of her land. This changed everything. When the Park Service learned of her request, Superintendent Jack Stark, determined to eradicate this development threat, placed a telephone call to Mary at her home in Laguna Beach, California, on July 1, 1981. It was not a friendly conversation. Stark informed Mary that her intention to build a home was in conflict with park policy, and if "they proceeded to secure a permit, I have no choice but to recommend condemnation of the property."[15] The threat of condemnation was Stark's mantra, one he repeated several times. He was never one to use a "feather approach." Stark's aggressive attitude made Mary feel that the park was trying to, as she put it, "clobber us." As she expressed to her son Roland, she informed Stark she only wished to provide "a home for [her] son. Again, Mr. Stark made the threat to condemn everything."[16]

This telephone conversation was the beginning of a contentious four years leading to condemnation and court proceedings. It was Mary's son, Roland, who had requested the building permit in his mother's name, and he received the approved permit on September 2, 1981, for a house, but not on 40 acres—rather on 10. He moved quickly. Completely ignoring Park Service protests, he built a foundation, and no sooner was the concrete dry than he trucked in a prefabricated house. He moved into his new home two weeks later.

The Park Service was outraged. John Pattie, chief of the Division of Land and Water Resources in the Denver Regional Office, took over negotiations with the McReynolds/Thompson representatives. For their part, Roland and his father, B. J. McReynolds, were equally aggravated, expressing their irritation by continually asking the Park Service for all correspondence dealing with their property, under the auspices of the Freedom of Information Act.[17] Furthermore, Lyle hired Jacobs Engineering to survey for a 40-acre subdivision. He did not file the subdivision with Teton County, but all those survey stakes certainly

got the attention of Superintendent Stark who now worked harder at negotiations with a certain urgency.

John Pattie now attempted to purchase the 80-acre Thompson parcel and the 70-acre McReynolds land. But he made an error when he hired an appraiser from Montana. Unfortunately he was unfamiliar with Jackson Hole and unable to comprehend the community's accelerating land values. His appraisal at $13,000 per acre was unrealistic, and when Pattie informed the McReynolds family of the appraisal, B. J. McReynolds wrote a vigorous and combative letter. He was incredulous, expressing to Pattie that "nobody but a 'damn fool' would sell at the NPS appraisal." Pattie, trying to save the situation, had long telephone conversations with both B. J. McReynolds and James Thompson. Obviously, the two had talked and knew they had the advantage. Pattie came away from these painful conversations knowing he could never get an agreement for less than $25,000 an acre. On March 28, 1984, B. J. McReynolds wrote to Regional Director Lorraine Mintzmeyer that "we are on a collision course." Mintzmeyer agreed, seeing no way to close the wide appraisal gap. She reluctantly informed B. J. that "the NPS will start condemnation proceedings and the filing of a declaration of taking of your property will be initiated."[18]

It should be noted that this "appraisal gap" was almost always the most critical obstacle to the park's process of purchasing inholdings. Anyone who has bought or sold land knows that property usually has two values: that of the seller and that of the buyer. Appraisers provide a more realistic value, but they provide no guarantee of agreement. Time and again, appraisers hired by the Park Service—but often jointly agreed upon—would come up with a figure acceptable to the Park Service but not to the seller. In the McReynolds case, son Lyle maintains that the choice of the appraiser was not agreed upon and with the gap so wide it could not be closed through compromise.

There were other mitigating factors. The Park Service's negotiating ability was limited by budgetary constraints. And sometimes landowners were contemptuous of the process and unwilling to reach a deal. In challenging letters B. J. McReynolds ridiculed the whole valuation method, stating that the Park Service should determine what they thought the property was worth, and then hire an appraiser to confirm their decision, thus reversing the process!

Another common theme obvious in many discussions was the seller's threat to develop the property. In one of his feisty letters, B.J. McReynolds finished with the following: "In the meantime we plan to fully pursue the possibility of subdivision to realize the proper value that the NPS has refused to negotiate." Pattie responded to B. J., acknowledging that "our greatest concern is, of course, your statement of intent to pursue subdivision and development of the property." It would do "irreparable harm."[19] B. J., of course, understood that it would do no harm to remind Pattie that the family needed only to file the Jacobs Engineering 40-acre subdivision and begin sales. This threat was a little mischievous, but an understandable strategy used by many other inholders.

The McReynolds/Thompson condemnation proceeding limped along. After a number of extensions the judge finally scheduled it for June 1987. In an effort to stay out of court, the Park Service raised its appraisal to a little over $19,000 per acre. But before the McReynolds family could consider the deal, a congressional committee "dashed" the proposal as "too high." There would be no settlement.

On June 22, 1987, the case commenced as "U.S. v. 163.94 acres of land, situated in Teton County, Wy., and Thompson et al., Civil No. C85-0567, Grand Teton National Park." After four days of testimony, much of it from appraisers, the jury reached its verdict. To the chagrin of Park Service administrators, the sum awarded to the McReynolds/Thompson families was $4,224,070, averaging $25,000 to $26,000 per acre. A Park Service employee transmitted the formal decision to Superintendent Jack Stark with a note: "For when you have trouble falling asleep."[20] Later a high ranking park official confessed to Lyle that the NPS blundered the whole issue from beginning to end.[21]

DORNAN'S

The Dornan family property is unquestionably the best-known inholding in the park. "Let's meet at Dornan's" is a refrain often heard from townspeople as well as park employees. Besides a restaurant, bar

DORNAN'S

and chuckwagon, it offers groceries, gasoline, fishing gear, raft trips, and fine wine. You can hear excellent folk music at Dornan's and rent one of their cabins on the Snake River. It is today an integral part of the park. It was not always that way.

Evelyn Dornan, a Philadelphia socialite, came to Jackson Hole at the conclusion of the Great War after divorcing her husband, John. Looking for adventure and a new life, she bought a train ticket to Jackson Hole in July 1918, for $128.35. She intended to visit her friend Maud Noble. With her came her 16-year-old son, Jack. As so often happens to people who arrive in Jackson Hole, the Tetons captured her heart. After an adventurous summer, the pair went back East. But they would return to Wyoming often. By 1922, Holiday Menor pointed out some abandoned land adjacent to his that was available as a homestead. It was only a touch over 20 acres but certainly more than enough for Evelyn's purposes. Evelyn filed a homestead claim on the scenic property and then returned to Philadelphia. Son Jack, tired of private schools and enamored with the West, stayed in Jackson on the homestead.[22]

In 1925, Evelyn informed the Land Office that she was ready to "prove up" on her land. The following summer, on August 21, 1926, C. S. Dietz from the Evanston General Land Office arrived to inspect

Evelyn's homestead. Dietz's specialty was mineral claims, but he was pleased, no doubt, to visit Jackson Hole in the summer. Dietz was a romantic, enthralled with both the Teton peaks and the spirited single women homesteaders he encountered in Jackson Hole. Earlier he had approved Geraldine Lucas' Desert Land Act entry on Cottonwood Creek, remarking that Geraldine was one of those "inspired authors and artists of the eastern cities [who] have abandoned their former visitations to the Alps, and at present, the local country is rapidly becoming known as the Switzerland of America."[23] Evelyn Dornan also benefited from Dietz's enchantment with Jackson Hole and what can be seen as a bias in favor of women homesteaders. In spite of discrepancies, Dietz approved Evelyn Dornan's patent for her homestead of some 20 acres in 1926. In perhaps one of the most remarkable homestead approval justifications penned by a land office bureaucrat, Dietz allowed a small garden as "agricultural improvement." As for her lack of livestock, Dietz reasoned that "instead of defiling the entered scenic land by grazing domestic stock therein, claimant has taken particular pains to see that only wild faunal life has direct access thereto." Evelyn based her homestead claim on her aesthetic and artistic sense. And Dietz, with good humor, agreed to the proposition, stating that Evelyn Dornan's "homestead entry is merely the final research laboratory or studio for the expression of her innate aesthetic abilities. Thereon, all articles of merely utilitarian value are entirely suppressed by objects of pure artistic worth."

From Dietz's dreamy perspective "no modern wire fence would dare mar the unrivaled wild effect of the local landscape." Furthermore, he observed, the "entrywomen's chalet are of original rustic design that blend with the magnificent wild region entered in a pleasing and mellifluous manner."[24] Apparently no land office superior challenged Dietz's assessment, for Evelyn received her homestead patent.

Son Jack shared his mother's enthusiasm for Jackson Hole and the homestead. He soon constructed a few cabins on the Spur Ranch, as she called her place. In October, 1927, Jack Dornan married Ellen Jones, the daughter of homesteader and neighbor Joe Jones. Ellen became adept at diplomacy, for husband Jack had opposed the land acquisition program of the Snake River Land Company and the ambitions of the National Park Service. Her father, Joe Jones was best friends with Struthers Burt and advocated park extension. As Ellen would say later in life, "Jack didn't have much use for the park." In her calm manner, she also recounted that Jack and her mother-in-law Evelyn "had a great deal of discord."[25]

The discord eventually worked to the advantage of the National Park Service. While the park constantly sought purchase of the Dornan land and structures with the possibility of removal, Jack continually sought control of his mother's 20 acres. In many respects, he had a right to it. It was Jack who had built the cabins and made numerous improvements on the land. He pleaded with his mother and in time "she deeded him the north half of the property in 1941."[26]

Jack believed that the remaining land should be his inheritance as well, but Evelyn had other ideas. In 1952, she approached the NPS with the thought of selling. On June 20, 1952, Mike Yokel submitted his appraisal for land and improvements at $28,000. Evelyn Dornan believed her property was worth much more. She wanted $32,000 plus a lifetime lease. If the government did not want it at that price, she intended to sell it to a private party.[27] Back in Washington, there was a sense of urgency. In early October 1952, Kenneth Chorley, who had been heavily involved with the struggle to create the park, advised Director Conrad Wirth to "act quickly." The director agreed and prepared a sales contract immediately. However, he had no idea where he would find the money. At that point, Chorley urged the director to go ahead, assuring him that the Jackson Hole Preserve would fund the purchase.[28]

Evelyn signed the contract on October 14, 1952, receiving the full $32,000 and her life lease. True to her contentious nature, she signed only after an offending paragraph was removed. Chief Ranger Paul Judge, who had been crucial in the negotiations, and Superintendent Edward Freeland acted as witnesses. Over 12 acres of land extending along the river bank just south of the present-day Dornans became the property of the federal government.

The case of Evelyn Dornan provides a glimpse into the park's decision-making process as well as the political dilemmas inherent in Jackson Hole. When Evelyn was in failing health, her guardian David Burns requested the park allow her to rent out her home to augment her deteriorating bank account. Son Jack opposed the idea. Superintendent Fred Fagergren was inclined to approve this variance of her lease, but hesitated, weighing his options. He realized that David Burns was "influential in a group who have been critical of the Service, but who during recent years have become more favorable toward us. On the other hand, if we accede to the request of Mrs. Dornan's son [to disapprove the variance], who was one of our most bitter critics but who has in recent years become more amicable, he [Burns] will become extremely upset." "Frankly," mused the superintendent, "we are caught in the middle, since we would like to maintain the improved relations that have developed in recent years by the good work of our employees with both parties."[29]

Fagergren found the perfect solution when he denied Evelyn's request to rent her home, but allowed the dying woman to give up her life lease for $2,000. Both sides were satisfied—a win-win situation. Every superintendent and his/her staff hopes to find such solutions in these difficult situations, knowing that the unraveling of an issue can initiate more bitterness. Furthermore, the Wyoming congressional delegation and their power to intervene is often just a letter away.

While negotiations with the Dornan and McReynolds families were drawn out and difficult, some of the purchases in the Moose area went smoothly.

THE ARTIST LELAND CURTIS SOLD HIS CABIN OFF THE MOOSE/WILSON ROAD WITH THE UNDERSTANDING HIS HOUSE WOULD BE REMOVED.

Artist Leland Curtis and his wife Elizabeth treasured their cabin and studio, located on 3.65 acres of sage-brush land just off the Moose-Wilson Road and perched on a bench overlooking the Snake River. It was difficult for them to part with their land, but Leland sold to the park in April 1980 for $72,000 and a life lease for himself. Leland made his intentions clear: "I strongly believe in a policy which would guarantee private or commercial interests would not be allowed to destroy the highest value for which the National Parks were established." Leland believed in a natural park, and he expected that the little cabin would be removed and the land would revert to nature.[30] He was successful in his wish. His cabin was moved over Teton Pass, and today only a few boards remain at the site.

CRAIGHEAD LAND

John and Frank Craighead were two top-flight wildlife biologists, who by 1960 had pioneered radio tracking of grizzly bears in Yellowstone National Park.

They were widely known, especially for their articles in *National Geographic* magazine. Wildlife biologists across the country admired their path-breaking work. In Park Service circles their views on grizzlies proved controversial in the late 1960s, but that issue is beyond the scope of this study. The concern here is their property in Jackson Hole.

The brothers first visited Jackson Hole and the West in 1937, when they drove an old Chevrolet from their home in Chevy Chase Heights, Pennsylvania. They loved the country and vowed to return when they were older and had a little money. When they graduated from Pennsylvania State University with degrees in science in 1939, they turned west. By 1943, they had settled in Jackson Hole and were considering buying 20 acres of barren sagebrush land on a bench above Blacktail Pond from pioneer John Moulton, a parcel of his holdings where, as Moulton put it, the land "ran out of topsoil."[31] Unlike Moulton, the brothers cared not for farming, but for the view. After pooling their resources with those of John's mother-in-law, Clara Smith, they met Moulton's asking price of $200 per acre.

In the years to follow, the 20-acre Smith-Craighead parcel would be the source of considerable strife. At the time, the park superintendent assured the handsome young twins that there would be no conflict between them and the park over this land. It was 1943 and the war was on. Furthermore, although President Roosevelt had established the Jackson Hole National Monument in the face of local hostility, it was unclear whether it would survive, or if the NPS would have any sort of hold on the east side of the Snake River. Though the initial investment drained the brothers' wallets, it soon paid off. Before long they subdivided and sold a few lots at a very reasonable price (such as the $1,000 lot to the earlier mentioned Robert Perkins). They retained 14 acres for themselves, and when the surrounding land became part of the park in 1950, they suddenly held a valuable inholding indeed.

William Craighead, first cousin to John and Frank, also dipped into real estate. He lived in Newtown, Pennsylvania, but spent as much time as possible fishing and enjoying the ambiance of Jackson Hole. He acted as a fishing guide for a few years and helped John and Frank with riparian studies. Eventually, he bought Lot 10 in the Inglis Plat, which was out in the sagebrush southwest of the NPS-owned McCollister property. He eventually put up a small shack, but the Park Service denied him automobile access to squelch a potential development. By the 1970s William realized that he simply could not support his family in Pennsylvania and have a cabin in Jackson Hole. He put his lot on the market and soon found a buyer who intended to build a large house.[32]

ALTHOUGH THE TWIN BROTHERS MADE GREAT CONTRIBUTIONS IN RADIO TRACKING OF GRIZZLY BEARS AND FAME FOR THEIR ARTICLES IN NATIONAL GEOGRAPHIC, THEY HAD SERIOUS DISAGREEMENTS REGARDING THE VALUE OF THEIR PARK LAND INHOLDINGS.

caused bitterness. While the park and the brothers should have been united in their advocacy for nature, the land came between them. John and Frank each owned three vacant lots, jointly totaling 13.6 acres. They had also built their own homes on adjoining lots, and sold lots to Reginald and Gladys Laubin and the Rudd family, who built homes on their lots as well. In the 1970s, park administrators were determined to forestall development on the remaining vacant lots, particularly because the property, sitting on a bench, was so visible from the main road. [34] The two brothers were quite amenable to selling, but only at what they considered a fair price. In May 1975, the superintendent offered Frank $123,000 for Tract 04-156 and $78,500 for Tract 04-118. In Frank's opinion, the offer was well below market value. He did not respond. In September 1977, Frank appeared before the county commissioners with a subdivision plan to split his 2.86-acre plot into three parcels. The park responded by threatening condemnation, but when he withdrew his plans, the condemnation threat disappeared.[35]

The Park Service considered William's potential sale unacceptable, and they offered $46,000 for the lot. William countered with a price of $100,000. The park anteed up to $50,000, and William reduced his price to $75,000, but they could not bridge the $25,000 difference. The park initiated condemnation proceedings. In September 1978, Judge Clarence Brimmer of the U.S. District Court heard the case and determined that just compensation for the lot was $79,500. William Craighead came out well, and the Park Service learned that perhaps the courts should be avoided. Their efforts did, of course, prevent any building on the sagebrush flats.[33]

Meanwhile, negotiations with John and Frank did not go well. In fact, it is fair to say that land issues

At the same time Frank was negotiating, the park expressed a desire to buy John's property. His three parcels were appraised at $50,000 for 04-128, $73,900 for 04-119, and $105,300 for 04-157. Superintendent Robert Kerr offered $250,000 and a 10-year lease for all three, but John refused the offer. In March 1977, he let the park know he had a buyer for 04-128 who wanted to build a large home. The park then reappraised the lot at $62,500. John was not interested and listed the property with a Jackson real estate agent to get a market-value price on it. The next few months produced a game of cat and mouse. John put the lot on the market twice, but then took it off, while Superintendent Kerr watched and threatened condemnation actions. According to Frank's son, Charlie Craighead, the two brothers had no interest in subdividing and selling to outsiders. The property division was intended to provide individual lots for their children.[36]

Both John and Frank felt they were being bullied to sell their parcels at less-than-fair value. They

THE CRAIGHEAD FAMILY LOOKS OUT ON THE VALLEY FROM BELOW THEIR LAND.

believed that the park had failed to account for the appreciation of the land. In October 1977, John, who was a professor of wildlife biology at the University of Montana, became outraged by a letter from NPS Land Acquisition Officer Robert Lunger. It threatened that if John did not accept the $62,500 offer for parcel 04-128, the NPS would initiate condemnation proceedings. John responded by appearing before the Teton County Planning Commission with a plan to subdivide his 4.86 acre parcel (04-157) into five lots. At the same time he wrote to his Montana senator, Lee Metcalf, and also to NPS Director William Whalen about his displeasure. He indicated that he did not really intend to sell the five lots but wanted to prove that the Park Service offer of $133,000 (up from $123,000) was unfair and undervalued.

It was clear that when pressed, the NPS would abandon the willing buyer/willing seller policy. If park administrators wanted the land, they could be aggressive and intimidating. Soon the controversy became public. Frank Craighead wrote a devastating opinion piece for the *Jackson Hole News* defending his individual rights against a bullying NPS. Meanwhile, John wrote another letter to Senator Metcalf:

> Lee, it is my considered opinion that if the United States Government can invoke eminent domain proceedings on the basis of assumptions by Federal employees, and if we are denied basic rights of offering property for sale in the open market, we have concentrated too much power in the federal government, allowing powerful bureaucrats to gradually destroy free enterprise and individual freedom.

John Craighead articulated a common complaint against federal power in the American West and his message played well in Jackson Hole. Park administrators backed off.[37] The drama continued. However, in the winter of 1978–79 a fire broke out in Frank's house and it burned to the ground. While no cause was ever established, of course rumors were rampant.

The fire seemed to dampen the issue. Frank Craighead constructed a new house, and the Park Service reconsidered its position. Finally in 1989, Assistant Superintendent Marshall Gingery took an informal tour of the property. The Craigheads were willing to sell 9.6 acres of open land. After appraisal, the deal went through with the understanding that the NPS would never build structures on it. The final park purchase was for just 1.5 acres of land that Charlie, his brother, and sister felt they did not need. Again, it was with the condition that the park would always keep it vacant.[38] Today trees hide Frank's and John's homes, and there are no building lots available. Yet the Laubin's and Rudd's homes, remodeled and enlarged, still present intrusions on the bench, which the Park Service must live with.

Incentives to Sell

Obviously many land owners were reluctant to give up their special patch of Jackson Hole property. They had become emotionally connected to the soil, the sky, the mountains and streams: in essence, the place. To give all this up was an agonizing decision, especially if the land was coupled with family memories. This was the case with Fred and Lila Abercrombie, who owned about 18 acres at Kelly Warm Springs, located at the start of the Gros Ventre River road. Around 1950, they built a guest ranch. Taking advantage of the warm-water springs, they set up a swimming pool and positioned a number of cabins around them. For some years the family ran the ranch successfully. However by the early 1970s, they decided that their land should become part of the park. When the park offered them $548,500, they agreed to sell.[39]

The Abercrombie family, however, could not bear to abandon altogether what had become a treasured part of their family heritage. Park administrators offered a 25-year term estate, in which the family would temporarily retain one acre, their main house, and that of the former caretaker. They could not engage in any commercial activity on the property. The two buildings were to be kept "in good repair," as were the fences and driveway. "Representatives of the United States" could enter at any time to inspect, and at the end of 25 years, the family would "peacefully surrender the reserved premises." At that termination, the Abercrombie family was expected to turn over the property "in the same condition as of the date of this agreement [allowing] for reasonable and ordinary wear and tear and damages by the elements, or by circumstances over which the VENDERS have no control."[40] Thus the family retained a foothold in their special place for 25 additional years. The park offered the Abercrombie family a very good price for their land and buildings, but without that "withdrawal period," it may not have been possible to acquire the parcel.

Sometimes families with inholdings aspired to continue occupation after their term estate with the Park Service ended. Such was the case with the Sky Ranch, located a stone's throw away from the White Grass Ranch. William and Ruth Balderson purchased the property in 1952. They put up a stylish house designed by a Philadelphia architect. For a number of years the family gathered at the ranch: an unsurpassed location, a secluded and peaceful Shangri-La with only wildlife and dude ranchers for neighbors. Then in 1979, for unknown reasons, the Baldersons sold their property to the park for the fair market price (land $309,000, improvements $167,000). However, they retained a 25-year lease, which lowered the take-home value to $445,850.

The Baldersons found how remarkably fast 25 years can fly by. As the date approached to turn over the Sky Ranch property once and for all, William made overtures to extend the lease, under pressure from the rest of the family to do so. In a letter to Superintendent Steve Martin, Balderson suggested the possibility of a land swap, or a material contribution to the nearby restoration of the White Grass Ranch, as compensation for extending the lease. What he thought were rather creative ideas, however, did not work. In early 2005, now Regional Director Martin indicated to Balderson that "there is no option to extend your term estate that expires August 27, 2005." The family regretted the decision made in

From the collections of Jackson Hole Historical Society & Museum

Bar BC Ranch Jackson Hole, Wyo.

THE BAR BC WITH SWIMMING HOLE.

Lazy or not, the family constructed a number of cabins, as well as a large lodge, but they used the place only as a summer family retreat. During World War II, Margaretta deeded the ranch to her daughter, Emily Frew Oliver. With the conclusion of the war, Emily and her husband, Henry, started what might be called a limited or selective dude ranch. Those selected were largely friends, and

1979, but the park held fast to the original agreement and in the process took control of an exceptional piece of property.

A similar situation happened with the 4 Lazy F Ranch, but with a much longer history of occupation. The ranch, located on the Snake River just north of the park's Moose headquarters, was homesteaded by Bryant Mears in 1914. He made the necessary improvements on the 135-acre tract to gain a patent, but sold his interest to William and Margaretta Frew in 1927. The Frew family, who had been introduced to Jackson Hole through Struthers Burt's Bar BC Dude Ranch, attached their name to the ranch by way of the appellation 4 Lazy F, which stood for the "four lazy Frews."

it was certainly not a money-making operation.

In 1967, Emily and Henry decided to sell to the park for the negotiated price of $650,000, retaining a joint life estate. This worked out well for the Olivers. There is a little joke in Jackson Hole that if you sell your property to the park with a life lease, it will guarantee you immortality—or at least a good long life. Henry did not live much longer, but Emily lived well into her 90s. She was still living in 2005 when her son Charles "Bucky" Oliver approached the park with the idea of terminating his mother's life lease. His motives seem unclear; they may have had something to do with inheritance tax. But there were considerations other than money. Conversations between Charles Oliver, Superintendent Mary Gibson Scott and Management Assistant Gary Pollock revealed that while the family was quite willing to relinquish the life lease, they still hoped to retain some sort of involvement in the ranch. Based on their long association with the 4 Lazy F, they suggested a creative form of "adaptive reuse" for the place and were willing to help with the funding. This was a new twist for the Park Service. Clearly this was an emotional event for the Oliver family, and Superintendent Scott recognized it as such. In a draft letter she expressed that "we recognize that letting go of the property is difficult, and we appreciate your sincere and heartfelt wishes to remain connected to it in some way." The park held some face-to-face discussions with the family, and the Olivers promised to bring in "people with significant influence and philanthropic interests to help." In spite of such talks, the family terminated their life lease on September 15, 2006, promising to remove or auction their personal property. In the end Superintendent Scott and others simply were not willing to have their hands tied to the hopes and desires of the Oliver family.[41] As of this writing, the final outcome for the land and buildings of the 4 Lazy F is yet to be determined, but the Historic Properties Management Plan (anticipated completion in 2014) proposes adaptive reuse of the ranch for seasonal volunteer housing.[42]

EACH SITUATION IS DIFFERENT

The National Park Service assisted by the Jackson Hole Preserve, Inc. proved extremely successful in acquiring private land west of the Snake River. By the 1990s, only one parcel of land remained in private hands, and that one acre belonged to the family of Senator Joe Clark of Pennsylvania. Clark fell in love with the country in the 1920s and decided to build the Double Diamond Ranch, a summer camp for boys (today it is the American Alpine Club's Climbers Ranch). About a mile from the camp, the senator moved one of the cabins for himself and his family. Only one acre in size, the property is tucked away near the Alpine Club facilities in the very heart of the park. When Clark died, his widow Iris thought of selling the place and using the proceeds to establish an endowed chair at Harvard University in memory of her husband. But the appraised value of the land ($900,000 to $1.1 million) and the cost of funding an endowed chair ($3 to $3.5 million) were at odds. Local realtor, Mike Wardell, showed the cabin to potential buyers a few times, and Iris provided the park with the right of first refusal. But nothing worked out, and finally Iris deeded the property to Harvard. The university then sold the cabin to Easterner, John Townsend. With the proceeds, Harvard established the Joseph S. Clark Chair of Ethics in Politics and Government. While Iris Clark achieved her objective, the Clark cabin represents the only private inholding on the west side of the Snake River.[43]

Gweneth Markham's money issues were different from Iris Clark's, but her situation worked to the benefit of the park. Gweneth divorced her husband Ed in 1958, and she needed to sell their Shadow Mountain Ranch in order to divide their assets equally. She needed to do this fast, for as she wrote Superintendent Oberhansley, Ed was "threatening [to take] back his shares of the ranch and making a great nuisance of himself as usual." She stressed that Ed's "devious mind is working overtime." The park staff went into high gear, and in short order they purchased the 123-acre parcel for $142,000, with a two-year lease.

Finding funds to make these purchases was always an issue for the Grand Teton staff. In an era before the Land and Water Conservation Fund of 1964 Act, there was no handy source for purchases. Even when money was available, the park often had to approach Congress, the Jackson Hole Preserve, Inc., or other private philanthropists, or squeeze the money from its own budget.

PAUL McCOLLISTER
PHOTO COURTESY JACKSON
HOLE MOUNTAIN RESORT

When Marvel Lesher indicated willingness to sell off 4.95 acres of her holdings on Cottonwood Creek, land acquisitions people jumped at the chance. On February 28, 1980, the two sides signed papers, agreeing to the $258,000 purchase price. There was only one problem; the park did not have the money. Acting Chief of Land Acquisition, Lloyd Garrison, wrote to Marvel asking for an extension of the option for another 60 days. A tough pioneer, Marvel was having none of it. She wrote to advise Garrison that the "government should be able to make up their minds on the offer of Feb. 28, 1980 by July 15, 1980." She gave Garrison 30 days. Notably, the Park Service got it done, thus acquiring a crucial west side property.[44]

Acquiring property out on Antelope Flats Road, east of the Snake River, did not have the urgency of Cottonwood Creek, but still the park goal remained to acquire all private land within its borders. Paul McCollister came to Jackson Hole in the 1940s and fell in love with the place. He purchased 21 acres just off the Antelope Flats Road and proceeded to build a cabin for his wife Ester and the children. An entrepreneur of considerable ability, he soon got involved with land and development activities on the west side of the river, and became the founder of the Jackson Hole Ski Corporation and Teton Village, the most important businessman in the valley. As his power and property expanded, it was clear that he could no longer live at his isolated cabin, especially in the winter when snow piled high and Park Service snowplows could not reach his place. In 1964, he sold the property and cabins to the park for $106,000, with a life lease.

McCollister had a shrewd business head, and he definitely pushed the envelope regarding his lease. It stipulated that the property could be used only for "residential purposes," but when he requested permission in 1971 to rent out his cabins, he received it. When he planned a wilderness training camp at his former property, he went too far. In a May 1973 letter, Superintendent Gary Everhardt informed McCollister that no wilderness training would be allowed.[45]

McCollister backed off, but continued to be a burr under the Park Service saddle. In 1983, Superintendent Jack Stark chastised him for having six horses on the property, whereas the lease allowed for a maximum of two. In his letter, Stark abruptly canceled the lease but stated that he would "honor my commitment to you for allowing two horses there under proper grazing use if you or your immediate family occupy the lease." There was a certain irony in the "occupy" provision, for Stark knew there was no chance that McCollister would move back to his old family dwelling.

ALEX MORLEY AND PAUL McCOLLISTER. PHOTO COURTESY JACKSON HOLE MOUNTAIN RESORT

Photo courtesy of Jackson Hole Mountain Resort

Evidently McCollister was able to restore his lease, for by 1990 Tom Rush and Renee Askins rented the place from McCollister for $28,000 a year. Rush was a nationally known folk singer, and Askins would gain a modicum of fame for her work on the restoration of wolves in Yellowstone.[46] With this idyllic setting and the whole sweep of the Teton Range before them, Rush and Askins would probably have loved to live out their lives writing and singing and sitting in their hot tub contemplating their mountain views and the passing of the seasons. But that was not to be. On April 14, 1999, Paul McCollister died. Superintendent Jack Neckels tried to move Rush and Askins off the property immediately. He had in mind selling the structures and removing them, but Askins was pregnant and expecting a baby in July. A letter from Dr. Bruce Hayse suggested that it would not be a good idea to force them to move at this time. Somewhat stymied, Neckels leased the place to Rush and Askins for $442 a month until June 1, 2000. After their baby arrived, Management Assistant George Helfrich

DUDES SWIMMING IN THE KELLY WARM SPRINGS POND.

negotiated with the couple and they finally vacated the property on September 5, 2000.

But what of Neckels' plan to remove or destroy McCollister's home and cabins? By that date advocates of historic preservation had mobilized, foiling Neckels' attempt to avoid evaluation of the property before removal or destruction. Independent historian Michael Cassity completed a Determination of Eligibility for the National Register of Historic Places, concluding that Paul McCollister "exercised unusual influence in the development of Jackson Hole," and therefore the property was eligible for the register. McCollister was arguably one of the most important business leaders in Jackson Hole, transforming the tourist trade from one to two seasons, perhaps three. Yet superintendents since 2000 have not forwarded the nomination to Washington. Today the site remains vacant and forlorn and the yet-to-be-released Historic Properties Management Plan proposes removal of the structures.[47]

OVER WITH THE YURTS

Most national parks contend with development over which they have no control. Residents of towns on park borders, for instance, often do not share or reflect NPS values and concerns. Gatlinburg at the entrance to Great Smoky Mountains National Park provides an example. These settlements are independent, not subject to the rules and regulations of a national park. At Grand Teton National Park the unincorporated town of Kelly, located at the southeastern corner of the park—but *within* its borders—is Jackson Hole's version of this dilemma. Few tourists see Kelly, and fewer still visit. It has never been a tourist town; historically it has been a place where middle- and working-class people could buy a small parcel of land, build a house (or move in a mobile home) and enjoy the amenities of Jackson Hole.

Over the years, the National Park Service has longed to rid the park of Kelly. Seen as an unregulated community where alternative lifestyles thrive, including in about 25 impermanent structures called yurts, the village has created an identity all its own. Those who defend Kelly note that it provides some the only affordable homes in all of Teton County and many of the residents have a deep attachment to the park and its values.

From a land ownership point of view, the real question is: Why was Kelly included within the park boundaries in the first place? Consisting of approximately 63 acres, it did not have to be within the park proper. So how did it end up within rather than outside Grand Teton National Park?

The answer is elusive, but I suspect the Snake River Land Company operatives reasoned that they wanted to include as much land as possible in the potential park, allowing the Park Service to resolve at a later date any problems that arose from that decision. By 1914 Kelly had developed several enterprises. It was particularly important for its bridge across the Gros Ventre River. By 1921, it had gained enough population and status to challenge Jackson for the county seat of Teton County.[48] Kelly's demise, however, came with the Gros Ventre landslide in 1925 and the subsequent flood in 1927. The torrent devastated the small town, drowning six residents, sweeping away the bridge and some 40 homes, and leaving fertile fields with a layer of gravel. It was Jackson Hole's greatest natural disaster. Most residents evacuated to begin their lives elsewhere. The Snake River Land Company had no desire to prey on the miseries of the survivors. The land company did step up, offering a land market for essentially worthless property. Many were happy to sell their acreage and surviving possessions. The Snake River Land Company then turned over the deeds to their Kelly land to the park in 1949. Without the flood, Kelly might well have remained outside of park boundaries, but once incorporated, the Park Service was reluctant to give up the land. Perhaps the public/private land issues might have been resolved had the Park Service possessed the resources of a Rockefeller. It did not, and when the Teton County commissioners approved the original plat, allowing cabin sites of one-tenth of an acre, it was easy to predict the outcome.[49]

In the 1970s, Kelly's unconventional ways attracted the attention of the very conventional Park Service. Perhaps it was because of the Kelly residents' independent views, their response to the hippie movement, and their sympathy with the growing radicalism surrounding the Vietnam War. The Park Service aggressively assaulted the Kelly community with an effort to remove the yurts and any other undesirable structures or residents. I use the military word *assault* deliberately because that word reflected residents' perception of park action. Correspondence between the Kelly residents and park officials during this era is all quite civil, but below the surface smoldered a layer of hostility and distrust that permeated the relationship.[50]

In 1975, the NPS determined to study the situation. In a letter from Secretary of the Interior Rogers C. B. Morton, the secretary instructed Grand Teton "to complete a comprehensive study of possible boundary extensions and land uses within and adjacent to Grand Teton National Park." Most of the study examined land that was far beyond the budget capacity of the park to acquire, but resolving the Kelly issue seemed achievable. When the NPS Director gave instructions, he emphasized that "particular attention [should be] given to the south boundary . . . and the town of Kelly."[51] In the study which followed, the team offered three alternatives for the town: 1) No action, 2) Federal Zoning by Legislation, and 3) Exclude Kelly from the Park Boundary. The no action option, suggested the report, would result in a "policy of opportunity [for NPS] purchase and condemnation," which would "probably result in acquiring the remaining 120 lots." So in actuality this option suggested *action,* and eventually gaining control of the town. The second alternative would "establish zoning standards for Kelly" thus "giving the Park Service more flexible control over the type of development on these inholdings." Finally, the third alternative would remove the town from the park boundaries. In this scenario, the Park Service "would have no control over the town of Kelly, and the 60 lots that it owns would be transferred to other ownership or sold to private interest."[52]

The study did not offer a "preferred alternative," nor did it address any political or economic concerns, even though Secretary of the Interior Morton asked that consideration should be given "to the Park's relationship to adjacent or nearby lands . . . and land use of contiguous private lands.[53] Although I found no memos regarding discussion by the superintendent and his staff, we may assume they quickly dismissed Alternative 2. It would have created a storm of opposition. In fact all three alternatives would have been controversial. Perhaps from a Kelly community view, Alternative 3, removal of Kelly from park jurisdiction would have been most acceptable, but it would have meant that the Park Service would have no control over its independent neighbor.

Secretary Morton asked that park personnel and its consultants make recommendations to him, and he would transmit the report and final recommendations to the Congress. It is questionable that any agreement could be reached on the town, and hence Alternative 1, to continue to acquire property, prevailed.

With a policy of acquisition, Grand Teton worked toward purchase of the 120 lots with limited success. The Park Service simply did not sympathize with residents such as James Beyer, who owned one-third of an acre but installed two long trailers and a small log cabin. The park initiated negotiations with Beyer and may verbally have threatened condemnation proceedings. In August 1977, the two sides came to agreement, and Beyers moved out of Kelly with $47,800 in his pocket, far more than he might have deserved.[54]

Park personnel did not appreciate "trailer trash," but neither did they feel any sympathy for land speculators. It seemed that in Kelly and Teton County sensible zoning had taken a permanent vacation. Dean and Iris Driskell split two 0.46-acre parcels into four lots. This action certainly concerned the Park Service, and the Driskells made a handy profit when the park bought all the parcels for $231,000.[55]

Park administrators were averse to new buildings, even though they might be attractive. In 1978, Rob Hinchee and his family decided it was time to build on their Kelly lot, which they had owned for many years. However, the Park Service threatened condemnation proceedings if they pressed on with their plans. Hinchee's response was to play the political card, a strategy commonly used by locals who felt injustice. He contacted U.S. Representative Dick Cheney, U.S. Senator Alan Simpson, Oregon Senator Mark Hatfield, Alaskan Senator Ted Stevens, and others. He also described his dilemma to NPS Director William Whalen, noting that he hoped "the Service will reconsider and realize that this action [condemnation] is not in the best interest of the National Park Service and will only serve as an additional embarrassment." Hinchee did not identify the other "embarrassments," but surely Whalen and his staff were aware of the difficulties in Grand Teton in general and Kelly specifically. The condemnation threat disappeared.[56]

One of Kelly's best-known residents was Lorraine Bonney. She and her husband, Orrin, wrote mountain climbing books, and Lorraine put together a fine Grand Teton National Park guidebook. She supported park values, particularly in limiting the airport, but when it came to private property, she was protective of her interests first. In 1977, she decided to sell her one-third-acre lot to the park for $27,000, retaining her house and land with a life lease.

LORRAINE BONNEY
SHE WROTE AN EXCELLENT GUIDE TO GTNP AND WAS A DETERMINED OPPONENT OF THE EXPANSION OF THE AIRPORT. WHEN IT CAME TO HER LAND IN KELLY, HOWEVER, SHE PAID LITTLE ATTENTION TO NPS REGULATION.

There are, of course, a number of restrictions on a life lease, but Bonney was not inclined to pay much attention to them. In June 1984, she allowed a friend to put up a yurt on her property. Clearly a violation of her lease, the yurt's presence provoked Superintendent Jack Stark to inform her that she must remove the yurt by the end of summer. Lorraine Bonney pleaded her case, maintaining that "one little yurt" could not be a problem and certainly could not be considered permanent. Perhaps giving a hint of the broader Kelly problem, Bonney argued that "only because of the trailer problem across the way did the park people realize there was a yurt here." Never one to mask her feelings, Bonney suggested to Stark and his administration: "I know you are not overly concerned with the NPS image in Kelly but this doesn't help it."

She was right. The superintendent was not sympathetic to her arguments. He reaffirmed his removal date of September 30. But then he went further, remarking that on closer inspection we "noted that a teepee had been erected on the lot and there appeared to be an automobile placed there which had not been moved for some time and was being utilized for storage." He requested that they be removed as well, and Bonney complied with all of Stark's requests. [57]

A RAPPROCHEMENT

By the 1990s, the park's aggressive attitude toward Kelly began to wane. With rising land values, it was clear that private land in Kelly was there to stay. It seemed unproductive to be in constant conflict with the good people of Kelly and their unorthodox ways. Kelly residents would dance to their own drummer. In 2007, Kelly's most prominent resident, author Ted Kerasote, wrote a best-selling book about his dog Merle.[58] As Kerasote describes him, Merle was a "free-thinking dog" that won the hearts of Kelly's citizenry.

MERLE AND KERASOTE

UP AT THE LAKE

A lake is always attractive, and lakeshore property is doubly so. Consequently the shoreline of Jackson Lake should have tempted cabin owners with its beauty and its recreational possibilities. Yet today, the shores of the lake have few structures. Why? A hostile winter environment and large expanses of willow flats and wetlands (looking out from Jackson Lake Lodge) discouraged home building. Moreover, Jackson Lake is misnamed. Although originally a glacially created lake, by 1907 a log crib dam stored reservoir water; it was soon to be replaced in 1911 with a substantial concrete dam. The Jackson Lake dam, enlarged in 1916, was part of the Bureau of Reclamation's Minidoka Project, designed to meet the needs of Idaho potato farmers.[59] There are always pros and cons in building a dam. Surely downstream irrigators profited, but the rising water in Jackson Lake inundated hundreds of acres of shoreline, creating a graveyard of unattractive dead trees. Maintaining an aesthetic shoreline was not among the Bureau of Reclamation priorities. In 1934, the young men of the Civilian Conservation Corps cut, piled and burned 17,000 cords of wood, but of course, they could not resolve the problem of a fluctuating water line.[60] Besides these environmental problems, the rather volatile relationship between the NPS and the U.S. Forest Service from 1920 to 1945 curtailed cabin building on the lake and elsewhere in northern Jackson Hole.

He roamed free and eventually became the unofficial "mayor" of the town. Of course, being within the park boundaries, Merle should have been on a leash, but he never knew the restraint of one, and no park ranger ever cited Kerasote or impounded Merle. In a way, Merle's life and relationship with the park symbolizes that of the human residents of Kelly, who respect the park but do not always feel constrained by its rules.

Today, figuring out who owns what in Kelly is difficult. Of the 63 original acres, 46 are in private hands, with the park owning the remaining 17 acres. The park continues to have a willing seller/willing buyer policy, but according to Grand Teton management assistant, Gary Pollock, buying up Kelly land is no longer a priority. Easing tensions has been good for both sides, and the failure to incorporate all of this private land can be attributed to mistakes and attitudes of many years ago.

JOHN DUDLEY SARGENT'S SECOND WIFE, EDITH SARGENT PLAYING VIOLIN AT THE MERYMERE LODGE. SHE LED A LONELY LIFE AT MERYMERE AND WAS KNOWN FOR SUNBATHING IN THE NUDE, OCCASIONALLY IN A TREE ON THE MILITARY ROAD TO YELLOWSTONE. SHE EVENTUALLY LEFT SARGENT AND MOVED TO CALIFORNIA.

There were some outposts of development. The town of Moran, located just below the dam, prospered briefly during construction then sank into oblivion. The Snake River Land Company eventually purchased Ben Sheffield's 106 slapdash Moran structures, either destroying or removing them. Today only a few foundation remnants remain.

The best known and most storied property on Jackson Lake was Merymere, homesteaded by John Sargent, an easterner and the illegitimate offspring of the painter John Singer Sargent. Given to drink and maniacal behavior, the family banished young Sargent to the West. There he turned his back on civilization, eventually laying claim to about 142 acres (proving up on his idyllic homestead in 1908), which now constitute the AMK Ranch. Sitting on a bluff overlooking Jackson Lake with the mountains spread to the south, the place, according to Struthers Burt, was "the finest for its view I have ever seen."[61]

No one can deny the truth of Burt's statement, yet the sublime view did not soothe Sargent's troubled mind. He had a few good years with his first wife, Adelaide, although her parents were very much opposed to the marriage.[62] When his friend Robert Hamilton visited, Sargent soon suspected an evolving love triangle with his wife. The outcome of that suspicion was that when Sargent and Hamilton were crossing the Snake River on horseback while looking for stray cattle, Hamilton took the wrong ford and drowned. A search party eventually found his body, signaling the others with a fire (and smoke) on the summit of a nearby hill—hence the name Signal Mountain.[63] There was much conjecture about murder, but Sargent was never brought to trial. He came under suspicion again when a soldier from Flagg Ranch stopped by Merymere and Sargent denied him entrance. He forced his way in to find Adelaide near death, seven months pregnant, and suffering two broken hips. She died in Rexburg, Idaho, after a toboggan ride to reach medical care in a severe snowstorm. Sargent was presumed to have flown into one of his rages, but he claimed the broken hips resulted from a ski injury. This time the strange man faced second degree murder charges, but in April 1900, the District Court in Evanston, Wyoming dismissed the case for lack of evidence.[64] Because there were no witnesses, Sargent again escaped prosecution. He soon left Merymere and did not return for seven years.

On his reappearance, the saga continued. Eventually, in 1906, he married Edith Drake, a woman who was mentally unstable. Rumor had it that her family paid Sargent to take care of her.[65] Whatever the case, she did have eccentric habits. Perhaps the most remembered was her penchant for sunbathing in the nude, occasionally sitting in a tree along the military road that led to Yellowstone. On the other hand, Edith was an accomplished violin player, and one of the most striking historical photographs from Jackson Hole is of her playing her instrument from their cabin verandawith the lake and mountains as backdrop. Edith was also sensible enough to leave Merymere for California, where she lived humbly, finally passing away in 1947.[66] Edith pleaded with John to come to California, but the despondent recluse could not pull himself away from his homestead. Sometime between June 27 and July 1, 1913, this sullen recluse rigged his Sharps 40-caliber rifle to fire into his mouth when he pressed the trigger with his toe. His death was probably on June 27, because when a discovery party entered his house, flies were numerous. According to Struthers Burt, they "had to use sulfur to get in."[67]

The future steps that led to the Park Service acquiring the AMK were less dramatic. William Johnson, a man of humble means who became an executive for the Hoover Vacuum Cleaner Company, picked up the property for back taxes. Although Edith and her daughter, Mary Sargent, contested his title, Johnson built a fine log home, which included a second-floor bedroom with a difficult stairway to accommodate his wife Mae, who feared bears. Johnson and his wife enjoyed the place, hunting, fishing, and horseback riding with friends and caretakers Slim and Verba Lawrence until 1931, when he died of a heart attack in New York City.

From 1931 until 1936, this secluded property remained part of the Johnson estate. Slim and Verba remained as caretakers, and if there was any constancy at the place, the two provided it. In 1936, Alfred Berolzheimer and his wife Madeleine purchased this storied property for $24,300. During the war years, Alfred changed the family name to Berol, and then proceeded to build the splendid Berol Lodge. As the president of the Eagle Pencil Company, Berol proved that if you make enough five-cent pencils, you can own an estate on the shores of Jackson Lake. It was not all fun, however. During this period Alfred began some rather frustrating, irrational correspondence with the Park Service. He worried about the erosion of the Jackson Lake shore below his lodge. Horace Albright disavowed responsibility, noting that the lake was under the jurisdiction of the Bureau of Reclamation, and he could do nothing. Berol also was apprehensive that the AMK might be condemned as part of the proposed extension of Grand Teton National Park. His fears were unfounded.[68]

AMK Ranch buildings

As a man of wealth, and never one to deny it, Berol used the lodge property for entertaining his eastern friends, and the lodge took on a very un-Jackson Hole appearance, with maids and cooks wearing uniforms which had to be clean, crisp, and pressed. This formality did not suit Slim and Verba Lawrence. Fortunately during the Berol years of 1936 to 1969, the family's average stay was two and a half months. The rest of the year, for all intents and purposes, it belonged to the Lawrences. Although they never owned land, Slim and Verba enjoyed the place without all the troubles and expenses of ownership.[69]

Meanwhile, the Park Service waited patiently for the chance to purchase the AMK property. That opportunity came in 1975, when Alfred's son Kenneth reached an agreement with the National Park Service. The selling price was $3.3 million for the 142-acre property. There were no conditions except that Ken Berol reserved a small house and one acre of land for Slim Lawrence to live out his life. He also made certain Slim would be buried on the property next to Verba.

But what to do with the magnificent buildings? Park officials produced a report outlining four options: (1) remove the buildings, (2) use them for government housing for summer employees, (3) convert them into a guest facility, or (4) turn them into a research and/or educational facility. Superintendent Robert Kerr favored option one, reasoning that this was the closest alternative "to a general NPS policy of removing buildings from acquired inholdings." Such a radical solution for this historic vacation retreat with such a rich history seemed unwarranted, and the "Regional Director . . . asked for a more varied list of alternatives to choose from." The park always needed seasonal housing, which represented a possibility. Some favored a guest facility, which might allow for the disestablishment of the Brinkerhoff unit further south on the shores of Jackson Lake, a cabin that offered little privacy or security for important guests.[70]

Use as a research and educational center won out, and today the University of Wyoming acts as a park partner to administer the center. Each summer the UW-NPS Research Center sponsors scientists from across the country involved with projects related to the park and the Greater Yellowstone area. To fulfill its educational imperative, each year Sue Consolo-Murphy, NPS Chief of Science and Resource Management, provides Director Hank Harlow with a "wish list" of possible projects for Grand Teton or the Greater Yellowstone area. Harlow does his best to bring in scientists who can help in the research and science mission of the park, although he is not restrained by the wish list. The park benefits, but so does the university and the public. Each Thursday evening the AMK Ranch hosts a scientific program along with a $5 hamburger dinner, which is always well attended by Jackson Hole people out for an evening ride and some intellectual stimulation in a spectacular setting. Professor Harlow retired in 2013, but the work of the research center will go on.

THE POLITICS OF DEVELOPMENT

Sometimes development or growth was not a matter of private land, but rather the policies of public land administrators. As is well known, there are two federal land agencies highly influential in the mountain West. The land surrounding Jackson Lake initially constituted part of the 829,440-acre Teton National Forest. In effect, it was the Forest Service that determined just how the land would be utilized and developed until 1943. They generally followed a policy of sustained yield, multiple use, with few strictures against commercial development. Early in the century, however, northern Jackson Hole was essentially a wilderness area with hunting, some cattle raising, and activities associated with the new Jackson Lake Dam. From the moment the soon-to-be NPS Director Stephen Mather and Assistant Director Horace Albright viewed the range in 1915, they set their sights on Jackson Hole as part of the National Park System. The Forest Service faced a formidable new agency with different ideas about Jackson Hole's values. In the next few years the two agencies developed an adversarial relationship. The National Park Service was aggressive, focusing on a preservation ethic, which often conflicted with the stance of the Forest Service regarding the same land. Olympic National Park, Grand Canyon National Park, Rocky Mountain National Park, and Grand Teton were all carved from lands once managed by the U.S. Forest Service.

In Jackson Hole, the NPS advocated for transfer of Forest Service lands to its care. In April 1918, NPS Director Mather and Assistant Director Albright prevailed on Congressman Frank Mondell of Wyoming to introduce H.R. 11661, a bill to extend Yellowstone National Park to the south. It would have placed the Teton Range, Jackson Lake, the smaller glacial lakes at the base of the mountains, and the land north of Buffalo Fork under the Yellowstone National Park umbrella. Congress took no action, but in February 1919, Mondell introduced a slightly revised bill (H.R. 13350). At the last moment, however, Senator John Nugent of Idaho objected, killing the bill.[71]

Although incorporation of the Tetons into a national park would have to wait another decade, the Park Service had gained an important foothold in the Jackson Lake area. In anticipation of passage of the 1918–19 bill, President Woodrow Wilson issued an executive order withdrawing all forms of private land entry or disposal of 600,000 acres within Teton National Forest. As mentioned, the bill failed, but Wilson did not rescind his executive order. The net effect was that the NPS had "veto power" over Forest Service plans in the area. Acting Chief Forester L. F. Kneipp vigorously protested this "right of review," but the Park Service refused to relinquish its advantage.[72]

In Jackson Hole, meanwhile, Forest Service Supervisor A. C. McCain was determined to fend off the NPS. His *modus operandi* was not to attack the NPS directly but to stress to local people the economic advantages of his agency's leadership. Trees could be harvested, minerals could be mined, and cows would graze. Most important was his advocacy of summer home leases along the shores of Jackson Lake. In his rashest moment, he estimated that some 6,000 summer cottages (not all on the lake), paying an average annual property tax of $14 a year, could bring in $84,000 a year for the cash-strapped county.[73]

Initiating this plan, of course, required the cooperation of the National Park Service, and McCain made it clear to locals that only the NPS stood in the way of summer cabins on Jackson Lake, producing a lower tax rate structure. To put it another way, only the resistance of the NPS prevented a situation where Jackson Lake might soon resemble a busy lake resort.

When the Park Service refused to endorse the summer home plan, a near catastrophe was averted. Although, Supervisor A. C. McCain did manage to issue six Forest Service leases before northern Jackson Hole became part of Jackson Hole National Monument in March 1943. The famous Hollywood film actor, Wallace Beery, received one in June 1942, but we know little about his lease or the fate of his cabin. The Forest Service issued another lease to Ben Sheffield, the former owner of the town of Moran, at a fee of $25 a year. In 1946, Sheffield transferred his lease to R. E. McConaughlin, who then conveyed the lease to Zack Brinkerhoff. Brinkerhoff tore down the existing shack and built an exceptional cabin that now occupies the site. Brinkerhoff made his money in oil, and when he moved from Casper to Denver in 1955, the cabin no longer met his needs. He was determined to sell, and when the park failed to meet his price, he placed an ad in a national real estate newsletter describing the cabin as a "Luxurious Lodge in Grand Teton National Park." It was offered at $70,000, a price that included a 33-foot Chris-Craft cabin cruiser and two speed boats. The ad also noted that "no more such sites are available." The threat of a private sale motivated the park. Eventually Brinkerhoff accepted their offer of $54,000. In a separate transaction, the Jackson Hole Preserve, Inc. purchased the Chris-Craft boats for $16,000. In a roundabout way, Zack Brinkerhoff received his asking price of $70,000. The cabin cruiser was renamed the *Queen* and became an attractive excursion boat for park visitors.[74]

Other purchases of the six Forest Service leases on the lake went very well. Josephine Brown's family built a modest cabin on their lease. In 1975, the family decided it was time to give up the place. At their departure, Josephine wrote to tell Superintendent Robert Kerr that she hoped the park could "salvage or use the old cabin in some way." In her heart of hearts, she knew that would not happen and that destruction would be the cabin's fate. In that case, she hoped, "all the wild life and flowers etc. will soon cover up the scars made by the use of man."[75]

From a legal perspective, the most interesting Forest Service lease on the lake is that of the Linderman family. The one-half-acre Linderman site had been issued in January 1940 to V. R. Madsen. Madsen died in 1948 and Katherine and D. H. Linderman became the new lease owners. In July 1949, the couple received a special use permit and prepared to build a cabin. Under the 1950 Act establishing the park, the new regulations guaranteed the family and their heirs the right to renew the lease. At that time Katherine and D. H. listed their two sons as their "natural issue" but also their three grandchildren, Shayne, Carol, and Catherine.

For many years, the family enjoyed the use of their Jackson Lake cabin. In time, the only listed family member still living was the youngest granddaughter, Catherine. In the 1990s, the park raised the question of whether she was entitled to have the lease renewed under her name. At issue was whether Catherine, born on August 6, 1950, legitimately squeaked under the established deadline of September 1950, and also whether she was indeed the "natural issue" of Katherine and D. H. Linderman. Could grandchildren be treated legally as "natural issue"?

The Park Service, for reasons not easily deciphered, decided that Catherine, a practicing anesthesiologist in Idaho Falls, had no legitimate claim for renewal of the lease. In 2000 and 2001, she corresponded regularly with Management Assistant George Helfrich, Acting Superintendent Steve Iobst, and Superintendent Jack Neckels. In the meantime, Catherine continued to enjoy her cabin and even made modest improvements. When it seemed apparent that the Park Service leaders were not going to back down, Catherine Linderman hired attorney Brad Mead of Jackson, and soon after, attorney Dave Nicholas of Laramie. Facing a formidable legal team, the park reconsidered its position.

In the summer of 2011 when I ran into Management Assistant Gary Pollock and Deputy Superintendent Bob Vogel, it was a good opportunity to ask about the Linderman case, since the written record had gone dry. They both explained that the case was on the so-called "back burner." Catherine Linderman continues to occupy her cabin, and the Park Service has chosen not to take action as of this writing. Linderman is in the enviable position of not paying any annual lease fee for her place, because the park cannot accept payment. To do so would be to admit that the lease is valid. Meanwhile, Catherine Linderman seems destined to enjoy her cabin for many more years.[76]

THERE IS A MISTAKEN ASSUMPTION that in 1950 the Snake River Land Company delivered the park as we know it today. No one would disparage the impressive gift that John, Jr. and his son Laurance

Rockefeller made to the nation, allowing dramatic expansion of the park. Yet there remained much work to be done in securing more privately owned land and state property within Grand Teton National Park in the years following transfer from monument to park status.

For more than 50 years, park superintendents and their staffs have purchased, negotiated, threatened, and compromised to bring private land into the park. Acquiring land and structures has usually been expensive. Often landowners have had the upper hand, able within reason to dictate their price. Most negotiated life leases, promising to hand over the land and structures in good shape but rarely doing so. Properties often came into federal control needing repair or replacement of the infrastructure. Such inconveniences notwithstanding, the life lease system allowed the park to acquire land and structures that might otherwise have been impossible to purchase. Today, some of the wonderful old ranches, such as the 4 Lazy F, are being partially restored for summer use. Many ranch sites remain unused because the Park Service lacks the funds to refurbish or rehabilitate them.

Although costly and sometimes frustrating, over the years the huge job of transforming the park's private lands into public lands has largely been achieved. Just a few private parcels remain, consisting of a total of 946 acres, plus two state school sections totaling 1,280 acres, or two square miles. To change from 13,296 acres in private land in 1950 to just 946 today is a positive success ratio. The largest private piece is the

450-acre Pinto Ranch, located in the northeast corner of the park. A family holding, it could impact the park should young members forsake livestock for tourist development or for a subdivision. Perhaps the most valuable private land holding is the 120-acre Moosehead Ranch, homesteaded in 1924 by Eva Topping and located in a superb position to view the Cathedral group of the Teton peaks. It is not likely that the park will be able to acquire this stunning property. Purchased in 1967, for $500,000 by the John Mettler family, it is managed as an upscale dude ranch. Such a use is certainly compatible with the

MOOSEHEAD RANCH GUESTS

mission of Grand Teton National Park; thus while there is no foreseeable risk, there are no guarantees. Management Assistant Gary Pollock is fully aware of the possibility of adjustments in ownership.

Farther south is the commercial enterprise of Dornans. As earlier noted, there have been plenty of disagreements between park administrators and the Dornan family, but they have smoothed out over the years, and the store, restaurants, and bar serve a useful role for visitors and local residents alike. The community of Kelly, with its interesting assortment of residents, also seems to have made peace with the park.

All in all, there exist only a few scattered parcels of private lands. They do not pose a problem, yet Grand Teton is not yet a perfect park. Gary Pollock believes that further opportunities to make the park whole may yet materialize.[77]

[1] This acreage figure comes from Superintendent Jack Stark who in 1981 testified that in 1950 13,296 acres were in private hands. In 1981 that figure was more than cut in half: 8,370 acres acquired, with 4,926 acres still in private hands. U.S. Congress, Senate, *Joint Hearing before the Subcommittee on Public Lands and Reserved Water of the Committee on Energy and Agricultural Taxation of the Committee on Finances*, 77th Cong., 1st Session, 1981, Jackson, Wyoming.

[2] Conrad L. Wirth, *Parks, Politics, and the People* (Norman: University of Oklahoma Press, 1980), 198.

[3] On Indiana Dunes National Lakeshore see *National Parks: Index, 1999–2001* (Washington, D.C.: U.S. Department of the Interior, 1999), 44. The Grand Teton National Park archives (hereafter cited as GTNP) contain 33 archival boxes of land records, plus a finding aid. They are superbly organized, as such important records should be. With such a volume of material, I was not able to examine every land transfer folder.

[4] Data from "Mission 66 Prospectus, Grand Teton National Park, April 20, 1956," copy in possession of the author. Given the date of this prospectus, it is mainly written in the future tense, but given the popularity of the program, I believe all these plans and protections were carried out. In regard to the discrepancies in private land holdings, I believe that the 6,468 acre figure did not include state lands,

[5] *Management Policies, 2006*, National Park Service, 1.4.1, 10.

[6] Frank Oberthansley, memo to Regional Director, August 29, 1955, GTNP, Land Records, box 16, series 1.4, folder 023.

[7] See *http://www.nps.gov/grte/historyculture/murie.htm*. The other national historic landmark is the Jackson Lake Lodge.

[8] Correspondence and notes are in GTNP, Land Records, box 16, series 1.4, folder 31, Clyde and Genevieve Kranenberg.

[9] GTNP, Land Records, box 16, series 1.4, folder 023, Robert and Katherine Perkins.

[10] For correspondence and documents see GTNP, Land Records, box 16, series 1.4, folder 034, William Fife and Francis Gordon.

[11] The Ridenour story is constructed from GTNP, Land Records, box 15, series 1.4, folder 025, Charles Ridenour.

[12] Albert Schwabacher was a wealthy San Franciscan who owned a parcel of land that is now the Lost Creek Ranch.

[13] "The Bet I Made With Uncle Sam," in J. R. Jones, *Preserving the Game in the Vanishing West* (Boise, Id.: Hemingway Western Studies Center, 1989), 95–108.

[14] Interviews with Lyle McReynolds by author, December 8, 2012, November 25, 2013; also GTNP, Land Records, series 1.4, folder 054.1, McReynolds et al.

[15] Jack Stark, Superintendent, Memo to the Files, July 1, 1981. We also have Mary McReynolds's recollection of this telephone conversation in a letter to her son Roland. Both are in GTNP, Land Records, series 1.4, folder 054.1, McReynolds et al.

[16] Stark memo and Mary McReynolds letter, GTNP, Land Records, series 1.4, folder 054.1, McReynolds et al.

[17] GTNP, Land Records, series 1.4, folder 054.1, McReynolds et al.

[18] John Pattie, February 7 and 9 memos to the files; B. J. McReynolds to Regional Director Lorraine Mintzmeyer, March 28, 1984; Mintzmeyer to B. J. McReynolds, April 9, 1984, all in GTNP, Land Records, series 1.4, folder 054.2, McReynolds et al.

[19] B. J. McReynolds to John Pattie, January 6, 1983; John Pattie to B. J. McReynolds, January 13, 1983, both in GTNP, Land Records, series 1.4, folder 054.1, McReynolds et al.

[20] More details of the decision can be found in Donald Rosendort, Attorney, Land Acquisition Section, U.S. Dept. of Justice, to David Watts, Assistant Solicitor, Parks and Recreation, Office of the Solicitor, Washington, July 20, 1987; note to Jack Start, both in GTNP, Land Records, series 1.4, folder 054.2, McReynolds et al.

[21] Interview with Lyle McReynolds by author, November 25, 2013.

[22] Bonnie Kreps, *Windows to the Past: Early Settlers in Jackson Hole* (Jackson: Jackson Hole Historical Society and Museum, 2006), 146-55.

[23] Sherry L. Smith, "A Woman's Life in the Teton Country: Geraldine L. Lucas," *Montana: The Magazine of Western History,* 44 (Summer 1994): 26–27.

[24] C. S. Dietz to Register and Receiver, United States Land Office, Evanston, Wyoming. Approved for Patent, March 26, 1927, Serial No. 09075, Patent No. 999739, General Land Office Records, National Archives.

[25] Ellen Dornan, interview by JoAnne Byrd (typescript), October 6, 1982, Jackson Hole Historical Society and Museum.

[26] Kreps, *Windows to the Past,* 158. For more of the relationship between Evelyn and her son Jack, see Kreps, 158, 162-3.

[27] Superintendent Edward Freeland to Director Conrad Wirth, September 29, 1952, in GTNP, Land Records, Series 1.4, Folder 041, Evelyn Dornan.

[28] Superintendent Edward Freeland to Regional Director Howard Baker, October 2, 1952; also Director Conrad Wirth to Reg. Director Howard Baker, November 3, 1952, in GTNP, Land Records, Series 1.4, Folder 041, Evelyn Dornan.

[29] Superintendent Fred Fagergren, Letter to Region Two, April 15, 1965, GTNP, Land Records, series 1.4, folder 041, Evelyn Dornan.

[30] GTNP, Land Records, series 1.3, folder 11, 12, Leland and Elizabeth Curtis. Unfortunately, Leland made a serious mistake when he put only himself as the retainer of a life lease. He died before Elizabeth, causing her to lose the place to the park before she would have wished.

[31] Charlie Craighead, interview by author, September 25, 2012.

[32] Ibid.

[33] GTNP, Land Records, box 13, series 1.4, folder 014, Craighead et al.

34 The Craigheads had sold at least two other lots to Reginald and Gladys Laubins, well-known for their Indian dancing, and the Rudd family. It should be mentioned that the Craighead property existed before the highway which bisected their view.

35 GTNP, Land Records, box 13, series 1.4, folder 017, Craighead et al.

36 Charlie Craighead, interview by author, September 25, 2012.

37 Ibid.

38 GTNP, Land Records, box 13, series 1.4, folder 009, Shirley Craighead; Charlie Craighead, interview by author, September 25, 2012.

39 GTNP, Land Records, box 1, series 1.1, folder 6, Fred and Lisa Abercrombie et al.

40 Ibid.

41 Constructed from GTNP, Land Records, box 17, series 1.4, folder 040, Emily Oliver. Also see GTNP, Cultural Landscapes Inventory 2011, 4 Lazy F Ranch.

42 Information from Katherine Longfield, Cultural Resources Specialist, January 16, 2013.

43 GTNP, Land Records, box 21, series 1.5, folder 018, Harvard College. In 2001 the family established the Senator Joseph S. Clark Chair of Ethics in Politics and Government, held at the time of writing by Nancy Lipton Rosenblum. See *http://scholar.harvard.edu/nrosenblum/*. Additional information from Management Assistant Gary Pollock and Cultural Resources Katherine Wonson.

44 GTNP, Land Records, box 21, series 1.5, folder 019, Marvel Lesher.

45 GTNP, Land Records, box 23, series 1.5, folder 028, Paul and Ester McCollister.

46 She also published a well received book on the subject. See Renee Askins, *Shadow Mountain: A Memoir of Wolves, a Woman, and the Wild* (New York: Doubleday, 2002).

47 GTNP, Land Records, box 23, series 1.5, folder 028, Paul and Ester McCollister. For Superintendent Stark's correspondence with McCollister see GTNP, Grazing, box 2, series 003.1, folder 013. Also information from Cultural Resources Specialist Katherine Longfield,

48 John Daugherty, *A Place Called Jackson Hole* (Moose: Grant Teton National Park, 1999), 210-12.

49 Gary Pollock, NPS, conversation with author, June 9, 2011.

50 Box 27 in the GTNP, Land Records contains 32 folders regarding Kelly land issues.

51 Secretary of the Interior Rogers C. B. Morton to NPS Director, April 25, 1975; Director to Regional Director, May 13, 1975, both in the appendix of "Boundary Study," Grand Teton National Park, September, 1975.

52 "Boundary Study," Grand Teton National Park, September, 1975, 44-5.

53 Secretary of the Interior Morton to Director, NPS, April 25, 1975, appendix to "Boundary Study."

54 GTNP, Land Records, box 27, series 1.7, folder 44, James Beyer.

55 GTNP, Land Records, box 27, series 1.7, folder 47, Dean and Iris Driskell.

56 GTNP, Land Records, box 32, series 1.9, folder 33, Rob Hinchee.

57 GTNP, Land Records, box 27, series 1.7, folder 45, Orrin and Lorraine Bonney.

58 Ted Kerasote, *Merle's Door: Lessons from a Freethinking Dog* (New York: Harcourt Books, 2007).

59 It should be noted that the Bureau of Reclamation regulates only the top 39 feet of Jackson Lake. Below that depth is controlled by the NPS.

60 See *www.usbr.gov/projects/Jackson Lake Dam*. Also Righter, *Crucible for Conservation*, 90

61 Maxwell Struthers Burt, *The Diary of a Dude-Wrangler* (1924; New York: Charles Scribner's Sons, 1938), 267.

62 Many of the details of Sargent and his wives and tragedies are told in Kenneth Lee Diem, Lenore L. Diem, and William C. Lawrence, *A Tale of Dough Gods, Bear Grease, Cantaloupe and Sucker Oil* Oil (Moran: University of Wyoming-National Park Research Center, 1986). Bizarre title notwithstanding, the authors revealed much new information on Sargent's life.

63 Daugherty, *A Place Called Jackson Hole*, 185.

64 Diem et al., *A Tale of Dough Gods*, 18.

65 Ibid., 29.

66 Burt, *Diary of a Dude Wrangler*, 274–77; Diem et al., *A Tale of Dough Gods*, 30–32.

67 Burt, *Diary of a Dude-Wrangler*, 277.

68 Diem et al., *A Tale of Dough Gods.*, 49–51; Sherry L. Smith, "A Woman's Life in the Teton Country," Annals of Wyoming, vol. 71 (Summer 1999), 35-43. By 1936 Horace Albright had resigned from the NPS, so perhaps he wrote Berol as a friend.

69 Smith, "A Woman's Life in the Teton Country," 35-43.

70 GTNP, Land Records, box 28, series 1.8, folder 06, Kenneth Berol. The NPS Berol Report is in folder 06.

71 See Robert W. Righter, *Crucible for Conservation: The Struggle for Grand Teton National Park* (Boulder: Colorado University Press, 1982; repr., Moose, Wyo.: Grand Teton Association, 2000) , 28.

72 Ibid.

73 Ibid., 68–69.

74 Compiled from GTNP, Land Records, box 30, series 1.8, folder 23, Zack and Jeanne Brinkerhoff.

75 GTNP, Land Records, box 33, series 1.10, folder 023, Brown et al. The smaller Chris-Craft boats were no doubt taken to the JY Ranch on Phelps Lake.

76 GTNP, Land Records, box 31, series 1.8, folders 30.1, 30.2, 30.3, Catherine L. Linderman.

77 Gary Pollock, NPS administrator, interview by author, June 9, 2011.

PEAKS, POLITICS, AND PASSION: GRAND TETON NATIONAL PARK COMES OF AGE

Chapter 3.

Private Rights on Public Land

IN DECEMBER 1972, a young Grand Teton National Park ranger published an article in the *Progressive* magazine titled "Senator Hansen's Cattle in the Park." Author Bernard Shanks' opening sentence read: "Cattle don't belong in the national parks, especially in Wyoming's Grand Teton National Park, one of the greatest landscapes of the West." The article lambasted U.S. Senator Cliff Hansen, claiming that he and "his cronies continued to graze their cattle on the park lands, using permits that were never legally established." In regard to the law, Shanks was wrong, but the article did bring from the shadows to the light another of the compromises and ongoing issues that has made Grand Teton a less-than-natural park.[1]

Shanks represented a new sensitivity and political activism toward the environment. Influenced by his friendship with the Muries, and honed by the emerging environmental movement, he could not restrain himself. The United States was changing, and if one were to pick a date to signal that change it would be April 22, 1970. On that first Earth Day, some 20 million Americans gathered to protest in cities across the country industrial pollution, gas-guzzling automobiles, the 1969 Santa Barbara oil spill, and a host of other abuses against nature and a sustainable environment. Grand Teton National Park was not immune from the new scrutiny. Whether insecticide spraying, highway construction, airport expansion, or cattle grazing, park policies would be questioned by advocates of the rising environmental movement. The park could never be an island to itself, separated from outside forces.

This chapter focuses on one of those issues: grazing. It examines cattlemen, their cows, their western image, their political power, and particularly their relationship to Grand Teton National Park. Once so prominent, cattle in the park have, with the passage of time, grown scarce and have now nearly disappeared. In the late nineteenth century, cattle barons, many of them English or Scottish, ruled the vast plains of Wyoming. The region was public domain, open to all who had the fortitude, power, and capital to spread vast cattle herds across vast landscapes. Cattlemen controlled not only the land, but also the political system in Cheyenne after Wyoming became

a state in 1890. Many of the governors, senators, and congressmen made their living from the range. They brought their skills, knowledge, and determination into the state capital.[2] Eventually the livestock industry had to share power with the mineral industry, but the two often view environmental issues and the national parks in a similar light.

GRAZING PRIVILEGES

In the first half of the 20th century the Wyoming cattle industry contributed impressively to the economy and shaped the character of Jackson Hole. After 1950, a declining market hurt the cattle ranchers. They began to lose their hold on the country, replaced by the vibrant tourist business. Yet, the cattle industry has continued to wield influence through tradition, its commitment to open space, and its appeal to advocates of the rugged outdoor lifestyle. The industry, its horses, cattle, and cowboys, has become synonymous with the state. But an icon does not necessarily pay the

bills. By the late 1940s, the business of tourism was burgeoning with alarming swiftness. A team of University of Wyoming economists in 1959 estimated that 72 percent of Teton County's income came from tourism.[3] Yet the cattle interests remained powerful. It has taken almost 60 years for Jackson Hole's indigenous wildlife to regain their share of the rangeland. Today elk, antelope, bison, bears and even wolves predominate, while cattle have been gradually eliminated.

There are, however, a large number of residents of Jackson Hole who believe that cattle grazing is a legitimate use of park land. In the year 2000, park officials invited the public to comment on their "Grazing Environmental Assessment" document. Although some agreed with the sentiments that "Grazing should not be allowed in GTNP; it violates the purpose and principles of a national park," many others disagreed. Here are a few of the views:

Continue grazing in Grand Teton National Park as an historic resource.

Extend all grazing permits as an important way of life, and as a means to preserve open space.

Ranchers need park lands to be viable. Ranching is a part of Jackson Hole's heritage.

Grazing is an acceptable use of park lands. Emphasize historic values and appreciation of ranching in the park.

Manage grazed lands in accordance with laws and considering the long-term interest in open space.[4]

All these thoughtful comments have legitimacy, but let us use the last comment as a segue into both history and the law. Starting in 1897 the U.S. Forest Service managed the Teton Range and northern Jackson Hole. They leased out grazing land to Jackson Hole ranchers. When in 1943 this land became part of the Jackson Hole National Monument, ranchers became concerned that they might lose their leases. So they defiantly drove their cattle across the national monument. They needn't have worried. The Park Service, the object of much hostility, had no intention of cancelling the Forest Service leases. In fact, at that time, NPS policy did not systematically oppose grazing. Grazing rights had been acknowledged in 1918, when Secretary of Interior Franklin Lane published a letter outlining the National Park Service basic creed. That letter, addressed to park supervisors, stated that in "all of the national parks except Yellowstone you may permit the grazing of cattle in isolated regions not frequented by visitors, and where no injury to the natural features of the park may result from such use."[5] One might quibble about whether the Teton's northern lands, mostly the "Potholes" region, were "frequented by visitors," but most reasonable people would agree that this open, sagebrush-covered region saw little visitation except on a drive-by basis.

The 1950 Grand Teton National Park Act, then, clarified and codified the rights of Jackson Hole ranchers to continue grazing in the newly expanded park. The act had, of course, been a bundle of compromises, and one of the key players in negotiations was the capable Teton County Commissioner Clifford Hansen. At a three-day conference in April 1949, a working committee of six people hammered out the most difficult issues of the park bill.[6] Grazing was not among the controversial ones. NPS Acting Director Arthur Demaray quickly conceded grazing privileges.[7] Thus the final act signed into law on September 14, 1950, guaranteed that all leases and permits issued by the Forest Service would be honored by the new park administration for 25 years. After that time they could be renewed during the lifetime of the lessee, as well as the lifetimes of "heirs, successors, or assigns but only if they were members of his immediate family on such dates, as determined by the Secretary of the Interior." The act specified that grazing rights for inholder ranchers would not be withdrawn until title to the land was vested to the United States. Until that occurred, if it ever did, the law guaranteed grazing rights in perpetuity.[8]

Arthur Demaray apparently saw grazing as a necessary concession, not an issue he would contest. The long, tedious, tortuous effort to get Grand Teton National Park into the system would not be sacrificed for any non-grazing principle. Demaray had long endured the struggle to establish the park and as the time of triumph drew near, he simply would not be deterred by the issue. Furthermore, Park Service personnel were not united either in opposition to or in support of grazing. Like former NPS Director Arno Cammerer, Demaray believed in the art of the possible and park legislation without grazing rights was impossible. In time the NPS would reassess its stance, but in 1950 cattle grazing would be allowed. When it was worked out, the park issued a total of 29 permits to ranchers, large and small.

From the outset, the rules allowed the park to retire a number of the leases. There would be no automatic transfer of grazing rights from one owner to another. Also, if the owner of a grazing right sold land before the 25-year time period was up, period was up, the remaining years transferred to the new owner, but that was it. The lease would be canceled after that time. Further, grazing fees were to be paid in advance. The annual fee policy conformed to that of Teton National Forest, calculated on the basis of animal unit months (AUMs), defined as "one animal grazing for thirty days, or one month." The park superintendent reserved the right to declare an overgrazing situation and reduce the number of grazing cattle for each permittee.[9]

In issuing the new grazing permits the park requested specific numbers of livestock for each rancher. It was the beginning of a new bureaucracy to which ranchers had to adjust. Some ranchers could provide the necessary data; others could not. Dude rancher Coulter Huyler confessed that he could not provide what the park wanted. Huyler, a friend to the park, admitted that he "was awfully sorry that I haven't the records necessary to fill in items 3 and 4 intelligently, except that during that period we have always run from thirty to fifty horses and for one or two years had a grazing permit for one hundred head of cattle." With his verbal assurances, Huyler received his permit, but it did not last long. In 1953, a memo to the superintendent of Grand Teton from Regional Director Howard Baker advised that after much research there was "no justification for giving further recognition to Mr. Huyler's grazing preference in the Park." Baker advised that the matter be discussed with Huyler, but by that time, his son Jack Huyler was running the operation and would soon sell to the park and give up the dude ranch business.[10]

The park administration was tougher on some residents than others. In a folder titled "Trespass Grazing, Jack D. Dornan," a memo from Acting Regional Director James Lloyd, dated June 22, 1950, commands the superintendent to get Dornan's cattle off federal land and remove them from the airport area, "where they were a hazard to aircraft using the runway." The memo further questions whether Dornan was entitled to any grazing preference. The superintendent asked Dornan to justify his claim.[11] Of course he could not, for although he frequently let his cattle roam north of the airport, there was no record of his owning any grazing leases on federal or Rockefeller land. This was just one of a number of disputes in which a fairly exacting bureaucracy began to impose restrictions on a formerly laissez-faire system.

Occasionally park leaders proved more amenable to working with lessees, even bending the grazing rules slightly if it suited their long-term objective of acquiring land. In one case, the NPS wished to acquire the Half Moon Ranch, a guest ranch inholding for young girls, pleasantly located on Cottonwood Creek. Anita Tarbell, an educator from the East, owned the place. Charles Guss, a friend and teacher unrelated to Tarbell, assisted her. Tarbell, an enterprising educator, lured the park administrators into special favors by suggesting that it would not be long before she relinquished the place, and she certainly would consider selling to the park. With such vague promises, she was able to increase her grazing allotment and also divert water by ditch to that allotment area. When a special water access problem surfaced on the ranch, she explained her need, and she soon received a letter from Conrad Wirth, Director of the NPS, assuring her that he would look into the matter by assigning a special water rights expert. Wirth ended his letter with an appeal that he was sure "you realize how deeply the Service feels that your ranch should eventually be made a part of the Park, and we, at the same time, appreciate your sincere interest in the Park and its objectives."[12]

Anita Tarbell died in 1963, still owner of the Half Moon Ranch. Her original grazing permits should have remained with the land in perpetuity. However the Park Service, transferred to Charles Guss both the revised grazing permit and a special use permit to use 300 acres adjacent to the ranch. Surely the Half Moon

HALF MOON RANCH ON COTTONWOOD CREEK

Ranch original grazing right was transferable to Guss, but the grazing changes and the 300-acre special use permit were questionable. Ranger Bernard Shanks reviewed the revised grazing permit and special use permit and determined they were not valid, so he recommended termination of the Half Moon Ranch grazing permits. However, as noted above, Superintendents Jack Anderson and Howard Chapman, as well as NPS Director Conrad Wirth, all wanted to buy the ranch, and the questionable grazing permits helped put pressure on Guss to sell.[13] In 1967, the park purchased the Half Moon Ranch land and cabins for $663,000.[14]

The Half Moon Ranch was a high priority property, and the price the park paid for it reflects its valuable west side location along a picturesque creek and near the current Bradley/Taggart Lakes parking lot. The NPS wanted restoration of the Cottonwood Creek bottom land, removal of all cows and other livestock, and permanent retirement of all grazing permits. By the mid-1960s, it was becoming obvious that livestock were not welcome, particularly in areas of high visitor density.

Up North in the Sagebrush

Cattle would primarily remain in the northern part of the park, encompassing the Potholes expanse, the Elk Ranch area, and the Moran region. In fact, the four largest permits were in the northern section. Bruce Porter, Ralph Gill, Arthur Brown, and Clifford Hansen grazed 1,154 cows on a vast 83,500-acre sagebrush-covered area known as the Potholes. These ranchers organized themselves into the Potholes-Moran Grazing Association. Rancher E. Cockrell, owner of the Pinto Ranch, also supported the association. Unlike these others, however, Cockrell's Pinto Ranch was located within the park boundary, so his permit was different. Under the 1950 Act, he and his heirs retained grazing privileges in perpetuity unless or until the ranch became park-owned. It remains privately owned to this day.

Throughout the 1950s, the Potholes-Moran ranchers drove their livestock each summer from south and west of Jackson into the northern Potholes region, southeast of Jackson Lake. The early summer and fall cattle drives were popular with tourists, providing a glimpse of the old West. But the arrangement in the Potholes was not working well. The ranchers were both critical and demanding of the Park Service. Fences needed to be built and repaired, cattle needed to be protected from the occasional predator, and marginal land needed to be improved. From the Park Service perspective, cattle spread over this vast region presented unique problems. Some tourists may have been disappointed to find cattle where they might reasonably expect to see such wildlife as elk, deer, coy-

Photo by Henry Holdsworth

ELK RANCH

otes, and an occasional bear. Clearly cattle offered competition with wildlife. Further, overgrazing occurred in some of the delicate vegetation, as well as on the dry sagebrush flats.

Given the situation, Grand Teton administrators approached the ranchers with a proposal. If they would give up the Potholes region, the park would provide fenced and irrigated pasture land elsewhere sufficient to support their cattle. The alternative lands would be mainly on the Elk Ranch, a level spread of hundreds of acres of well-watered grassland east of the Snake River. The trade was agreeable to the ranchers, for the abundant grass would certainly fatten the cattle, and they could keep track of their roaming herds better than in the wilds of the Potholes region.[15] Cattle would now be in full view of tourists traveling the main highway, but in an irrigated setting.

The relationship between the park and the ranchers, however, did not improve with the new grazing pasture. In essence, the two sides viewed the grazing arrangement differently. As noted, ranchers referred to their permits as rights, while park personnel preferred to call them privileges. The distinction had no legal meaning, but it could color a conversation or alter an attitude. In response to rancher criticism, Superintendent Harthon L. Bill wrote to Hansen, Porter, and Brown that he hoped they realized the added expense of moving the lease from "open range" to "fenced pasture." He assured the ranchers that Grand Teton would make every effort to carry out its obligations, but funds were short. Such a general statement meant that mending fences or clearing irrigation ditches might happen on the park's timetable, not theirs. He did assure the grazers of his confidence that "in the future [adjustments] can be mutually and cooperatively arranged."[16] But civility and necessity both characterized and prompted the letter. Ranchers knew that all the cards were not in their hands, and probably a few were aware that the 1962 park master plan had called for continued grazing only "until it can be eliminated entirely," signaling a sea change in attitude that had not characterized earlier interactions.[17]

Tensions percolated at the meeting of the Pothole-Moran Grazing Association in August 1967. The ranchers had "not been pleased with the current arrangement" at the Elk Ranch area. Unless their list of grievances was met, they warned, "they may give serious consideration to returning to the Pot Holes Allotment." The Park Service representative did not take kindly to this veiled threat, pointing out to them that "throughout the life of this permit the Service had invested approximately $260,000 in providing irrigated fenced pasture," while the "fees collected on the first nine years totaled approximately $30,750." By any scale, this was an impressive commitment of public funds to benefit private economic interests. In regard to the fences, the government built them, but condition #14 of their agreement stated that permittees were supposed to maintain them. They had not done so. The minutes of their meeting suggested that the park would have to raise permit fees. Whether they did or not is not clear.[18]

COWS, POLITICS, AND THE LAW

Further inflaming the relationship, Ranger Bernard Shanks began reviewing the Potholes-Moran Grazing Association permits. Shanks was brilliant, relentless, committed, unafraid, and perhaps a little reckless. After reviewing Arthur Brown's livestock permit in 1967, he concluded that Brown had "no apparent legal basis for [his] permit." It apparently resulted from local hostilities toward the monument, political pressure and war production efforts. Honoring this permit had cost the government over $200,000. Shanks recommended that it should be "reduced or terminated."[19] It is not likely that Shanks' recommendation was ever made public, for Brown continued to graze his cattle in the park. But in 1978, he subdivided and sold his ranch land which was located outside the park, thus terminating his grazing privilege.[20]

Disappointed with the park administrator's failure to take action on the Brown permit, Shanks took an independent course when his review of grazing permits revealed discrepancies. He would "go public" as he did with the *Progressive* article. This would be a dangerous move, but Shanks was a young idealist who worked hard, loved the mountains, and embraced the Park Service mission to protect its resources. He took up mountain climbing when he was in college, then worked as a smoke jumper for the Forest Service in Alaska. While in Alaska he met Mardy Murie, and also her husband Olaus' brother, Adolph. They encouraged him to apply to Grand Teton as a ranger. No doubt they also told him of the long controversy to establish the park, as well as his ethical responsibility to expose any wrongdoing.[21]

Even before Shanks' article appeared in the *Progressive,* former Governor and U.S. Senator Cliff Hansen faced scrutiny for his cattle interests in the park from the developing environmental movement. In response to hard questions from David Brower's environmental group Friends of the Earth, Grand Teton Superintendent Howard Chapman explained and defended Senator Hansen's legal right based on the transfer of his Forest Service permit to that of the Park Service, as defined in the 1950 legislation.[22] Shanks, of course, was reading the record differently. He did not believe that the transfer of Hansen's lease from the Forest Service to the Park Service was legal, and he said so, though he failed to explain why. Shanks' attack against Senator Hansen, flawed as it was, reflected a much larger issue. In the eyes of many, cattlemen had inordinate political power in Wyoming and the West. In his article, the unyielding ranger accused Hansen of advocating "cattle grazing activities and schemes [which] have benefited not only himself but the entire Western livestock industry." Hansen, he claimed, opposed any reasonable increase on grazing fees. In fact, there was "no stronger opponent in the U.S. Senate than Clifford Hansen." This was the opening salvo in the growing disillusionment of the NPS with cattle grazing on its land.

Of course, Senator Hansen was engaged in doing what any politician does—defending and protecting the interests of some of his constituents. He supported the ranching community. In pleading the cause of the cattle industry he was simply representing his neighbors...and himself.

Shanks wanted his article to transcend the narrow topic of grazing in Grand Teton. His was one of the first responses to the growing "Sagebrush Rebellion," a movement reflecting the irritation of cattlemen, especially in Nevada and Utah, with management by the Bureau of Land Management and the Forest

Service. They argued that grazing fees were too high, regulations were too onerous, and if the federal government did not wish to turn the public lands over to the states, then at least they should allow the respective states to manage these vast lands. The themes of the Sagebrush Rebellion were common enough in the West. But Shanks and other defenders of the public domain believed that cattle interests ignored the greater public interest. In Grand Teton National Park, Shanks aimed his barbs at Hansen, charging that the senator was profiting from federal funds used to construct miles of irrigation ditches and to hire the labor of park employees that irrigated and tended to his cattle. Privately owned cattle consumed tons of forage needed to support publicly owned animals such as elk, deer, and moose during the long winter season. Furthermore, the irrigation program resulted in serious erosion, carrying mud, manure, and pollutants into the prime trout fishing waters of the Snake River.[23] Simply put, for Shanks and the more vocal environmental groups such as Friends of the Earth, there was no place for cattle in a national park.

Senator Hansen, always known for his gentlemanly manner, chose not to respond publically to the shrill *Progressive* article. He did, however, reply privately to a concerned citizen, stating that he was simply one of a number of ranchers with valid Forest Service permits on land now incorporated into the national park. He noted that the Park Service recognized private homes and dude ranches and allowed hunting at times. In regard to the relocation of his 569 cattle to irrigated land, he observed that this was at the request of the Park Service. Hansen made no apologies.[24]

In the meantime, park administrators conducted damage control. According to Michael Frome, Shanks was taken to task by the chief ranger and told: "I don't care what you find in the records. As long as Cliff Hansen sits on the Senate Interior Committee, we're not going to touch his cows."[25] But that response ignores the fact that the park could not touch Hansen's cattle because he had every legal right to be there. Of course, the chief ranger's admonition suggests fear that Hansen might cut the park's operating funds. Would Senator Hansen penalize Grand Teton National Park? It seems doubtful for he was not a vindictive man. But why take the chance? Cattle on park pasture could be endured, but cuts to the budget would cripple the park's larger mission.

Superintendent Gary Everhardt, who would eventually become NPS Director, kept a low profile during the controversy. In response to a letter criticizing the grazing policy, Everhardt stated that he personally agreed with much of Shanks' position, but then noted: "It is not a matter of choice on the part of the National Park Service that grazing continues at Grand Teton, but instead, it is the exercise of rights granted by the Act of September 14, 1950, which established the present boundaries." Everhardt stated that he hoped to discontinue the practice at the earliest date possible but expected it to continue "until approximately 2030 or 2040."[26]

By 1974, the issue had calmed down, mainly due to the efforts of Everhardt and others, who concluded it was simply not worth alienating Hansen, the Senate, and the Jackson Hole residents who sympathized with the ranchers. Bernard Shanks quit the National Park Service, feeling that his efforts as a whistleblower were not appreciated.[27] Shanks' departure meant the end of national publicity, but the grazing controversy did not disappear. Finally in 1986, Clifford Hansen and Ralph Gill suggested a possible buyout of their grazing rights. This was an idea that could have been achieved more easily in the 1960s, but by the 1980s the price would be difficult to negotiate. Assistant Superintendent William Schenk examined the situation and shared his findings with the Rocky Mountain regional director. The two ranchers had permits for 13,150 acres. The youngest of the family members was 50, and figuring on actuarial statistics, they could hold the lease for another 25 years. Schenk reported that the average yearly cost of upkeep of the grazing leases was $44,000, while the fees collected totaled $5,000. He seemed to favor negotiations to retire the two leases, but the record suggests that the park never pursued the matter further. The park would simply continue its grazing policy based on the 1950 Act.

SAVING THE "OUTSIDE" RANCH LANDS

When Jack Neckels became superintendent in 1991, relationships with grazing lessees improved. Neckels believed that supporting ranchers with grazing rights would help prevent the loss of open space outside the park. Land prices in Jackson Hole had increased dramatically after World War II, and this upward trajectory showed no signs of slowing. Neckels thought that grazing leases in the park would relieve the pressure on ranchers to sell their ranch land outside the park.[28]

However Neckels, who often thought of the park as part of the entire Jackson Hole community, had more confidence in the ranchers' dedication to their lifestyle than proved warranted. Earlier, in June 1978, a joint congressional committee on public lands visited the town of Jackson to listen to testimony on an important bill. The bill would provide $200 million to purchase scenic easements and development rights on land south and east of the park. The reason was clear. Grand Teton park visitation had skyrocketed to over 3 million visitors annually, and the county was in the midst of a gigantic real estate boom. The sprawl was creeping north from the town. Ranchers, such as Stanley Resor and Paul Walton, did not want to subdivide their pastures, but the cost-benefit ratio of managing this valuable property as ranch land made no sense. The temptation to cash in on the real estate boom was powerful. The bill would resolve the problem by paying ranch owners about 65 percent of the appraised valuation of their ranches. They would still own the ranch land and be able to pass it on to their heirs—minus the development rights. The Citizens Committee for Jackson Hole pushed the bill. Mardy Murie, a prominent member, testified that if a rancher could receive so much money and still have the ranch to hand down to heirs, "I should feel that life had dealt kindly with me."[29]

But a number of ranchers did not agree. Why remains a mystery, beyond the usual pronouncements about absolute property rights and those who, as William Everhart put it, had "unkind things to say about perceived imperfections of the federal bureaucracy."[30] I attended this hearing, and like many others, could not understand the ranchers' opposition. Not every livestock owner was opposed, but there was enough disapproval to discourage the congressional committee. After the hearing, I spoke to one of the congressmen, suggesting that the park staff and most in the community strongly favored the bill. He looked at me with a quizzical expression, saying: "We want to provide them with $200 million to save their land, and they don't want it." The bill died.

However, the defeat of the bill was not that simple. The committee still probably would have advanced the bill, but there were lingering fears within the Jackson Hole ranching community. The bill stressed that purchase of ranch easement rights would depend on the guiding principle of willing buyer/willing seller. But ranchers were leery of this supposed policy. They had seen the condemnation threats in the town

of Kelly and followed the McReynolds ongoing condemnation proceeding in the early 1980s (See Chapter 2). If the government held certain easement rights, could they not use that right to condemn those easement rights and acquire the land by that method? It seems unlikely, but for years the government had, to their minds, plotted against private land holders. A group of ranchers flew to Washington to express their fears to Senator Hansen. They asked him to withdraw his support, and he did.[31]

Some ranchers simply believed that the park would continue a policy of grazing to support ranching in Jackson Hole, even though the evidence was to the contrary. Paul Walton, one of the valley's largest ranchers with more than 1,800 acres, had lost his park grazing permit in 1975. In a high-minded move he placed his ranch under a conservation easement with the Jackson Hole Land Trust, guaranteeing that it would remain as grazing land in perpetuity.[1] In a letter to Superintendent Jack Stark, he noted that other ranchers were subdividing and "going out of the ranching business," thus losing their park permits. "This should leave room for others to graze cattle in the park," reasoned Walton. He wanted to be one of them, and he requested that Superintendent Stark give his "request serious consideration."[32] Walton seemed to think that Grand Teton National Park had established a cattle "carrying capacity," and that as one rancher's cattle were removed, another's could fill the vacuum. Although he must have known it,

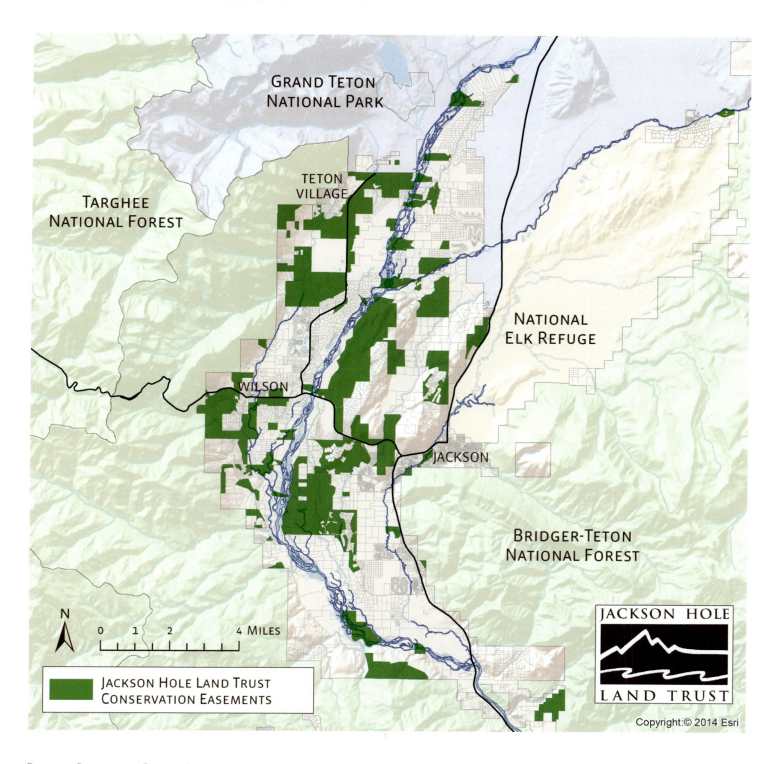

GRAND TETON
NATIONAL PARK

TARGHEE
NATIONAL FOREST

TETON
VILLAGE

NATIONAL
ELK REFUGE

WILSON

JACKSON

BRIDGER-TETON
NATIONAL FOREST

N

0   1   2   4 MILES

JACKSON HOLE
LAND TRUST

JACKSON HOLE LAND TRUST
CONSERVATION EASEMENTS

Copyright:© 2014 Esri

Walton did not admit that the park ultimately wanted to remove *all* livestock in favor of wildlife.

Paul Walton, however, made a remarkably generous "gift" to the community. He donated his development rights to his 1800-acre ranch to the Jackson Hole Land Trust, and because of technicalities, he even had to forfeit a tax deduction on a parcel of his land. This was a major gift to the Jackson Hole Land Trust, an organization created by Story Clark and Jean Hocker as a positive response to the failure to secure federal funds. The trust, one of the earliest in the country, has been highly successful in placing conservation easements on 23,000 acres of western Wyoming private lands, convincing some large landowners that selling developmental rights for either cash or sizable tax benefits represented a sensible move. Not only could they remain in the cattle business, but their heirs could, as well.[33]

The land trust has been workable in Jackson Hole, but national parks elsewhere looked to other methods to protect the integrity of adjacent lands. Ron Foresta notes in *America's National Parks and Their Keepers* that the Grant-Kohrs Ranch National Historic Site in Montana owns a mere 216 acres in fee simple, but has maintained almost five times that acreage in open space by purchasing the developmental rights on surrounding private lands. Sometimes it is more feasible simply to use federal funds to purchase the land.[34] In the case of Jackson Hole, Congress was prepared to make a huge investment. Inexplicably, landowners refused this generous offer. At Grant-Kohrs, the NPS maintains open space, while in Jackson Hole, the Land Trust takes on that role, seeing that the land adjacent to the park remains free of development, thus benefiting the park and the community.

TWO DUDE RANCHES

Dude ranching and cattle ranching are different ways to make a living. Both activities have used Grand Teton National Park: One for its grassy pastures, the other for its scenery. And both are part of the Grand Teton heritage, and as such, have a legitimacy not enjoyed by many other park enterprises.

Guest ranches have also played a significant role in the tradition of Jackson Hole, established well before a national park was in place. Once there were many; today there are only two. One is on private land, while the other represents the only working dude ranch on federal land in the nation. Each uses the public land and has concession agreements with the park, and each has a rich history of association with the National Park Service.

EARLY PROMOTIONAL PICTURE FOR MOOSEHEAD RANCH, 1950S

THE MOOSEHEAD RANCH

The 120-acre Moosehead Ranch, homesteaded by young school teacher Eva Sanford, remains a private inholding. Eva came to northern Jackson Hole in 1924 to accept a teaching position at $100 a month (plus an extra $5.00 for janitorial duties). Not long after filing for her homestead on Spread Creek, she married a local cowboy named Fred Topping. The two combined their talents to create a dude ranch. In the 1930s they struggled, with Eva eking out a living by hosting summer guests at very reasonable prices. In the fall months, Fred guided hunters. Eva's life was one of constant toil. She survived the Depression years, especially when she secured the Postal Service contract to manage the tiny office at Elk (which was at the Moosehead). In time, Fred's health declined, his body fading through hard work and also from excessive drinking. Eva could no longer maintain the place alone.

In the meantime, the park made overtures in the 1930s to purchase the Moosehead. Neither Eva nor Fred had any affection for Grand Teton National Park. Fred, who at one time served as Teton County commissioner, developed a deep resentment toward anyone in a national park uniform, partly because he believed the NPS conspired with the General Land Office (in Evanston, Wyoming) to deny Eva's homestead claim. The truth of this charge is unclear, and certainly never put in writing. The Toppings refused to sell to the government at any price.

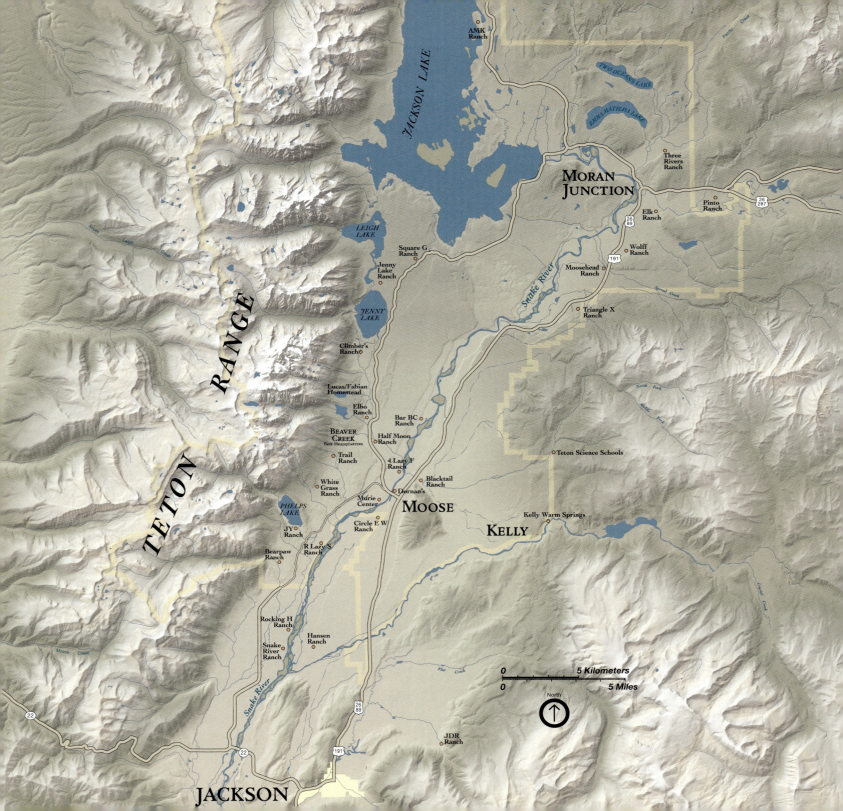

In 1965 Eva was tempted. She and Fred had put the Moosehead on the market for $600,000. NPS Regional Director Fred Fagergren wrote the new Grand Teton Superintendent Jack Anderson that one of the rangers had "cultivated a warm relationship" with both Eva and Fred, and purchase might be possible. Fagergren estimated the NPS could buy the place for around $500,000.[35]

Unfortunately, the Park Service representatives who negotiated with Eva Topping did not really understand her. She cared little about money, but cared rather deeply about the Moosehead Ranch. When she wrote Ray Roberts, a potential buyer, she revealed her true feelings. She believed:

> the Park Service would take this place in a
> minute if we say the word—they would tear it
> down, bull doze it under, government style, and
> we feel like the public can still enjoy it and the
> area if the place can be put to further use.[36]

This was a key point, one that the park negotiators never seemed to realize. Sale to the park would mean the destruction of thousands of hours of Eva's loving labor. It would, in a metaphorical sense, mean the eradication of her life work.

Eva searched for a buyer and found one in the Mettler family of Florida. On December 8, 1967, the Toppings sold the Moosehead to John W. Mettler. The price was $500,000. Considering that this gorgeous piece of property had originally cost Eva a ten-dollar homestead filing fee, her homestead may be the most profitable ever for a continuous owner. Although the Mettler family would soon remove most of the Toppings' cabins to build comfortable new ones, the Moosehead still operates today as a guest ranch. In contrast to the Toppings' middle-class clientele, the Moosehead Ranch is now definitely on the high end. Along with the Pinto Ranch and Dornans, it is the most valuable private property within the park.

Today the contact between the Moosehead Ranch and the park has been very cordial, and Superintendent Mary Gibson Scott intends that it will stay that way. The present proprietor, Louise Davenport, has a grazing privilege with the park for 284 horses but no cattle. On the surface, the horse permit seems excessive, although running their type of guest operation requires plenty of four-legged animals of varied ages and temperaments. Also, the Moosehead under the 1950 law is guaranteed its grazing right until such time as the Moosehead becomes the property of the federal government. This is not likely in the near future, as there is no sign that a change of ownership might be possible. Even if they had the funds, the park has no strong desire to obtain the land.[37] One might regret that park administrators were not more perceptive to Eva Toppings' wishes in 1967, but on the other hand, today's Moosehead Ranch serves a need that is consistent with the values of the park.

THE TRIANGLE X RANCH

The Triangle X, just two miles south of the Moosehead, is a very different operation with a distinctive history. John S. Turner, the family patriarch, purchased the 160-acre homestead in 1926 for $1,000, then purchased another 160 acres at a price of $3,655, putting up a rustic ranch house and six dude cabins. It was a good start, but when Harold Fabian, representing the Snake River Land Company, offered the Turners $20,000 for the expanded homestead, they took it, a move they probably later regretted. After the sale John S. and Matie Turner moved north to the Buffalo River and, with relatives, established the Turpin Meadows Ranch. Their son, John C. Turner, and his wife, Louise, however, stayed on the Triangle X Ranch, signing a lease with Harold Fabian, who represented the Snake River Land Company. The lease, signed in March 1930, called for perpetuation of the ranch primarily as a dude operation. The agreement contained 14 conditions regarding farming, irrigation, buildings, and livestock. The Turners would be expected to keep good records and would pay the Snake River Land Company 10 percent of gross receipts from all operations, including their dude business.[38]

The lease between John C. and Louise Turner and the Snake River Land Company seemed to operate smoothly. When the company conveyed the Triangle X Ranch property to the Park Service, along with more than 33,000 acres of Rockefeller land in 1949, it was with the stipulation that "existing lease agreements would be honored through the term of the lease." The transference of title to the Park Service made the Triangle X unique. It is the only working dude ranch owned by the United States government. The lease extended to January 1, 1952, at which time it was renewed with the NPS. A Triangle X Forest Service permit for cattle grazing, transferred to the NPS, did not go so well. That permit allowed grazing for 75 cows and a number of horses south of the Triangle X Ranch (in the Hedricks Pond area) and on toward Antelope Flats. In 1966, Ranger Bernard Shanks found discrepancies that caused Superintendent Jack Anderson to write to the NPS regional director that he could "find no valid reason for extending the [grazing] permit beyond the current year." Thus permit No. 14-10-0232-1106 expired on January 1, 1967.[39] But the "discrepancies" were never spelled out to the family, and to this day they feel that the cancelation was unjust. In particular, the loss of the lease worked a hardship because the Turner family used the cattle as collateral for bank loans to carry the Triangle X through the winter. It was particularly difficult for a tourist operation owned by the government to secure loans.[40]

In 1960, John C. Turner died and the Triangle X lease came to Louise. A year later, she married a World War II navy captain, Robert S. Bertschy. The two, along with Louise's sons, Donald, Harold, and John, continued to run a successful dude operation.

TRIANGLE X RANCH

Families fell in love with the Triangle X Ranch with exposure to its warm personalities, cordial hospitality, horseback rides along the river, and guitar music and stories around the campfire. Like Struthers Burt and the earlier Bar BC, the Turners and the Triangle X Ranch drew guests who became so enamored with Jackson Hole that many eventually became residents themselves.

Although relations between the Triangle X and the Park Service went generally well, John and his brother Donald decided to purchase a nearby 5.74-acre lot for possible future family homes. The National Park Service was not pleased with this purchase, since it represented another inholding that could result in two additional houses within park lines. On reflection, both Donald and John decided that they preferred their private homes to be outside the park. They decided to sell their recent purchase to the Park Service. At first, negotiations with John F. Pattie, chief of the NPS Division of Land and Water Resources, proved frustrating. But by 1983, both sides had moved toward finalizing the sale, with Pattie writing to John Turner on September 12 that "it has been a pleasure to work with you." After additional phone calls and discussions, Pattie's mood changed, and just 10 days later, he wrote that "the failure of negotiations coupled with the threat of use of your property for purposes incompatible with the land acquisition policy would lead to the acquisition of your property by condemnation." Whatever glitch happened went unexplained in the record, but both sides ultimately wanted the sale to go through. It did, and on October 18, 1983, the federal government assumed the parcel for a consideration of $228,600.[41]

Throughout the 1980s, a number of issues arose between Louise and her sons on one side and Superintendent Jack Stark on the other. These were common enough issues between the federal government as manager of the land and the lessees, who occasionally felt harassed by regulations and requests. One situation occurred when Ellie Talbot, who had a life lease on the Aspen Ridge Ranch (off the Antelope Flat road), died in 1987. For many years, the Turners had rented the ranch fields for hay. When the NPS took ownership, Stark informed John Turner that the park would have to reconsider the rental agreement between Ellie Talbot and the Triangle X. In doing so the superintendent asked for detailed financial records on the cost of irrigation, field maintenance, baling of hay, and even statistics on the number of paying guests at the Triangle X Ranch. On the surface, requesting such detail seemed to border on harassment.[42] This long-standing rental agreement could simply have been renewed.

From the federal policy point of view, however, Stark was doing his job. The Washington office instructed superintendents that in managing such concessions, they must protect the natural and historic resources, provide quality visitor services at reasonable cost, and provide concessionaires with a reasonable opportunity for profit and a "fair return on fees, investments and services to the government." These conditions surely benefited the Triangle X. On the downside, the government was expected to "provide competition in concession contracting," a condition which would prove increasingly awkward and difficult with respect to the Triangle X Ranch. Providing competition in a dude ranch concession was certainly different from doing so for a restaurant or almost any other kind of concession because of the personalized and specialized nature of dude ranch service. Yet the Washington-based Park Service officials made no distinction.

When the time came, renewal of the Triangle X operation contract would be open to public bidding, even though such free competition could result in a disastrous change in management, undermining the whole dude ranch experience which relies so heavily on personal relationships built up over years between hosts and guests.[43] In some businesses, a regulated monopoly is surely more sensible than open competition.

As the decade of the 1980s progressed, the relationship between Superintendent Stark and the Triangle X Ranch deteriorated. Each side tended to read the lease through different lenses, with the Turners minimizing some lease requirements while park administrators maximized many conditions. The different perspectives came to a head in August 1991. Superintendent Stark retired and, in doing so, shot off a letter complaining to NPS Director James Ridenour that the Turners' grazing violations had "plagued him." He asserted that their 265 horses and mules had trampled and eaten native vegetation intended for wildlife. He also charged that the ranch had mined gravel on park land without authorization and, perhaps more serious, illegally buried trash. Furthermore, they had allowed camping and campfires down along the river, a privilege denied to all other river users. All these lease violations, according to Superintendent Stark, contravened principles to preserve the park "in absolutely unimpaired form," as well as a park superintendent's mandate to follow "the national interest."[44]

The Triangle X community was stunned, particularly when Stark's letter was later published. The two sides had their differences, and the Turners were not averse to criticizing Stark's efforts to destroy or remove historic buildings from the park, his refusal to manage exotic weeds and plants, and his snail-like approval of needed improvements and upgrades at the Triangle X. Superintendent Stark sometimes lacked grace in dealing with those who might differ with his policies. He believed the Turner brothers were "arrogant," according to John Turner, perhaps simply because they disagreed with him.[45]

Harold Turner, in high dudgeon, contested all Stark's charges, stating that "about the only thing factual in this [letter] is the date our lease expires." From Washington, John Turner, tapped by President George H. W. Bush to serve as Director of the U.S. Fish and Wildlife Service, refused comment. Angus Thuermer, editor of the *Jackson Hole Guide*, expressed their concern: "What rankles the family most is that John, Director of the U. S. Fish and Wildlife Service, was dragged into the issue even though he swore off involvement in Triangle X operations when he took the federal post in 1989."[46] Soon enough the rumor mill in Washington, D. C. discovered the story, with one paper headline proclaiming: "Teton Park Director Blasts Wildlife Chief." Forty-five papers across the country carried the story.

In time the Turners addressed Stark's charges. The gravel pit had been started much earlier by homesteaders and then continued by those involved with construction of the Jackson Hole Highway. Furthermore, throughout the park there were scattered gravel pits either maintained by the park or authorized for road use and repair. The Turners vehemently denied that they grazed 265 horses in 1991. They challenged Stark's contention that the

Triangle X allowed campfires and camping along the river as inaccurate and said whatever overnight camping or campfire/cookout sites they used, the park had authorized.

Perhaps the most serious accusation was that Harold Turner had buried trash on park land. For a number of years he operated a backhoe to excavate a trench, then dumped ranch refuse in it, including refrigerators and car batteries, without concerns for toxicity or anything else. Harold Turner did not deny that he buried trash, defending his actions on ranch precedent: "I don't know what to say here. I don't guess I believe in doing things the way the park does. Burying stuff is the way it's been done in this country for 101 years."[47] Turner was exactly right on one level. Ranch yards in Wyoming are often strewn with old cars and farm equipment, rusting away in a kind of mechanical morgue. But some ranchers did recycle them, in a sense. Vehicles became makeshift septic tanks, filled with rock and gravel. If an old truck was not buried, it might be driven into a stream bank to prevent erosion. Harold Turner simply reflected the environmental ethics of the ranching community in Wyoming. Ranchers buried castoffs as a more aesthetic solution than leaving it in the ranch yard for the world to watch it rust. From Harold Turner's view, he would be violating ranching tradition by *not* burying his refuse.[48] The secret is not to allow any toxic chemicals, batteries, paint, or similar products into the informal landfill. Turner admitted that this did not always happen. From a Park Service viewpoint,

Harold Turner's rationale was understandable but inexcusable: "The concessioner's operations appear to be patterned after long-term habits which, while they may be common to ranches in the West, are not acceptable on National Park Service lands."[49]

There is no way to evaluate Stark's accusations completely, but the National Park Service, embarrassed by Stark's aggressive memo, called for a three-person Park Service fact-finding team from Washington, which was also endorsed by the Turner family. In the middle of September they submitted their report. They concluded there had been some illegal tree cutting, buried garbage, mined gravel, and small oil spills. They found no overgrazing. The panel concluded that "none of these incidents [should result] in the initiation of termination proceedings."[50] Later a team of professors from the University of Wyoming's Department of Range Management examined the Triangle X pasture and declared that it had received only "light to moderate use overall."[51]

Of course, Stark's letter and the fallout that followed were all preparatory to a negotiation in 1992 for a new Triangle X lease. In the court of public opinion, the Triangle X Ranch had the advantage. Not only had the former superintendent acted waspishly, but many believed that park officials were intentionally raising the Triangle X issue to bolster their campaign for a natural park, free from historic buildings and dude ranches. Carl Oksanen of Jackson wrote that "we no longer have the White Grass, The Bar BC, The Double Diamond, The Elbo, The Old R Lazy S, or the Jackson Hole Ranch." He saw the attack against the Triangle X Ranch as one more strike against "our Western heritage."[52]

In fact, the Triangle X issue served as a catalyst to examine the purpose and mission of the park. In an editorial, the *Jackson Hole Guide* called the Triangle X Ranch a "major contributor to the character of the valley and the most important concession in the park. Forty-one Jackson Hole families fell in love with the valley as guests of the Triangle X. It is intertwined with the valley's past and one of a diminishing number of historic sites." The *Guide* then touched on the sensitive subject of cultural resources, stating that "it is distressing to think that, in their unyielding quest for 'naturalness' this demise [of the Triangle X Ranch] could be the goal of some Park Service officials."[53]

The new superintendent, Jack Neckels, quickly distanced himself from Stark's views. Although he was generally in the "naturalness" camp, he could see nothing to be gained by confronting one of the two dude ranches remaining in the park. Nor did he wish to challenge a family so well respected and one with significant political accomplishments and power.[54] On a personal level, he was more sympathetic to the Triangle X's needs, among them finding the long overdue funds ($850,000) to complete a new sewage system. The Turners also made a number of concessions. Grazing would be confined to 920 acres stocked with a maximum of 120 horses necessary for the dude ranch operation. The many horses and mules involved with the Triangle X backcountry hunting camp (in the Two Ocean Pass and Thorofare region) would be pastured outside park lands. The overnight camp on riparian lands of the Snake River would be relocated. This new management plan would be in effect for ten years.[55] Although management plans come and go, a 1995 letter from Harold and Don Turner and their mother, Louise Bertschy, to Superintendent Jack Neckels seemed to exude friendship and future cooperation.[56]

Issues with the Triangle X Ranch nevertheless continue. By 2007, the 10-year concessions contract expired and Grand Teton issued extensions to authorize continued operation of the dude ranch. Pursuant to the NPS Concessions Management Improvement Act of 1998, the agency must provide competition for concession contracts. The NPS developed a prospectus for a new 13-year contract to begin in 2012. The Turner family contested the NPS intention to open the Triangle X Ranch concession to full competition. Their attorney took the position that when John S. Turner, the patriarch of the family, sold his land to the Snake River Land Company in 1929, and when all parties signed the lease in 1930, it was with the understanding that the family, and particularly the three brothers—Don, Harold, and John—could live at and operate the ranch for the remainder of their lives.[57] The potential for a court case dissolved when the Park Service asked for bids to run the Triangle X Ranch, as required by the 1998 law. The Turner fam-

Photo by Christine Paige

IN LOCATIONS WHERE CATTLE NO LONGER GRAZE WITHIN THE PARK, BARBED WIRE FENCES HAVE BEEN REMOVED. IN OTHER LOCATIONS, FENCES HAVE BEEN MODIFIED TO REDUCE THE CHANCE OF WILDLIFE ENTANGLEMENTS.

experience. They will continue to do so for the foreseeable future. With the Triangle X, the disputes regarding the running of the ranch can be attributed to the difficulties of dual management: one party is a bureaucracy with rigid but necessary rules, and the other derives from the pioneer West dominated by handshakes, not contracts, and given to the belief that nature is to be used but not abused. At times, the park and the Triangle X Ranch have differed about what abuse means. Whatever their differences, these days they are in general agreement that traditions should carry on within the framework of a new environmental ethic.

FROM 1950 ONWARD, Grand Teton National Park faced issues that were slowly but successfully resolved. Livestock grazing in the park, initially acceptable but inappropriate today, has ended with expiration of the 1950 leases. Only the Pinto Ranch cattle lease remains, and that has changed. When Pinto Ranch cattle were suffering loss from grizzly bears and wolves in their Pacific Creek allotment, the park negotiated a new agreement to move the livestock to more protected and fenced Elk Ranch pasture. The agreement included the retirement of a Bridger-Teton National Forest cattle lease, through which Grand Teton assumed the ALMS that had been accommodated on USFS land.[59] Although confusing, the prevailing agreement indicated cooperation by all parties.

ily bid for the concession, and they won.[58] A family and a ranch whose origins far precede the jurisdiction of Grand Teton National Park will continue to offer a service that is in the tradition of both the park and Jackson Hole.

The dude ranch tradition lives on at the Triangle X and Moosehead ranches, offering a unique Western

The annual cattle trail drive from south of Jackson to the north region of Grand Teton National Park is now a thing of the past. The old trail has grown over with grass and sagebrush. Its disappearance is symbolic of the demise of cattle grazing in the park, an activity reminiscent of the old West but at odds with park objectives. Cattle have access to 90 percent of the American West; it makes sense for wildlife to have primacy in the national parks. Thus, after a 100-year hiatus, fences have come down with the volunteer effort of the Jackson Hole Wildlife Foundation and the rangeland is once again in the total possession of wildlife.

[1] Grand Teton National Park archives (hereafter cited as GTNP), Grazing, box 2, folder 009, series 00.

[2] Much has been written about Wyoming and cattlemen. One could start with T.A. Larson's *History of Wyoming* (Lincoln: University of Nebraska Press, 1990) and *Wyoming: A History* (New York: W.W. Norton, 1984); also see Gene Gressley, *Bankers and Cattlemen* (New York: Alfred A. Knopf, 1966). The most informative is Michael Cassity's *Wyoming Will Be Your New Home: Ranching, Farming, and Homesteading in Wyoming, 1860-1960* (Cheyenne: Wyoming State Historic Preservation Office, 2011). For Jackson Hole, see John Daugherty, *A Place Called Jackson Hole* (Moose: Grand Teton Association, 1999).

[3] Floyd K. Harmston, Richard E. Lund, and J. Richard Williams, *A Study of the Resources, People, and Economy of Teton County, Wyoming* (Laramie: University of Wyoming, 1959), 32, 75.

[4] "Grazing Environmental Assessment," 2000, GTNP, Steve Cain Files, file cabinet #4.

[5] See Horace M. Albright, *The Birth of the National Park Service* (Salt Lake City: Howe Brothers, 1985), 69.

[6] An account of the meeting may be found in "Memorandum to the Director" from Conrad Wirth, April 21, 1949 in Dieterich, Compendium, II: 4, Exhibit 56.

[7] Robert W. Righter, *Crucible for Conservation: The Struggle for Grand Teton National Park* Park (Boulder: Colorado University Press, 1982; repr., Moose: Grand Teton Association, 2000), 138.

[8] *An Act to Establish a New Grand Teton National Park*, Public Law 81-787, 64 Statute 849 (1950), Sec 4.0. Aside from the Moosehead Ranch, today the only ranch to retain a large grazing right is the Pinto Ranch in the extreme northeast corner of the park. I have never heard an explanation of why it was included within the park boundaries, but the park is relatively small and including as much acreage as possible was a sensible objective.

[9] Grazing policy document from GTNP, Historic Records Collection, CAT#GRTE, box 8 of 10, folder 58, Grazing General File #1.

[10] GTNP, Historic Records Collection, CAT#GRTE, box 8 of 10, file 76, Coulter Huyler.

[11] Acting Regional Director James Lloyd, memo to Grand Teton superintendent, June 22, 1950, in the folder "Trespass Grazing, Jack D. Dornan."

[12] NPS Director Conrad Wirth to Anita Tarbell, March 2, 1953, GTNP, Historic Records Collection, CAT#48002, box 8 of 10, folder 69, Half Moon Ranch.

[13] Memo to the grazing files by Special Services Ranger Bernie Shanks, March 28, 1967, GTNP, Historic Records Collection, CAT#48002, box 8 of 10, folder 69, Half Moon Ranch.

[14] GTNP, Land Records, box 22, series 1.5, folders 023.1–023.4, Half Moon Ranch. Workers moved the cabins to Colter Bay and today no remains of the ranch are visible.

[15] This relinquishment of the potholes region occurred in the mid- 1950s.

[16] Superintendent Harthon L. Bill to Clifford Hansen, Bruce Porter, and Arthur Brown, August 26, 1960, GTNP, Grazing, box 1, series 003.1, folder 006.

[17] Master Plan for the Preservation and Use of Grand Teton National Park: Objectives and Policies, April 1962.

[18] Minutes of the meeting of the Potholes-Moran Grazing Association, August 1, 1967, GTNP, Grazing, box 1, series 0031, folder 007.

[19] Memo from Bernard Shanks, Special Service Ranger, to Grazing Files, February 27, 1967, GTNP, Grazing, Solicitor's Records, box 12, folder 26. I cannot say if this recommendation was ever made public.

[20] Ibid.

[21] The details of Bernard Shanks's life come from national park observer Michael Frome's book *Regreening the National Parks* (Tucson: University of Arizona Press, 1992), 132–37.

[22] Superintendent Howard Chapman to Friends of the Earth, Albuquerque, N.M., May 6, 1971, GTNP, Grazing, box 2, series 003.1, folder 009.

[23] See "A Big Slice of National Parkland Serves as a Ranch for 569 Head of Cattle Owned by a U.S. Senator," in "Econotes," *Audubon* (January 1973).

[24] Senator Clifford Hansen to John C. Osterling, February 8, 1973, GTNP, Grazing, box 2, series 003.1, folder 009.

[25] Frome, *Regreening the National Parks,* 136. Frome interviewed Shanks, and while I doubt that this is a word for word quote, it surely expresses Shanks's memory of the conversation.

[26] Superintendent Gary Everhardt to Mrs. A. A. Luckenback, November 27, 1972, GTNP, Grazing, box 1, series 003.1, folder 004. Probably Everhardt's guess as to when Hansen's grazing permit would end was based on the presumed lifespan of Mary Mead, his daughter. However, a tragic horse accident that took her life changed the situation.

[27] After leaving the National Park Service Bernard Shanks earned a Ph.D., taught at Utah State University, and was an active opponent of the "Sagebrush Rebellion." He ended his academic career at Sacramento State University, where he was director of California Studies.

[28] I did not consider myself a good friend or confidant of Superintendent Neckels, although I and three others approached him about forming a "friends of Teton Park" group to support projects. This did not materialize, but one day he telephoned and asked me a question: "If the extension of grazing rights in the park would save ranches and extend open space outside of the park, would I extend rights?" Surprised, I took a moment, and then responded that I thought the superintendent's job was to protect the core of the park, and nothing should dilute that mission. He thanked me for my opinion.

[29] See William Everhart, *The National Park Service* (Boulder: Westview Press, 1983), 84-86.

[30] Ibid., 86.

[31] Telephone interview with Story Clark by author, August 30, 2012. Story Clark was then much involved with the Citizens Committee for Jackson Hole. She and Jean Hocker then founded the Jackson Hole Conservation Alliance where Story served as Director for 8 years. Jean Hocker set up and directed the Jackson Hole Land Trust.

[32] Paul Walton to Superintendent Jack Stark, April 6, 1984, GTNP, Grazing, box 2, series 003.1, folder 013.

[33] Jackson Hole Land Trust, *2011 Annual Report*. Interview with Story Clark by author, October 5, 2013

[34] Ron Foresta, *America's National Parks and Their Keepers* (Washington, D.C.: Resources for the Future, 1984), 240-41.

[35] Fred Fagergren, Regional Director, to Jack K. Anderson, Superintendent, GTNP, in GTNP Archives, unorganized in early 1990s.

[36] Mrs. Fred Topping to Ray N. Roberts, Pascagoula, Mississippi, January 14, 1967, in Eva Topping Papers, Teton County Historical and Museum Center, Jackson. This account of Eva Topping is from an unpublished 27 page typescript by the author. It is based on the Eva Topping Papers in the archives of the Teton County Historical Society and Museum.

37 GTNP, Grazing, box 8, series 003.2, folder 15.2, 18, John Mettler. Conversation with Superintendent Mary Gibson Scott, January 29, 2013.

38 GTNP, Grazing, box 9, series 003.2, folder 25.9, John S. Turner. Also see Daugherty, A Place Called Jackson Hole, 242–43.

39 Superintendent Jack Anderson to Regional Director, November 15, 1966, GTNP, Grazing, box 9, series 003.2, folder 25.8.

40 John Turner, memo to the author, November 8, 2012. John was helpful in sorting out his family relations for me. He also provided a Turner-family perspective of the NPS–Triangle X relations. With his help I hope I have provided a fair and balanced view.

41 The story of the Wolff Road property is constructed from notes and letters in GTNP, Land Records, box 29, series 1.8, folder 13, John and Mary Turner.

42 Superintendent Jack Stark to John Turner, January 8, 1987, GTNP, Grazing, box 9, series 003.2, folder 25.7.

43 The park's obligations in managing the Triangle X concession were laid out in a letter from David Moffitt, Acting Associate Director, NPS, to Louise N. Bertschy, July 17, 1991. However, in his memo to the author of November 8, 2012, John Turner stated that a satisfactory concession had a "preferential right of renewal of their contract."

44 Memo to Director [Ridenour]of the National Park Service from Superintendent [Stark], August 2, 1991, GTNP, Grazing, box 9, series 003.2, folder 25.3. Also see Jackson Hole Guide, August 21, 1991. A whole folder of clippings on the Stark-Turner grazing fight is in GTNP, Grazing, box 9, series 3.2, folder 25.5.

45 John Turner, memo to the author, November 8, 2012.

46 Jackson Hole Guide, August 21, 1991.

47 Ibid. See also John Turner memo, November 8, 2012.

48 In new home construction in Jackson Hole—of which there was plenty—contractors would dig a hole, throw in all the trash, burn it, and what did not burn was covered over and buried. That practice is no longer allowed, a response to new environmental attitudes.

49 Quoted from the Casper Star-Tribune, August 21, 1991.

50 GTNP, Grazing, box 9, series 003.2, folder 25.5; also see Casper Star-Tribune, September, 20, 1991.

51 Jackson Hole Guide, March 12, 1993.

52 Jackson Hole Guide, August 28,1991.

53 Ibid.

54 For another view on the Triangle X political influence, see Gary Ferguson, Hawk's Rest: A Season in the Remote Heart of Yellowstone (Washington, D.C.: National Geographic Adventure Press, 2003), 121.

55 "Triangle X Ranch Concession Management Plan," approved August 1992, GTNP, Grazing, box 9, series 003.2, folder 25.2.

56 Louise Bertschy and Harold and Don to Superintendent Jack Neckels, February 9, 1995. The letter promises full support in grazing matters, so long an issue.

57 Information on the new lease provided by Mallory Smith, Grand Teton Chief of Business Resources; also see Cory Hatch, "Family Sues to Stay on Ranch," Jackson Hole News and Guide, October 19, 2011.

58 Phone interview with Mallory Smith by the author, February 19, 2013.

59 Memorandum on "Pacific Creek grazing allotment," from superintendent to the files, May 28, 2009.

PEAKS, POLITICS, AND PASSION: GRAND TETON NATIONAL PARK COMES OF AGE

Chapter 4

Protecting People and Resources

AT 1:00 A.M. RANGER PETE MUCHMORE and his wife were playing a game of cards with Ranger Eliot Davis and his wife when a knock came at the front door. This was unusual, not only for the hour, but for the place. Muchmore and his wife lived at the Jackson Lake Ranger Station, and on January 11, 1953, there were few places in Jackson Hole so isolated.

He opened the door to face a young blond-headed boy. The lad explained that he and his two friends needed help. Their car had slid off the road into a snow bank. They could not budge it—nothing but spinning tires. Although no doubt dismayed at the thought of a rescue effort at that time of night, the two rangers hopped in their pickup trucks and went to the scene, a little east and across the Buffalo Fork bridge. They hooked a chain to the car and asked the boy to start his car. They became suspicious when he reached under the dashboard. Obviously it had to be hotwired. The mood changed from helping two boys in distress to dealing with a possible criminal act. They started asking a few questions while the chain was still attached to the suspect's car. The other boy panicked and suddenly reached under the front seat, pulled out a .38 caliber pistol, and fired two shots at Ranger Davis. One shot found Davis' chest.[1]

What happened next is a little confusing, but the two boys and one very scared girl freed the car, unhooked the chain, and fled toward Jackson. Muchmore attended Davis and then radioed ahead to Chief Ranger Paul Judge, who set up a roadblock at Moose and eventually apprehended the three fugitives. In Jackson, Dr. MacLeod received the call for help and was soon driving north to meet the injured ranger.

Happily, Ranger Eliot Davis survived and was proud to carry the bullet on a necklace the rest of his life.[2] All three of the fugitives were from Dallas, where they had stolen the car with the intention of driving to Idaho to see friends. Billy Pamplin, the shooter, was already on parole. The federal government tried him for attempted murder in the U.S. District Court in Cheyenne. Since he was still a juvenile, he received a lenient sentence of three years and six months.[3]

Until the Pamplin incident, no one had ever been shot in Grand Teton. The park did not lack for enemies who might have liked to harass Park Service leaders, but verbal abuse and occasional fisticuffs were the extent of the local animosity. Certainly pistols and rifles were not strangers to Jackson Hole. It is doubtful that any small community was better armed than the citizenry of Jackson Hole, but gun cabinets contained tools for hunting wildlife, not shooting people. Yes, there had been gunplay in Jackson Hole, such as the local posse at the Cunningham homestead who killed two supposed horse thieves. But that legendary episode belonged to the late 19th century, just as today's tourist-inspired "shootout" in downtown Jackson is historical in flavor.[4]

But by 1953, modern America had arrived in the Tetons. The young men and their girlfriend represented an urban criminal element invading a national park, confronting a ranger staff unprepared to face desperate and unscrupulous people. The whole incident seemed an anomaly that would not happen again. That would not be the case. As this chapter will show, incidents would occur requiring rangers to be vigilant against lawbreakers, while helpful to visitors who made bad decisions. Although park rangers must deal with dangers inherent in the mountains, the river, and winter itself, over the years their duties have expanded and become more uncertain. In their commitment to the traveling and vacationing public, rangers must have more and more specialized training. In the early days, a ranger seemed to be a "jack of all trades." The flip side was that he/she was the "master of none." In today's more complicated park with more than three million diverse visitors a year, rangers have had to become masters of many new skills. Clearly more specialized training was necessary to serve the public and protect the park. This chapter focuses on the evolution of the ranger force toward professionalization and specialization. It stresses that the Park Service is constantly changing to meet new situations and challenges. Change over time is as prevalent a theme in the NPS as it is in society.

KEEPING THE PEACE

On reflection, Deputy Chief Ranger Jack Davis recalled that he and Chief Ranger Doug McClaren were "woefully unprepared" for what happened to them on a late October, 1962 evening. Their lack of training, recalled Davis, made them fearful and could have cost them their lives.[5]

It happened in the midst of an early snowstorm. Ranger Davis pulled his patrol car alongside a vehicle stopped without lights. Davis was on "poaching patrol" and was suspicious. The two men in the vehicle claimed they were having trouble with their headlights. They wanted to go over Togwotee Pass, but Davis strongly advised against it. Instead, Davis volunteered for them to follow his patrol car to a shop in Jackson where they could have the headlights repaired. After a few miles, the car disappeared. Jack Davis retraced his way and found the car in a snow bank, well off the highway. He went to headquarters at Moose, picked up Chief Ranger Doug McClaren, and returned to the now abandoned car. While figuring out what happened, a tow truck with driver and one of the men arrived to tow the car to the Chevrolet dealer garage. Davis and McClaren followed, and on the way, they radioed their concerns to the Teton County Deputy Sherriff, feeling that the man and his partner were running from the law. They all met at the Chevrolet garage. In the midst of questioning, Allen Bullock, 34, of Canada, pulled a .22 caliber Ruger semi-automatic pistol. While seemingly yelling to his partner to shoot anyone who moved, he successfully tied up all four from head to toe.[6] Taking their money, Bullock and his accomplice then fled in the NPS patrol car. The two had no idea where they were, thus they drove up the narrow cemetery road and managed to high center the ranger vehicle. They then fled on foot. In the meantime, Ranger Russ Dickenson as well as Wyoming Game and Fish employees and highway patrolmen all joined the search. The *Jackson Hole Guide* reported that the next morning "the townspeople saw more guns being carried around than had ever been seen at once except in the old Western movies on TV." The next morning two school children, Fred Joy and Rich Hughes, spotted Bullock hiding in some bushes and told their teacher, who then alerted the police. Bullock was apprehended as well as his younger partner. They were both escaped prisoners on a rampage of robberies in Oregon, Idaho, and Wyoming.[7]

Both Rangers Jack Davis and Doug McClaren received a letter of commendation from NPS Director George Hartzog for their work and their courage. Hartzog noted that the rangers had not been armed and were fortunate to escape serious injury. The director observed: "It is unfortunate but nevertheless true that rangers cannot approach every car suspected of illegal operation with guns, but such precautions must await the overt act of other confirmations of their suspicions."[8] Clearly, in an increasingly dangerous world, rangers were at a serious disadvantage. Hartzog seemed to suggest it was time to reassess the ranger's law enforcement role in the park.

TROUBLE IN YOSEMITE

Such incidents had little immediate effect on national policy or even that of Grand Teton National Park. Dramatic change in all parks would come later following an incident hundreds of miles away. Yosemite National Park, one of the Park Service's acknowledged "crown jewels," is by no means an urban park, but its proximity to Los Angeles and San Francisco make it a convenient weekend retreat that receives enormous visitation. The urban atmosphere is enhanced by the fact that most of its visitors are concentrated in a small but spectacular valley.

The beautiful setting could not keep 1960s social tensions at bay. Discontent over the Vietnam War and racism merged with drugs, alcohol, and sex to create a volatile situation. Whereas many thousands of youths had gathered peacefully in the summer of 1969 at Woodstock, New York, the July 4th Yosemite Riot of 1970 brought out the worst in people.

Hippies, motorcycle riders, drug users, and a cluster of hard drinkers assembled in Stoneman's Meadow, a fragile area featuring dramatic views of Yosemite Falls. The revelers seemed less interested in the scenery than in their menu of drugs, alcohol, and rebellious and noisy activity, which disturbed the campers at Camp 14, designated a family campground. Rangers tried to persuade the rowdy group to move to the more secluded Sentinel Beach, but that attempt failed.

The night of July 4th, Independence Day, rioting broke out at Stoneman's Meadow as park rangers, mounted on horses, tried to disperse the unruly crowd. The rioters attacked Park Service cars, showering them with rocks and breaking the windows. Eventually there were more than a 100 arrests, several injuries, and considerable wanton destruction of property. It was an unprecedented event in a national park.[9]

The ranger staff was ill prepared to deal with a crisis that involved anger, insults, crowds of boisterous youth, and total disrespect for authority. The parks had so far been spared the 1960s unrest, but now Yosemite seemed to have joined in the general turbulence that swept the country.

Historian Al Runte noted that few incidents were more repulsive to the Park Service or more prophetic.[10] Changes would have to come in law enforcement. In the early 1960s the methods of law enforcement were relaxed. Rangers had no formal training in crowd control or what might be termed "anger management." Some rangers wore firearms, but they were not required to do so. Generally policy seemed to emanate from the view of a particular superintendent and the location of the park. That changed, particularly in 1973 when Ranger Ken Patrick was shot and killed at Point Reyes National Seashore. In 1976, the Park Service issued Circular NPS-9 and Congress passed Public Law 94-1588 on July 7, 1976. If one were to pick a year when rangers became law enforcement officers, this would be it. The "fern fondlers" (naturalists) were disappearing, which prompted NPS naturalist Paul Schullery in 1980 to speak of the "requiem for the ranger."[11] Edward Abbey, always dismissive of authority, acknowledged that Yosemite Valley might not be the proper place for a youth festival, but just as surely it was not "a proper place for a jail, for administrators, for police wearing park ranger uniforms."[12]

NPS Director George Hartzog agreed. The director went undercover during the riots in Yosemite to see for himself what was going on. He joined a circle of hippies in Stoneman's Meadow, declining a joint and instead offering cigarettes. For a few hours he joined the party. The next evening he met with these counterculture types in a different role—as director of the National Park Service. He recalled that the questions were fast and furious, but one became "etched in my mind:"

Why would you prohibit us from sitting in the meadow, mashing down the grass when you are cutting down 150-year old Douglas fir trees to expand a campground for recreational motor vehicles?

Hartzog had to admit they had a good point. As he later articulated their stance: "Whose parks are these? What are their purposes?"[13]

These were legitimate questions, and ones that Hartzog believed must be asked continually. In the case of the Stoneman's Meadow riot there was the additional issue of order and respect. If the revelers had approached the Yosemite rangers requesting a permit for a meadow party, perhaps they would have been denied the Stoneman's Meadow site but accommodated elsewhere. Instead, they chose to defy the law altogether. They were not interested in asking permission or applying for a permit. Ignoring legitimate authority, of course, produced a response. The problem was that the National Park Service was not prepared to respond to this challenge in a professional manner. They needed new tools, and these tools represented a serious shift in the way of maintaining order and protecting visitors. That is exactly what happened.

Since the 1976 NPS-9 regulation, new rules have strengthened the original directive. Now any ranger or person involved with law enforcement must wear a sidearm while on duty, and most rangers wear Kevlar bullet-proof vests.[14] They are also required to spend considerable time in training at the Federal Law Enforcement Training Center, which was established in 1970. Law enforcement rangers today are armed and, while outwardly friendly, are not always received as welcoming. Visitors may react with caution, depending on their individual response to a revolver.[15] Certainly when Horace Albright penned *"Oh, Ranger!"* in 1947—a narrative about the kindly, thoughtful ranger—he did not have a gun-toting ranger in mind.[16]

LAW OFFICERS IN YELLOWSTONE

But perhaps Albright idealized the gentle qualities of the ranger. Let us look at Yellowstone in a different era when law enforcement was part of the NPS tradition. Although the U. S. Army provided the first effective law enforcement in Yellowstone, a frontiersman named Harry Yount is credited with being the father of the ranger service. Describe as "rough, tough, and intelligent," Yount held various jobs within Wyoming Territory ("bull whacker," buffalo hunter, guide and scout) before Superintendent Philetus W. Norris found $1000 in his 1880 budget to hire Yount with the title "gamekeeper." He was the first white person to winter in Yellowstone, and soon complained that policing the park was far more than one person could accomplish. He recommended a "small active police

force," and in a way the U. S. Army, taking up quarters in 1886, fulfilled his request.[17] When Congress established Yellowstone National Park in 1872 it failed to provide an adequate budget to administer the park, a common case of creation without appropriation. By 1886, Congress still provided only miniscule funds. In that year Secretary of the Interior L. Q. Lamar invoked an 1883 memo of understanding with the Secretary of War to bring in troops. Thus on August 20, 1886, Captain Moses Harris moved into the superintendent's office in Mammoth to take control. Army administration of Yellowstone lasted for 30 years.[18] A visit to Mammoth Hot Springs today reveals ample evidence of the army's tenure in the form of permanent officers' and enlisted mens' quarters as well as the extensive stables related to the cavalry days at Fort Yellowstone. In truth, aside from Yount, the troopers of the U.S. Army were the first national park rangers not only in Yellowstone, but also in Yosemite and Sequoia National Parks.

How did the army perform as protector of Yellowstone? Very well, is the appraisal of historians. The officers and troops were above political issues and simply did what they were superbly qualified to do. They protected the thermal resources against foolish tourist stunts, and they were fearless in tracking down poachers and arresting them or ejecting them from the park. They performed equally well in Yosemite. Wilderness advocate John Muir sang their praises: "In pleasing contrast to the noisy, ever changing management, or mismanagement, of blustering, blundering, plundering, money-making vote-sellers who receive their places from boss politicians as purchased goods, the soldiers do their duty so quietly that the traveler is scarcely aware of their presence."[19]

In Yosemite Lieutenant Colonel S. B. M. Young, undeterred by the political implications, arrested a prominent San Franciscan and his camping party for carrying a loaded rifle in the park and flaunting the rules, essentially ruining their camping trip. Besides their egalitarian attitude, the troopers were particularly good at finding illegal sheep grazing and then driving them out of the park. Again, Muir sang the praises of the soldiers, declaring "blessings on Uncle Sam's soldiers! They have done their job well, and every pine tree is waving its arms for joy."[20] Historian H. Duane Hampton gives them high praise for their work to the point of saying they "saved" our national parks.[21] After the Great War (WWI), some of the veterans mustered out of the army to become some of the best superintendents and rangers in the Park Service.[22]

TODAY'S CALLING

Today's commissioned law enforcement ranger is not much different from those Army soldiers of more than 100 years ago. They still ferret out poachers in the parks. According to the *Management Policies, 2006* manual, the ranger's task is to prevent "criminal activities through resource education, public safety efforts, and deterrence," and the law enforcement division must investigate, apprehend, and prosecute criminals. In Grand Teton, rangers must also protect natural and cultural resources.[23] Law enforcement rangers are commissioned and highly trained for their jobs, and yet every employee is responsible for rules enforcement and education, because, as the *Management Policies* manual puts it, "effective enforcement requires a cooperative community effort." Therefore, employees without a commission are also responsible for both the protection of park resources and the safety of visitors. Every employee should be on the alert for violations of park regulations or for any criminal acts. They should record what they see, but a "citizen arrest" or any sort of confrontation should be avoided.[24]

There is no doubt that greater security concerns and more rigid regulations have developed over the last 20 years. These new regulations were not limited to Grand Teton, but rather applied across the National Park System. We live in a more complex and fearful world, and that apprehension is evident in the print and internet news, on television, in our homes, and in the national parks. Change is the constant, though we may long for a 1950s-style park. In a conversation about how security has changed, former Grand Teton National Park Chief Ranger Andy Fisher gave me wise words to remember: "We all long for a day that is no longer here."[25]

Search and Rescue

All law enforcement rangers deal with criminals or those who violate regulations. But they also work with visitors who may get themselves into trouble while hiking or climbing or floating the Snake River. In the mountains the task of finding and rescuing visitors falls to the rangers who make up the search and rescue team for the park. This may simply mean returning a lost child to parents, but sometimes it means searching out climbers who are lost or have fallen on snow or rock. Rangers doing this kind of work garner publicity and sometimes fame, for they perform complicated and dangerous feats in the course of aiding lost hikers or taking forays of life-saving "short-haul" rescues to help injured climbers. Some of their duties are not so pleasant, such as the retrieval of a climber's body after a fatal accident.

The climbing rangers who also conduct search and rescue operations have a long and distinguished record. It would be impossible to recount all of their activities. Perhaps however, the 1967 rescue on the North Face of the Grand Teton is representative. Two experienced climbers, Gaylord Campbell and Lorrie Hough, were high on a ledge after being struck by falling rocks. Lorrie was in good shape, but Gaylord suffered a compound fracture of his leg and required a difficult rescue. A young Ralph Tingey led the rescue preparations. While the details are fascinating, with limited space we can only suggest the difficulties he encountered. [26] A crucial decision had to be

CLIMBING RANGERS PERFORM A 'SHORT-HAUL' RESCUE.

made. Stranded on a ledge at 13,000 feet, Gaylord could only be raised or lowered. With the advice of expert climbers Leigh Ortenberger and Bob Irvine, who were actually climbing on the mountain at the time, the decision was made to descend. As Tingey related, "no one knew the mountain, and particularly the North Face, like Ortenberger, and although not a Park Service employee, he spent every summer in the Tetons and was the key to the route finding on the rescue." Ortenberger and the rangers determined they needed to lower Gaylord by a Stokes litter down close to 2,000 feet of sheer cliff, while other rangers escorted Lorrie to the Upper Saddle of the Grand Teton and eventually to safety by helicopter evacuation from the lower saddle.[27] Then began the three-day effort to save Gaylord by lowering his litter from one difficult ledge to another while he received injections of morphine. Ortenberger "hopped off like an elf to find a route and a ledge." In spite of the difficult odds, the rescue was a success. Later Tingey would call "The Impossible Rescue" the "most complex and difficult" rescue in North America. All seven members of the rescue team received the Department of the Interior's Valor Award, presented in 1968 by Secretary of the Interior Stewart Udall.[28]

In the years to follow, the Grand Teton rescue team went their separate ways, most earning PhDs in various disciplines. But the comradeship shaped by three days on the North Face of the Grand provided the bonds of trust and fellowship which continued. Much later, Ralph Tingey summed up the life-long bond: "These guys were my best friends, the type of friendship that only depending on each others' lives at the end of a rope could forge, like in battle. The experience of working with them shaped my thoughts and actions for the rest of my life."[29]

That spirit of service and friendship has continued into the new century. Renny Jackson is one of the most admired rangers in Grand Teton National Park's history. Both competent and compassionate, he has been intimately involved with many rescues. Jackson's career reveals something about the semi-independent world of climbing rangers. He was a climber first and a ranger second. In 1976, he joined the park as a seasonal ranger, and he remained in that role for a number of years. He then decided that he wanted a permanent ranger position. He applied, and after his standard forms cleared the park personnel office, administrators forwarded his application to the climbing rangers group. Unlike most other park positions, the applicant must be qualified not only from the point of view of

RENNY JACKSON

the Washington personnel office, but also must pass the hurdle of approval from the Jenny Lake climbing rangers themselves. The superintendent and chief ranger will make the choice, but in conjunction with the climbing rangers. There is a reason for this process: this is life and death work. Rescuers must depend on their partners, and so each member of the group must be chosen with care. A climbing ranger must act as part of a team, and thus physical ability is crucial, but so is mental makeup.[30] Scott Guenther, head of the Jenny Lake climbing rangers, put it well: When considering a new hire, his team looks closely at "how well he plays in the sandbox."[31] The same care is taken in choosing rescue helicopter pilots. Pilots are under contract with private companies and all are proficient in aerial support for fire fighting operations. To qualify for mountain rescue, pilots must also pass the trial of lowering a litter 150 feet into a 10-foot circle—just the thing that would be necessary in a difficult short-haul rescue.[32]

The climbing rangers have achieved a distinctive status in the mountaineering world because the Grand Teton peak is iconic. Every rock climber knows of it and for those who have not yet climbed it, it is on their life list. Still, the rugged peak has a hazy history. Some believe that James Stevenson and Nathanial Langford, both associated with the Ferdinand Hayden Survey in 1872 made the first ascent. The preponderance of opinion, however, credits the William Owen party's ascent in 1898, documented with writings and photographs.[33] The National Park Service keeps a record of the thousands who have climbed the Grand Teton.[34] Most climbers reach the summit and return without incident. Others occasionally run into trouble. Those cases attract attention and sometimes tax the resources of the park rescue team.

In 1997, two University of Wyoming professors of statistics, George Montopoli and Ken Gerow, completed an informative study that featured analysis of backcountry accidents in the park.[35] Both climbers themselves, they discovered that between 1950 and 1996, the park had 609 significant backcountry accidents, for an average of 13 incidents a year, with an average of two being fatal. Many mishaps resulted in falls on rocks (195) or on snow (155). The mountains are never stable. Falling rocks or icefalls caused 41 accidents. Of course, not all accidents took place on the highest peaks. Seventy-four occurred during hiking rather than climbing situations. Fifty-six incidents were a result of illness. The great majority of accidents occurred while visitors were approaching, climbing, or retreating from the Grand Teton.

Among all these statistics are real lives, drama, heroism, and occasionally foolishness and cowardice. The backcountry rangers have seen it all, human emotions at their most intense. Quite often, tragedy is a result of hubris. In August 1957, two young men from South Carolina and Florida had summited Teewinot Mountain but became overconfident on the descent. A loosened boulder knocked "both boys off their feet" and swept them down the mountain, then struck and killed one of them. The other suffered a fractured leg and spent a cold night with his dead friend, but he did survive.[36]

By 1960, the number of climbers had increased dramatically at Grand Teton National Park and also across the country. Young people were discovering the excitement and sense of accomplishment in ascending a peak for the first time or pioneering a new route on an old mountain.[37] In Yosemite National Park, a whole group of "dirt bag" climbers scaled vertical big walls such as El Capitan and Half Dome. They developed new technology that revolutionized the sport.[38] Teton pioneer climbers such as Paul Petzoldt and Glenn Exum, who began their ascents in the 1920s, approached the mountains with a rope and a sturdy pair of boots. Those days of minimal technology were over by the 60s.

So also were the days when the injured were laboriously carried off the mountain on a hand-held stretcher. In the 1960s, climbing rangers began using helicopters for mountain rescues. The helicopter would land at an acceptably level site while rangers lowered the victim off the mountainside and then carried him by stretcher to the waiting helicopter for an aerial evacuation. This rescue method was surely better than pre-helicopter days, but eventually even better techniques, perfected in Europe, came into use. The "short-haul" method, common by 1990, depended on a skilled helicopter pilot hovering above the location of the injured climber. A ranger and basket litter would be lowered by rope and the injured person stabilized and then lifted into the evacuation litter. Once ready, the helicopter returned, delivering the end of the short-haul line to the ranger. The ranger gave a signal and the rescuer and victim swung away from the cliff in tandem, then lowered thousands of feet to land at the location of the search and rescue

cache at Lupine Meadows, soon to be transported to St. John's Medical Center in Jackson.[39] Such a rescue is both dramatic and dangerous. Because of the continual freezing and thawing of water, rocks fall from the mountains with regularity. Not only do these rock missiles pose risks for climbers, but there is always the possibility of collision with a helicopter rotor.[40]

Sometimes, the ranger's challenge is not rescuing but locating a stranded or injured climber. Forty-nine-year-old Dwight Bishop was a well-known climber who had followed his passion all over the world. On Friday, July 16, 2004, he headed into the mountains alone to do the "Grand Traverse," a technical climbing route that involved summiting 11 major peaks. When no one heard from him after four days, 20 climbers mounted a major search. The next day another 50 joined, for a total of 70 searchers plus five dog teams. The park put out a missing persons flyer with Bishop's physical description. This extensive effort came to a sad conclusion when a search team found Bishop's body a couple of thousand feet below a 5.8 rated pitch, where he presumably fell to his death on the North Ridge of the Grand Teton.

What complicated the situation was Bishop's "free soloing." He was alone, and no one knew where he was. The search and rescue report from the Bishop case outlined the advantages and the decided disadvantages of Bishop's style:

> The free soloist sacrifices the safety that is normally afforded the climber who is belaying or who is belayed by a partner, for a lighter-weight and swifter style of climbing that has its own set of unique advantages. However, if anything goes wrong as in this particular case, the results are usually catastrophic. A momentary distraction, a hand or foot hold breaking, a slip on an unnoticed wet or icy spot, or an objective hazard such as rock fall, can all contribute to a loss of the all-important focus that the free soloist relies upon for success.[41]

BISHOP'S DECISION TO GO ALONE ended his life, but it also raised questions. The effort to find and retrieve Bishop's body cost $57,561. Some asked: Should free solo climbing be banned? Renny Jackson remembered that the superintendent did ban it briefly, but then rescinded the decision. Jackson was of the opinion that free soloist climbers will do what they want, regardless of the rules. Regrettably, it can be costly, in this case to the taxpayer, since the money came from a national account.[42]

Most climbing incidents result from poor judgment. Joe and Beth Hestick from West Virginia survived two nights in a cave near the summit of the Grand Teton. When caught in a blizzard in late August, 2003, they lost all visibility. They finally tried to descend, but Joe, suffering from frostbite and exhaustion, fell 50 feet. Rangers evacuated them by helicopter. Climbing ranger Dan Burgette questioned their judgment: "For us, it's a no-brainer that you shouldn't be high on the mountain, especially when it's spitting snow."[43] What Burgette and other climbing rangers rarely say is that their own lives are often in jeopardy because of the foolish or irrational decisions of inexperienced climbers.

When you combine poor judgment with poor equipment, you greatly increase the chances that the climbing rangers will become involved. In July 2000, the Jones party, two groups of four, signed out at the Jenny Lake Ranger Station to climb Skillet Glacier on Mt. Moran. On July 4, they attempted to cross choppy water on Jackson Lake in two small runabouts. Wind-blown waves swamped the boats and they had to be rescued by lake patrol rangers. Besides the danger to themselves, they lost considerable equipment. The next day, a pontoon boat dropped them off at Bearpaw Bay. They climbed the glacier, presumably with ice crampons, but on the descent, one of the party fell some 500 feet, "tumbling head over heels down the Skillet Glacier, hitting rocks with the side of his body." He wore no helmet, for he had lost it in Jackson Lake the day before, and he had not bothered to strap on his crampons. He was alive, but unconscious. Rangers called for a helicopter to assist in the rescue operation.[44] Such rescues are a result of a lack of judgment that leaves the climbing rangers shaking their heads in disbelief.

The largest rescue in park history occurred on Wednesday, July 21, 2010. A severe lightning storm was the culprit. Seventeen climbers in three parties were all on the Grand Teton above the Upper Saddle when a severe storm hit at 12:30 p.m., with lightning, hail, and snow battering the mountain peak for two hours. The climbers, who ranged in age from 21 to 67, were using two of the most popular routes, the Exum Ridge and the Owen-Spaulding. One group of eight was descending the "belly roll" of the Owen-Spaulding route when the lightning hit. Brandon Oldenkamp, age 21, died when he fell about 2,000 feet after being knocked off a ledge by a violent strike. The seven survivors descended to the Lower Saddle under their own power. At that point, a medic checked them for injuries, then a hovering helicopter flew them to Lupine Meadows on the floor of the valley. The other two parties of four and five climbers, some "hobbled

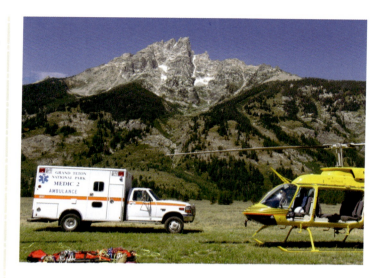

by injuries and all suffering from shock, both electrical and otherwise," were in bad shape. Both rangers and helicopters were kept busy as they short-hauled a total of 16 affected climbers from the upper mountain.

It was the most complex mountain rescue ever in Grand Teton National Park. Two helicopters, 15 Jenny Lake climbing rangers, and eight other rangers were in the air or assisting on the ground. One journalist praised the Jenny Lake Rangers as an elite team "with plenty of loners and mountain men, but…also …people who've done law-enforcement training—a mix of type As and poets that works."[45]

Others from the park and local community participated as well, including 24 emergency medical workers, among them two doctors and 13 members of the Jackson Hole Fire/EMS volunteer team. A total of more than 80 people worked on the rescue.[46] When there is a crisis, or as one ranger put it, "a bus wreck" in the mountains, the park must recruit all trained first responders. There were plenty of heroes in this story, and in March 2012, Secretary of the Interior Ken Salazar presented awards for valor and citizen bravery to seven Grand Teton National Park rangers and six civilians for their part in this major rescue operation.[47]

At the time of rescue, no one considers the financial cost. All attention and effort focuses on saving lives and sparing people's suffering. However, rescues are costly and bills eventually arrive. The July 2010 logistical operation cost $52,000. Who would pay? If the people rescued made errors in judgment, is it logical that the victims should be financially responsible? The 17 lightning casualties in 2010 placed themselves in a precarious position, since climbers should summit the mountain by noon and begin their descent before mid-day thunderstorms develop, a common occurrence during summer months. Significantly, no guided parties were caught in this intense lightning storm. They were all off the peak and no longer vulnerable. Many other rescues can be attributed to human error, and with the Park Service strapped for cash, it seems reasonable that those who caused the problem should shoulder the cost. However, because the climbing rangers fear that those in danger might not call for assistance if they knew they would have to pay for their own rescue, the policy remains that a mountain rescue—or any rescue in the park, for that matter—will not be billed. There is a special account designated as Jenny Lake Rangers Fund, and those who have appreciated the help or owe their lives to the rangers may contribute. Renny Jackson revealed to me that all the 2010 climbers who were rescued during the lightning disaster were made aware of the fund.[48] Perhaps in the future "trip insurance" may become part of the Teton climbing experience.

As with so many functions of Grand Teton National Park, change over time has provided new challenges for park management. There are many more people in the mountains today than decades ago, and if they encounter a problem, they expect that climbing rangers or backcountry volunteers will help them. In 1950, mountain operations and management were simple procedures because participants had to assume more personal responsibility. The Jenny Lake Rangers were few, and without cell phones, radios, and particularly helicopters, climbers who became lost or injured relied on their own resilience and courage. In the last 60 years, the Teton Range has remained geologically inviting, and our visual excitement at observing these jagged peaks has not lessened. What has changed is people's desire to have a life-changing adventure in the Tetons. That has consequently accelerated use and increased the climbing accidents. The climbing rangers, however, will always encourage mountaineering while knowing that it complicates their job.

IN THE SUMMER RANGERS ARE ON THE RIVER EVERYDAY.

RIVER RESCUES

Along with the mountains, the Snake River is a chief attraction of the park. And like climbing, the number of visitors floating the river has increased exponentially over the last 60 years. The Snake River gathers several tributaries of the Yellowstone country and flows south into Jackson Lake. Below the Jackson Lake Dam, the Snake, as of 2009 designated as a Wild and Scenic River, flows through Grand Teton for some 20 miles, bisecting the valley with its swift, clear-running waters. It is a stunningly scenic river, attracting thousands of tourists annually. Most visitors take a raft trip with one of a half dozen commercial companies, putting in at Deadmans Bar and exiting the river ten miles downstream at Moose landing. The river guides are well-trained, and as park concessionaires, the companies must conform to safety regulations. Rafting companies share the river with fishing guides and private boaters. Private rafters must have a permit, and they are warned at entry points that the river is swift and should not be attempted by the inexperienced.

While thousands of visitors enjoy the river today, it is a rather recent phenomenon. Before World War II, there were no adequate rafts available. The kayaks used today did not exist, and canoe owners generally found the piedmont lakes a more pleasant experience. Stories of fur trappers struggling to cross the river in "bull boats," or of early river running such as by explorer Lieutenant Gustavus Doane during November–December of 1876, were a matter of necessity, not recreation. Some of these early river expeditions ended in ruin.[49] In our modern era, it should be no surprise that the first river fatalities resulted from an automobile accident. Albert Oakley, 38, a foreman with the Peterson Construction Company, was returning to his trailer at Moose on Sunday evening, December 14, 1956, with his wife and four children. Oakley and his workers were constructing the bridge that would kill him and his family—a bridge that still spans the river. It was December and a blizzard obscured his vision. As he approached the bridge, he lost control of his car, which reportedly "whipped back and forth." His vehicle hit the left

wing of the new bridge, careened into a concrete center post and plunged into the river because the bridge lacked a guardrail. Traffic was practically non-existent, and even if someone had come along, the swirling snow had covered his tire tracks. It was not until noon the next day that two children playing on the riverbank noticed the overturned car and told their parents, who then alerted park rangers. What they found was not pretty. Albert, his wife, Marguerite, and their four children were all dead.[50]

Ironically enough, one of the worst mishaps related to the river involved rangers on patrol in the back country. In March 1960, Assistant Chief Ranger Stan Spurgeon and rangers Gale Wilcox and John Fonda were on their way to the west side of Jackson Lake on a three-day ski trip to check the Survey Creek cabin, shovel it free of snow, and record any wildlife sightings. They took a snow plane up Jackson Lake and, when near the head of the lake, they prepared to cross the ice. Where the river current enters the lake, the ice was thin and not safe, so they moved southeast a few hundred yards where they found a crossing with seemingly solid ice. Spurgeon cautiously slid off the 5-foot bank onto the ice, testing it with his ski pole. When about half way across, he quickly poled to the western shore. Gale Wilcox followed, closely matching Spurgeon's tracks. Then John Fonda, an experience mountaineer who had climbed most of the park's peaks and served with the search and rescue rangers for eight years, began to cross. Spurgeon was looking west when he heard the ice crack. He spun around to see a head above the water about 15 feet from the east shore. Both men raced back on their skis. Wilcox dropped to his stomach and extended his ski pole to Fonda, as Spurgeon held Wilcox's by his ski.

The rescue effort was futile. The ice broke and Wilcox also went in the water. Both Wilcox and Fonda had used Arlberg leather safety straps to keep from losing a ski in deep snow. Unfortunately, in the frigid water it was nearly impossible to release their heavy wooden skis. With sheer determination, Sturgeon and Wilcox broke the safety straps on his skis and Spurgeon managed to pull Wilcox onto the ice and away from the hole. But Fonda was lost. Spurgeon later recalled that "John's head bobbed under. I yelled at him to hang on. He came up on at least two occasions before he stayed under." Spurgeon attended to Wilcox who was in deep hypothermia and unable to walk. Finally Spurgeon determined the only chance to save Wilcox was to push on to the Lower Berry Creek cabin, warm up a little, and return with a sleeping bag for Wilcox. Exhausted and hypothermic himself, it took considerable time before Spurgeon returned, and discovered that Wilcox had died of exposure.[51]

Two experienced, fit rangers had died, and the third barely survived. The Department of the Interior awarded posthumous Citations of Valor for John Fonda and Gale Wilcox. Ranger Stanley Spurgeon received the Citation of Valor in April, 1961, as well as a Bronze Medal by the Carnegie Hero Commission. Today, the lake's northeast promontory is called Fonda Point, and the landing spot near Berry Creek is named Wilcox Point.

Visitors do not normally experience a river float trip in winter, but in the summer, the Snake River is incredibly beautiful, scenic and popular to boat. However in any season, the Snake can be risky. While there are no rapids in the park section, the river is very braided and the water is cold and flows swiftly. Entering the wrong channel can be perilous. Spring runoff in May and June may require quick thinking, strength, and techniques that inexperienced rafters may not possess . The greatest danger is from logjams and debris or from trees dislodging from the bank, floating down the river, and then creating unexpected barriers across the main current or a side channel. These cottonwoods and lodgepole pines often settle in the middle of a channel. This was the situation on June 2, 2006, when a commercial raft rounded a curve in the "maze" region, a multi-channeled section halfway between Deadmans Bar and Moose, to confront a large recently fallen tree lodged in the middle of the current. With the weight of 13 elderly people aboard, the raft was not easily maneuvered. The guide tried to avoid the obstacle, but the raft hit the tree trunk, turned over, and dumped all passengers into the icy stream. What followed was a major rescue effort by search and rescue rangers on foot, in a jet boat, and by helicopter. All the passengers were wearing life preservers and most were able to make their way to shore. However, three guests were trapped by tree roots and branches below the water line and drowned.[52]

Drownings have occurred on a regular basis in the Snake River rapids below Jackson on Bridger-Teton National Forest land (jurisdiction), but this was the worst river accident in Grand Teton's history.

Although there was nothing the river rangers could have done to prevent the mishap in this case, having an official park presence is essential. River use must be managed. Some "Sunday rafters" neglect to buy a permit. Others neglect to take life preservers, insist on taking their dog, or are simply inexperienced and unaware of the natural dangers of the river. Novices attempt to canoe the river, sometimes with disastrous results during high water. A wrong move can easily swamp a canoe, resulting in damage or loss of the boat, a cold dunking, and possible hypothermia. Along most of the 20-mile route, the river flows at least a quarter to a half mile from the nearest road, thus help is not readily or quickly available. Commercial or private parties will help a river runner in distress, but the park river ranger is often a welcome sight, especially on a cold spring day when the potential for hypothermia is the greatest.

Perhaps the most bizarre river death occurred on June 28, 1974. Jim Wyatt, a boatman for the Grand Teton Lodge Company, was entertaining his passengers with stories on this clear day. Among his guests were Beaumont Newhall, a well-known photographer, and his wife Nancy. She had won a certain fame as the editor or author of a dozen books on photography and was working closely with Ansel Adams on his autobiography. The couple had so enjoyed a morning float with Wyatt from Pacific Creek to Deadmans Bar that they decided to accompany him on the lower half of the river, putting in at 3:20 p.m. at the lodge's picnic area just south of Deadmans Bar. About 20 minutes downstream, the Newhalls asked Wyatt to show the other guests the erosive effects of high water on the banks of the river. Wyatt obliged, with an 80-foot-high leaning spruce tree providing the example. A brisk wind came up, and as he was talking, the tree tipped and fell. Wyatt could not row the raft quickly enough to evade it, and the huge tree crashed onto the raft. Some were thrown overboard and swept down river as far as a mile and a half. Nancy Newhall took the full brunt of the falling spruce, and hidden in the limbs, she was unconscious and badly hurt. There was a moment of chaos. One of the group, a Mrs. Newman, was in "a state of hysteria" concerning Nancy Newhall, and she was screaming and being totally disruptive. Wyatt had to yell at her to shut up, since she was "becoming a threat to the state of order and control being maintained by everyone else."[53]

Fortunately, Wyatt's raft was the first of three floating in tandem down the river. The other two boatmen helped in the rescue of those swept downriver: the Carroll family (parents and two children) and the rest of the Newman family (parents, and three children). Beyond cuts and bruises, they suffered only mild hypothermia. Wyatt meanwhile wanted to take Nancy Newhall overland to the road, perhaps a quarter of a mile distant, and flag down a car. The other two boatmen thought better of that plan. They lashed

Wyatt's raft to one of their boats, made Newhall as comfortable as possible, and rowed for the Moose Landing take out. They arrived at 5:47 p.m. where an ambulance awaited to take Nancy Newhall to St. John's hospital. She never recovered, having suffered a partially severed leg, broken ribs, internal injuries, possible fractured vertebra, and likely concussion. She died in the hospital on July 7, 1958.

Ranger Edward Wilson investigated the accident on June 28 and 29. After composing his description of the incident, he wrote his opinion: "From my investigation and six years of river patrol experience, I feel that the accident and/or injuries were caused by NO negligence on part of the boatman (Jim Wyatt) or the Grand Teton Lodge Company float operation. Wyatt was operating the craft in a normal manner, when the combined set of circumstances of timing, high water, wind, leaning tree, and bank erosion caused the accident." No one could really take issue with such a freak accident. Yet, with the unfair advantage of hindsight, we might note that the report indicated "a strong wind (15–25MPH)." Given that the water was high and fast, and it was the "falling tree season," Wyatt might have kept his raft farther away from the eastern shoreline.

Ansel Adams took the news of Nancy Newhall's death hard. The Newhalls were among his closest friends. Furthermore, her death took place close to the location of his iconic Teton photograph with the river in the foreground, shot near today's Snake River Overlook turnout. Later, in his autobiography,

Adams wrote about the irony and implausibility of Newhall's death:

It is difficult to understand the extraordinary coincidence of time and place; a tree, standing perhaps for centuries, weakens and falls at the precise moment a raft glides beneath it. The physical event is disturbing in itself but the fact that Nancy Newhall, a dedicated writer and scholar, devoted to the wilderness, should have been the victim of this fearful moment in time is hard to accept without questioning the decisions of the gods in time and space.[54]

MOST OF THE RIVER INCIDENTS, fatal and otherwise, have taken place in the area known as the Maze, a stretch about five miles down river from Deadmans Bar, where the Snake braids into multiple channels. Downed trees seem to congregate there, new ones each year, blocking channels and creating sudden barriers. This was the case on July 4, 1992, when Harvey Cohen, his wife, Gail, and his friends, Desmond McCarthy and his wife, Cezanna Philippon arrived from Colorado, rented an Avon raft, and headed for Deadmans Bar. Cohen had rafted the river a few times, but only from Schwabachers Landing (an entry point rarely available today), thus avoiding the more hazardous Maze portion. They left at 10:05 a.m. with Cohen on the oars. According to the official board of inquiry, all occupants of the raft placed their personal flotation devices on the seats "and were sitting on them." As they approached the Maze the strong current swept Cohen into the wrong channel. A log blocked his path. About to hit it, he swung the raft to the left, which inevitably dipped the right side and caused the raft to flip. All four passengers fell out. After struggling to the surface, Cohen hung onto the offending log. Gail did as well, while Cezanna passed under the logjam and emerged in two feet of water. Desmond McCarthy, however, did not surface. After the shock of the accident passed, Cohen and Gail searched the logjam, and about five minutes later they spotted him underwater. They were unsuccessful in their effort to free McCarthy from his entangled clothes. After a 10-minute struggle he slipped from their grasp leaving them with only his windbreaker.

Ranger Chalfant arrived 40 minutes after the accident. McCarthy could not be found. Chalfant requested a helicopter with divers and chainsaws. Search operations continued on July 5 and 6, without success. Finally, search dogs alerted the rangers that McCarthy might be submerged beneath the logjam. The situation called for an unusual meeting. Representatives of the NPS, Forest Service, Bureau of Reclamation, and Wyoming Game and Fish Department met to discuss lowering the river at its exit from the Jackson Lake Dam. This would be the only way to recover McCarthy's body. They decided to lower the dam outflow incrementally, beginning at noon on July 7. Park divers quickly found his body on the downstream side of the logjam in five feet of water. But still McCarthy's body could not be freed until the Bureau of Reclamation further lowered flows, at which time park personnel pulled his body to shore.[55]

The board of inquiry determined that wearing a life jacket could have saved McCarthy's life. It was foolish for Cohen not to insist that his passengers wear and secure their life jackets. The most unusual aspect of this episode was the cooperation among the federal agencies in lowering the river. Although there is no record of the actual meeting, there could have been disagreement about whether to reduce the river flow, for clearly McCarthy was dead. In the end, all apparently agreed to take this step to recover his body.

For every recorded incident on the Snake River, there are dozens that do not result in death. Some of these tales end up in the *Jackson Hole News and Guide*, reminding us that we will always have incidents in the Teton Range and on the Snake River as a result of accidents, inexperience, ignorance, disregard of regulations, or just plain hubris. In those cases, the people of Grand Teton's search and rescue teams stand ready to do their best to keep visitors safe.

ONE COULD CONCLUDE that Grand Teton National Park is a dangerous place to take a vacation, whether climbing in the mountains, rafting on the river, or hiking the scenic trails. Hundreds of thousands of visitors have had enjoyable, safe, and memorable experiences and promise that they will be back. The mountains sear one's memory. The river is equally impressive, and a raft trip is often a high point of a park visit. Most come away with positive stories and memories of their Grand Teton vacation. However, it is well to remember that Grand Teton National Park is not a theme park where paying guests intentionally engage in fear-inducing rides created by humans. There are real risks and moderate dangers attached to some national park activities. Normal precautions should dictate the adventurer's choice of activities, and there are park rangers to monitor bear sightings, conduct nature walks, and provide cautionary advice, all with the intent of ensuring an exciting but a safe and educational experience.

There is no mystery about the reasons for the park's turn toward more intensive law enforcement, more sophisticated mountain rescues, or efforts to keep people safe on the river. Hardly a day goes by when the law enforcement rangers do not resolve a life-threatening crisis, often on the highways. Why? In the case of Grand Teton, the answer is partly a matter of increased use. In 1945, visitation to Grand Teton National Park and the Jackson Hole National Monument was 41,349 persons. By the 1970s, visitation exceeded three million people a year, reflecting tremendous growth in the popularity of the park. Just as a good-sized city must increase its services and protections with increased population, Grand Teton has responded by doing the same. Today there are new activities and new dangers, but rangers are professionals, well trained in new technologies. The intent is to educate the visitors to use the park safely. If that does not work, they are prepared to do more and, if necessary, rescue.

[1] Official Report Concerning the Shooting of District Park Ranger Eliot Davis, January 11, 1953, Grand Teton National Park archives (hereafter cited as GTNP), Elk Studies 1950, Leases, Boundary Changes 1930s, file no. 801-01. Obviously this report was misfiled.

[2] This story is according to Jack Huyler.

[3] Official Report, January 11, 1953

[4] For an account of the Cunningham homestead shootout, see Robert B. Betts, *Along the Ramparts of the Tetons: The Saga of Jackson Hole*, Wyoming (Boulder: Colorado Associated University Press, 1978), 170-74.

[5] Interview with retired ranger Jack Davis by author, February 11, 2013. Davis continued his career as superintendent of Grand Canyon National Park, and retired as Ass't Director of the NPS. Also see the *Jackson Hole Guide*, October 25, 1962.

[6] His partner was not in the garage, but according to Davis the fugitive had been an actor, and convinced them that if they moved they would be shot.

[7] Ranger Jack Davis interview by author, February 11, 2013. Also see the *Jackson Hole Guide*, October 25, 1962.

[8] This account is taken from a chronological summary of incidents involving deadly force in Paul D. Berkowitz, *The History of Law Enforcement in the Federal Conservation and Land Management Agencies* (n.p., revised 1992), 48. The incident took place on October 22, 1962. GTNP Chief Ranger Michael Nash provided the author with a copy of the summary.

[9] Much of the detail of the riot is from Laura Avedisian, "The Yosemite Riot: Changes in Policy and Management in the National Park Service," M.A. thesis, San Jose State University, 1998.

[10] Alfred Runte, *Yosemite: The Embattled Wilderness* (Lincoln: University of Nebraska Press, 1990), 202.

[11] Paul Schullery, *Mountain Time* (New York: Nick Lyon Books, 1984), 141–54.

12 Avedisian, "Yosemite Riot," 82, quoting from Abbey, The Journey Home, 144–45.

13 George B. Hartzog Jr., *Battling for the National Parks* (Mt. Kisco, N.Y.: Moyer Bell, 1988), 1–3.

14 Interview with Assistant Chief Ranger Ira Blitzblau by author, January 29, 1913

15 Obviously this judgment is based on my own reactions.

16 Horace M. Albright and Frank J. Taylor, *"Oh, Ranger!"* (New York: Dodd, Mead, 1947).

17 A short biographical sketch of Yount can be found at *www.cv.nps.gov/history/hisnps/npshistory/yount.htm#35*. Yount has been further honored by the NPS, which named a prestigious award after him. The Harry Yount Award honors each year a ranger who "have the skills to perform a wide scope of ranger duties—protecting resources and serving visitors. " See www.nps.gov/aboutus/harry-yount-award.htm

18 John Ise, *Our National Park Policy: A Critical History* (Baltimore: Johns Hopkins University Press, 1961), 44–45.

19 Ibid., 45, quoting Muir.

20 Quoted in Robert W. Righter, *The Battle Over Hetch Hetchy: America's Most Controversial Dam and the Birth of Modern Environmentalism* (New York: Oxford University Press, 2005), 114.

21 H. Duane Hampton, *How the United States Cavalry Saved the National Parks* (Bloomington: Indiana University Press, 1971).

22 See Horace M. Albright, *The Birth of the National Park Service* (Salt Lake City: Howe Brothers, 1985), 91–93.

23 National Park Service, *Management Policies, 2006* (Washington, D. C.: Government Printing Office, 2006), 108. This 168-page book provides guidelines for decision making, a book that Superintendent Mary Gilson Scott and her staff consult with great regularity when problems emerge.

24 Ibid.

25 Ranger Andy Fisher, discussion with author, August 8, 2012.

26 Ranger Ralph Tingey later wrote in some detail of the rescue. His four part account can be found at the following internet address: http://outerlocal.com/climbing/the-impossibe-rescue-outpost#.UTEXOPc21pw.emailC

27 Ortenberger was a physicist, but a historian and climber who wrote the classic book on climbing in the Tetons: Leigh Ortenberger, *A Climber's Guide to the Teton Range* (San Francisco: Sierra Club, 1965). The most recent edition of *A Climber's Guide* is co-written with Renny Jackson. Ortenberger may be considered a pioneer climber along with Paul Petzoldt, Glenn Exum, and Fritiof Fryxell.

28 Ralph Tingey, "The Impossible Rescue, Part IV. " In 2009 the team reassembled and filmed a limited reenactment of the rescue, directed by Jackson Hole filmmaker Peter Pilafian. It should be available by the summer of 2014.,

29 Ibid.

30 Renny Jackson, interview by author, November 1, 2011. Jackson is now retired but is active as a climber and heading community projects. As a member of the Jackson community he worked with the team that worked to fund and then construct the climbers' rocks and memorial at the Jackson City Park which can be attributed to his hard work and foresight.

31 Telephone interview with Jenny Lake Ranger Scott Guenther by author, March 8, 13, 2013

32 Ibid., March 13, 2013. Film makers produced a very enlightening film detailing the mountain rescue techniques. It is called Acceptable Risk and is available in the Teton County Public Library.

33 There is a rich and controversial climbing history of the Tetons in print. For a starter, see Orrin H. Bonney and Lorraine Bonney, *The Grand Controversy* (New York: American Alpine Club, 2000). The Stevenson and Langford first ascent claim, for example, has been contested by climbers and scholars.

34 To see a listing of all those who have climbed the Grand Teton as well as a number of other peaks in the range, see: *www.tetonclimbinghistory.com*.

35 George Montopoli and Ken Gerow, "An Analysis of Backcountry Accidents in Grand Teton National Park," (35-page typescript), University of Wyoming–National Park Service Research Center, 1997.

36 *Jackson Hole Guide*, August 1, 1957, in "Accidents" vertical file, Jackson Hole Historical Society and Museum.

37 In 1965 Leigh Ortenburger published *A Climber's Guide to the Teton Range* (San Francisco: Sierra Club, 1965). Ortenburger's guide sold well and has gone through a number of editions. The latest editions have been co-authored with Renny Jackson.

38 See Joseph Taylor, *Pilgrims of the Vertical: Yosemite Rock Climbing and Modern Environmental Cultures* (Cambridge: Harvard University Press, 2010).

39 Renny Jackson interview, November 1, 2011.

40 Scott Guenther interview, March 13, 2013.

41 2004 Major SARS Reports, GTNP, "Bishop Fatality" folder.

42 Information from Jenny Lake Ranger Scott Guenther.

43 *Jackson Hole News and Guide*, September 3, 2003.

44 2000 Major SARS Reports, "Jones Party," GTNP.

45 Brad Wieners, "Countdown to Tragedy," *Sports Illustrated*, July 18, 2011.

46 Angus Thuermer Jr. and Kelsey Dayton, "Climbers Were Retreating," *Jackson Hole Daily*, July 26, 2010.

47 *Jackson Hole News and Guide*, March 7, 2012, 2A.

48 Renny Jackson interview, November 1, 2011.

49 Doane's foolhardy exploration down the Snake River is recounted in Frank Calkins, *Jackson Hole* (New York: Alfred A. Knopf, 1973), 89–107.

50 *Jackson Hole Guide*, December 20, 1956.

51 I constructed this account from the NPS Search and Rescue Report and Charles R. Farabee, *Death, Daring, and Disaster: Search and Rescue in the National Parks* (New York: Rowman & Littlefield, 2005) 241-2. Also see *Jackson Hole Guide* and the *Jackson Hole Courier*, March 17, 1960 for newspaper accounts. The *Courier* noted that it had been "well below zero" the night before. For days the temperature had been very low, so the question became, why did the ice break? The best answer came from Chief Ranger Doug McClaren who believed that the water kept flowing out of the dam, creating an air pocket between water and ice.

52 See Superintendent's Report, 2006, GTNP.

53 This account is based on the "Case Incident Record," June 28, 1974, (Boat Accident Investigation—Verbal Report), GTNP, Dispatch Office, SARS Record.

54 Ansel Adams, *Ansel Adams: An Autobiography* (Boston: Little, Brown, 1985).

55 "Accidental Death of Desmond C. McCarthy," July 4, 1992, GTNP, Dispatch Department Files, Death Records.

Peaks, Politics, and Passion: Grand Teton National Park Comes of Age

Chapter 5.

Protecting the Natural Environment

PROTECTING THE NATURAL ENVIRONMENT is at the very heart of the charge and custodial mission for the staff at Grand Teton National Park. While aspects of this broad topic can be found throughout the book, this chapter focuses on fire policy, a misguided effort to place wild animals behind a fenced enclosure, and the park's more recent effort to create some balance or sustainability for wildlife and their habitats. In protecting the park from fire, whether caused by human actions or natural forces, again we see changes in official attitudes. In the effort to create a wildlife park, we see a strong conflict between scientific thought which supported wildlife for its own sake, and those who believed park wildlife existed primarily for tourist enjoyment.

In recent years, the park's wildlife philosophy has evolved toward an emphasis on the "rights of wildlife," with humans honoring those rights and acting simply as facilitators. The wildlife picture in Grand Teton is constantly changing, particularly in the relationships between predator and prey. The park's wildlife biologists must constantly modify policies in seeking sustainability and balance between preservation of resources and human activities. In a small park such as Grand Teton, such a goal is not easy. Wildlife require significant and essential space and tourists expect unfettered access. Scientists embrace a natural system concepts, but while that might be their ultimate a goal, for now they must balance between human behavior and those of nature.

FIRE POLICY

James Sterba, a reporter for the *New York Times,* was puzzled. He was watching the Waterfall Fire in October 1974 as it burned on the western shore of Jackson Lake, sending up plumes of smoke. With him were five men, two of them park rangers. What perplexed Sterba was the group's inactivity. He noted that it was "a strange feeling to stand in the middle of a slow-burning fire and do nothing but watch it burn. It could have been easily stopped, but nobody moved."[1] Sterba was understandably baffled by a new fire policy that allowed fires to burn naturally without suppression efforts. Why not snuff it out? The answer was that the peculiar policy represented a revolutionary reversal of fire suppression strategy in national parks. Science now advocated an alternative approach which acknowledged fire as a natural process upon the landscape.

When we think about fire in Grand Teton National Park, we imagine those chaotic blazes we call wildfires—fires that cannot be controlled. Even "controlled burns," those fires deliberately set by the Park Service as an ecological tool, have sometimes turned into unmanageable wildfires. The best-laid plans can go astray; wind is a capricious and an often uncooperative catalyst.

Fire can be both a threat and an asset. "For as long as humans have experienced fire, they have embraced and fought it with equal ardor."[2] One of the first European visitors to Grand Teton did neither—he ran. When William A. Baillie-Grohman, an aristocratic Englishman, entered Jackson Hole in 1880 he had every intention of enjoying the valley. He later explained that "we stayed for 10 days in the Basin, and probably would have remained another fortnight had not a great forest fire, raging in the timbered regions north of us, the smoke of which we had seen for a week, threatened to invade the Basin." So, he left. The adventurous Englishman intended to return, but this was not to be. Neither was his plan to climb the Grand Teton. As he put it, "Most annoying was one of the consequences entailed by the fire, namely, that I was prevented ascending quite to the summit of the great Peak."[3] Not only did the fire represent danger,

THE WATERFALL CANYON FIRE

but the blueblood explorer observed that other lightning-caused fires had left their distinctive mark on the landscape. Blackened tree trunks told the story of past fire encounters. Baillie-Grohman's descriptive account reminds us that fire has always been a natural feature of the Jackson Hole landscape. In 1876, for instance, the pioneer photographer William H. Jackson, documented a significant fire on Signal Mountain through his glass plate exposure of the charred landscape. Although a source of fear, these early fires were altogether natural and, we now know, in many ways beneficial.

Early settlers, explorers, and park advocates, did not regard fire as beneficial. Only the deceitful did; those who used fire to their advantage. North of the Tetons, "unscrupulous hunters" torched Yellowstone Park lands to push wildlife beyond the Yellowstone boundaries to the south (now the John D. Rockefeller, Jr. Memorial Parkway). After the army assumed control of Yellowstone in August 1886, the company unit stationed at Flagg Ranch was committed to extinguishing natural or human-caused wildfires, but lacked staffing to adequately do the job. Lightning ignited many of the fires while errant hunters and/or careless campers were accountable for others. Mark Twain may have been a typical example of a careless camper, although his experience happened in California, rather than Wyoming. When camped on the shore of Lake Tahoe, he neglected his campfire and soon "saw that my fire was galloping all over the premises." He was forced to take to the lake waters to avoid being incinerated by his own irresponsible blunder.[4]

In southern Yellowstone National Park, Twain's anecdote would have amused people, but nothing could change the helplessness of the military firefighters confronted with these periodic blazes. In the 19th century, few Americans were even aware of fires in the West. What transformed the national attitude was the "big burn" of 1910 when wind-driven wildfires consumed over 3.1 million acres of forest land in Idaho, Montana, and eastern Washington. The massive conflagration monopolized newspaper headlines across the nation as the blazes swept away both lives and timber wealth. This national drama was the largest fire disaster in the country's recorded history, taking the lives of 78 firefighters. According to one historian, the fire also assured the ascendency of the U.S. Forest Service as the protector of the extensive national forest lands—a portion of which would soon become part of Grand Teton National Park.[5]

Before the park materialized, Teton National Forest employees were on alert, keeping a sharp eye for fires from the ground or from lookouts such as those at Spalding Bay, and on Signal Mountain and Blacktail Butte. In the 1930s, these lookouts were an important element of fire protection. In Jackson Hole, they were manned by young men from the Civilian Conservation Corps who worked for $1.50 an hour.[6] Records list 87 fires between 1910 and 1920, but all seem to have been minor blazes conflagrations and quickly suppressed. In those days, it was unproven that cigarettes caused cancer, but the records show that they certainly ignited fires.

With the arrival of the National Park Service, the established record of fire suppression continued. Between 1929 and 1938, rangers reported 62 fires, of which 48 were human-caused. They were all small, and the average "corral time" was 54 minutes.[7] Surely this record illustrated the tremendous success in the park's objective when it came to fires at that time. The 1939 perspective is worth quoting:

Fire constitutes the greatest menace to the park. It is therefore essential that fires be prevented so far as possible, and those that do start shall be detected and extinguished with the greatest possible dispatch. Our objective in suppression is to confine every fire to the smallest possible acreage, and in no case fail to control the fire before the heat of the second day. The number of men necessary to attain this objective will be the govern-ing factor in determining the number of men to be sent to any fire."[8]

THE STATEMENT REVEALED a certain hubris, assuming that park personnel could manage any fire within two days. It helped, of course, that many of these small fires were the result of careless disposal of cigarettes by individuals, while lightning-caused fires, of course, were a natural occurrence. The policy suggested that with a quick, forceful response, any fire could be controlled. It is a mode of management that speaks to human dominance and the helplessness of nature in resisting our will. Second, the policy assumed that all wildfires were harmful, both to people and to the natural environment. This policy reflected the ideas of John D. Coffman, a one-time Forest Service fire expert and then the fire guru of the National Park Service. He espoused the philosophy that fire was the enemy, and "the park's job was to put it out as soon as possible."[9]

A New View

More recent fire experts eventually challenged Coffman's position that all fires were evil and detrimental to the park and people. In the 1950s and 1960s, new ideas and revelations in science began to gain the ascendency in fire management philosophy. After 50 years of fire suppression, science interceded and significantly revised our understanding of the role of fire—basically from a negative to a positive mindset. At Grand Teton National Park, the fire management staff began considering natural and prescribed burn plans. They were part of a small group determined to follow the 1968 *Green Book* of administrative policy for NPS natural areas. The policy suggested that "the presence or absence of natural fire within a given habitat is recognized as one of the ecological factors contributing to the perpetuation of plants and animals native to that habitat."[10] In short, fire could be a good thing for the natural environment, particularly in managing the accumulation of hazardous fuels, and restoring natural vegetation. Small controlled fires might prevent a future big burn like that of 1910. A 1974 plan underscored this evolving understanding: "Grand Teton National Park is not being managed to preserve natural ecosystems unless fire is allowed to play its natural ecological role. Without fire, marked changes have occurred and will continue to occur, in patterns of vegetation."[11] This was a revolutionary statement in that it acknowledged that 50 to 70 years of fire suppression had been creating an ecologically

artificial park, one that inhibited diversity in plant and tree life. Furthermore, the report indicated that a "no fire policy" meant increased fuel reserves. A large fire could lead to a catastrophic burn, like the explosion of a full gasoline tank versus a near empty one. It should be noted that Grand Teton was in the vanguard of the revised national fire policy. This was not the case in many other parks. Historian Richard Sellers noted that, "through much of the 1960s, the goal of total suppression of forest fires in the parks remained in effect." Not until 1978 did the official Park Service *Management Policies* embrace fires as "natural phenomena which must be permitted to continue to influence the ecosystem if truly natural systems are to be perpetuated."[12]

To implement the new policy, the staff at Grand Teton established three specific fire sections. In Zone 1, the northern reaches of the park, wildfires would be allowed to burn naturally. In Zone 2, the central area, particularly the Potholes region, the park's fire management team would determine the response, if any. In Zone 3, the heart of the park from Moose to Jenny Lake and east of the Snake River, all fires would be suppressed. The plan also noted that, "the concept of wilderness [Zone 1], where natural forces are dominant, and man is only an observer, may in time become farcical with total fire suppression."[13]

The plan was largely the work of Lloyd L. Loope, research biologist at Grand Teton. Not only did he delineate the three sections, but he also strongly defended the plan's prescribed, or controlled, burn policy. He did not want to "turn back the clock so that the landscape appears exactly as it did in 1808 when John Colter arrived. The important consideration is that natural ecological forces must be allowed to operate, subjecting animal and plant communities to the same processes of selection which have influenced them for thousands or millions of years." Loope, in essence, invited wildfires back as one of the forces of a natural ecosystem.[14]

Meanwhile, fire policy was slowly changing in other places. NPS Director George Hartzog chided Edward Cliff, chief of the Forest Service, that "various park people have suggested to me that the fire protection message, especially as presented by Smokey Bear, might be improved." Of course the Park Service had little to teach the Forest Service about wildfires, although it did adopt a prescribed burn policy several years in advance of the Forest Service. But Hartzog wished to remind his fellow bureaucrat that "fire is not the devastating destructive agent it has been said to be. It kills some life but it makes conditions for many forms of life possible." Writing in a somewhat jocular vein, Hartzog suggested that Smokey's message be revised to "don't let wildfires be your fault."[15] Not very catchy, but it would be a more ecologically correct message.

Beyond changing policy regarding natural wildfires, Grand Teton National Park also advocated and implemented prescribed burns; that is, actually identifying areas to ignite purposely. This idea faced some criticism. Wyoming Governor Stan Hathaway admitted he did not fully understand the program, but he did "have a gut feeling that the public may misunderstand or have apprehension about man-made forest fires."[16] His view certainly represented the thoughts of many. Even local environmental activist, Mardy Murie, and her half-sister, Louise Murie, expressed doubts from an ecological viewpoint. They suggested that this sort of experimentation should not be carried out on park land. Wildlife biologist Adolph Murie chimed in that fire chiefs ought to be "guardians, not gardeners." If anywhere, testing should be conducted on Forest Service land, which "has a different sort of mandate." The park should "keep the ecosystem in as pristine a state as possible, with a minimum of 'management.'" Whereas park fire experts considered prescribed burns as a human-induced return to the natural, the Muries saw such fires as an artificial manipulation of nature.[17]

In spite of such reservations, the park implemented the prescribed burn policy in 1973. The first to be scheduled was a 20-acre burn on the very visible Blacktail Butte, but wet weather intervened, causing postponement and eventual cancellation. The second planned burn took place at Uhl Hill in late August. Conditions were not perfect, and the park instituted some additional protective measures. To keep the 100-acre burn in hand, the park employed 56 workers and a D-7 Caterpillar bulldozer to clear a one mile fire line. Fear that the fire would get out of their control proved unfounded. In fact, the fire only burned approximately 30 acres. Although questionable, park officials declared the Uhl Hill fire a success. As one internal account put it: "In the most basic terms, Grand Teton had started a fire, monitored it, and achieved some resource management goals without incurring the ire of the community."[18]

Soon, the Park Service did incur public wrath over a lightning-caused fire. A logical, scientific policy hammered out in the conference room may not always work in the field. The Waterfall Fire demonstrated this. Lightning struck on July 17, 1974, igniting a timbered region on the west side of Jackson Lake. The blaze was clearly in Zone 1, thus park officials routinely checked its location, monitored it, and let it burn naturally. Since the smoke was visible, the park informed the public as much as possible. However, an unanticipated problem soon arose. The fire did not go out, but neither did it spread rapidly. In six weeks, it slowly consumed about 200 acres. On September 18, the wind picked up and pushed the acreage to 1,300 acres. The next day it expanded to 1,900 acres. Although increasing acreage was evident, the larger problem was smoke. The smoky haze did not dissipate in the valley, but became thicker and stagnant. Tourists expecting to see a grand mountain view, the magnificent feature of the park, were sorely disappointed as heavy smoke obscured the very peaks they had come to see. Obviously natural clouds and storms can screen the mountains, but smoke was another matter—particularly one that was created by purposeful choice. Townspeople were equally annoyed with the constant smoke, which seemed to migrate in all directions.

Slowly the so-called "let it burn" policy began to erode. It was simply counterintuitive to everything that had been drilled over decades into the American public regarding fire. By September 26, a paid advertisement appeared in the Jackson Hole newspapers demanding that the fire be extinguished and the policy changed. Articles appeared in the *Denver Post, New York Times,* and *Christian Science Monitor,* as well as in regional papers in the West. Tourists became more outspoken. The North District Office filed a "case incident" by Mac Porter from Grand Rapids, Michigan. Porter marched into the office and announced that he was a personal friend of Gerald Ford (a former seasonal ranger) and planned to send a telegram to the vice president complaining about the Waterfall Canyon fire. He announced that "he didn't know who was responsible for letting the fire go but that he should be in jail." The ranger attempted to explain the policy, but Porter left in a huff, announcing he "wasn't going to listen to any explanation."[19]

Later, park personnel put together a pamphlet called "The Anatomy of a Public Issue." The account noted that "not much of anyone was interested in fire management last year…Not much of anybody, that is, until a shaft of lightning struck a tree in isolated Waterfall Canyon in Grand Teton National Park."[20] Park fire leaders withstood the negative publicity. The fire expanded to a perimeter of 3,700 acres before nature intervened. When snow covered the area late in the year, the park staff finally declared the fire extinguished. The Waterfalls Canyon fire came down to a choice—put it out and make the people happy or follow science and ecological rules and validate current management policy. Science won. The park withstood an inflamed public opinion and was not swayed during the three-month ordeal.

In the years to follow, the National Park Service continued to develop a workable fire policy under the leadership of Director Russell Dickenson. In October 1982, Associate Director James Dempsey informed 10 superintendents, among them the Grand Teton chief, that they would be part of the FIREPRO system, a new fire management program. The plan identified and tailored "a program to meet [the park's] needs for fire management activities."[21] Under this system, park managers could systematically analyze and quantify management needs "for appropriate levels of personnel, training, equipment, and supplies to achieve resource management goals." Although loaded with jargon, FIREPRO addressed the crucial problem of wildfire funding, which often depleted the annual Grand Teton park budget. The plan established a core account that could be used for fire fighting.[22]

It came none too soon. Fires were incinerating not only larger and larger sections of land, but also the federal and park budgets. For instance, the 1985 Beaver Creek fire bled $650,000 from a tight budget as it destroyed seven buildings at the Climbers' Ranch, threatened park housing and other facilities at Beaver Creek, and scorched 1,152 acres. Setting up a system that provided money to fight fires through a central fund would allow Grand Teton administrators to

sleep better during the riskiest months of August, September, and October.

Financing was a problem, but so was management. On September 2, 1987, the Dave Adams Hill fire broke out on the northern boundary of the park, spreading to the John D. Rockefeller, Jr. Memorial Parkway. It was in the Zone 1 "let it burn" area. At first the fire languished, burning only 25 acres by September 21. Then on September 22, the catalyst arrived: gusty and erratic winds. On September 25, a strong cold front hit, accompanied by winds exceeding 70 miles per hour. Almost immediately, the Fire Management Committee (composed of the superintendent, the chief ranger, and various other park leaders) met. After discussing the changing conditions, they modified the let-burn policy, authorizing use of two air tankers and three helicopters, while 10 ground crews established fire lines. Fire monitors feared the blaze might threaten power corridors and/or jump the Snake River and endanger the Flagg Ranch lodge and outbuildings. Furthermore, officials from Bridger-Teton National Forest did not wish to "accept" the fire into the Teton Wilderness. Eventually, the fire slowed and came within "behavior parameters." It blackened 2,350 acres and cost the park approximately $400,000.[23] But the significance of the Dave Adams Hill fire lay with management and decision-making regarding the blaze. Clearly in a let-burn zone, the policy was fine—until it was not. When things went wrong, the management team was quick to abandon the policy. Changed conditions led to

ACTIVE FIRE BEHAVIOR ON THE BEARPAW BAY FIRE ON SEPT. 26, 2009, AS SEEN FROM JACKSON LAKE. THE FIRE WAS IGNITED BY LIGHTNING AUG. 30 ON THE SOUTHWEST SHORE OF JACKSON LAKE.

changed tactics. Fires provoke fear, and can force those in charge to question a policy born of science, which does not necessarily take into account practical considerations such as saving important structures or peoples' livelihoods. Although it makes sense to have a general fire policy, the idea of a plan that can be followed unfailingly is unrealistic. Each fire is an individual event. Each must be evaluated on its own terms. Action must be flexible and must be decided by a series of factors, including weather, structures endangered, wildlife considerations, and occasionally even public opinion.

YELLOWSTONE, 1988

All the fires in Grand Teton paled in significance compared to the great Yellowstone National Park fires of 1988. That year, the Yellowstone conflagrations attracted national attention, and Superintendent Bob Barbee became a lightning rod for Park Service detractors. The premier park, the crown jewel, was burning up and administrators could do little to stop it. Whereas Grand Teton largely avoided the limelight and the often hostile media publicity, its location adjacent to Yellowstone made it a center for many reporters who descended on the region to cover a national story. In spite of much evidence that humans often fail at controlling nature (in tornados, hurricanes, and floods, for example), some reporters, perhaps to enhance their stories, suggested that the National Park Service could have controlled the Yellowstone fires, but simply chose not to. Although he admitted in hindsight that he might have taken action on a couple of the early fires, Yellowstone Superintendent Bob Barbee had it right when he noted that the park as a whole was in a condition of explosively dry fuels that were "then choreographed by the wind, the wind, the wind, the wind."[24]

In this dramatic story, Grand Teton was a mere footnote. Yet Yellowstone's needs depleted Grand Teton's capacity to respond with "initial attack capabilities" to its own fires. The staff was worn out supporting Yellowstone, working seven days a week, with days off canceled for extended periods.

Fortunately, increased "aerial detection flights" in Grand Teton snuffed out fires early, and ultimately, only two fires got out of hand. The Hunter Fire started on August 20 and spread to 15 acres, threatening structures at the Teton Science School's Kelly campus. It moved into Bridger-Teton National Forest and consumed 4,400 acres before it was finally "controlled." The Huck Fire took off on the same date in the Rockefeller Parkway. It moved toward Flagg Ranch Resort, but veered into Bridger-Teton National Forest, and became part of the Mink complex that charred 96,300 acres.[25]

Perhaps the most noteworthy action was the partial abandonment of the fire management plan featuring the three zones (let-burn, conditional, and suppression). In theory, a fire's location should determine the park's response. However, the 1988 fires, and the subsequent *political* heat, modified that policy. The Grand Teton Fire Management committee became more flexible, recommending to the superintendent a strategy based on location, weather, wind, availability of resources, and weather forecasts. The Forellen Fire, a small lightning-caused fire in a remote area of the northern Teton Range, that broke out on July 27, 1988, reflected this new elastic policy. Although it was clearly in a let-burn zone, the Fire Management committee recommended suppression based on their limited fire resources and the fact that Targhee National Forest officials informed park managers that they "would not accept fires across their boundary under the current fire danger conditions."[26]

The Yellowstone fires, of course, were a political event as well as a natural one. The National Park System as well as other agencies reexamined their fire policy. The NPS suspended established fire policies and Congress recommended that all agency fire principles and procedures be reviewed. The legislators provided direction in the 1995 Federal Lands Wild Lands Fire Policy document. Those agencies under the wing of the Department of Agriculture (U.S. Forest Service) and the Department of the Interior (NPS, Bureau of Land Management, U.S. Fish and Wildlife Service, and Department of Indian Affairs) were expected to sit down together, review past policies, and hammer out new strategies.[27]

NEW FIRE POLICIES EMERGE

As a result of this process, today there is much more coordination among the various federal agencies. The Greater Yellowstone Coordinating Committee, consisting of the superintendents and supervisors of the affected land areas, meets twice a year to discuss issues common to all federal land managers, including fire policy. Also at least twice a year, the fire managers of the various Greater Yellowstone area meet to review policies regarding such conservation activities as non-suppression regions and proposed controlled burn areas. Perhaps the most important change is the response to wildfires. Agencies coordinate. Fire managers in both the national parks and national forests are in constant communication, and available manpower and equipment are always on call, ready to assist wherever needed.[28]

Another agonizing issue has been the tremendous cost in fighting a major wildfire. In earlier days, Grand Teton National Park had to absorb the costs, at times analogous to squeezing blood from a turnip. Today, if a fire in the park requires men, women and equipment, this significant outlay is borne by the interagency fire management group, with the costs assumed by the Interior Department's Wild Fire Appropriations fund.

Thus, as we look at wildfire suppression today, the old problems of coordination and funding are understood and in place. Unfortunately, they will never completely resolve the issues and potential tragedy of wildfires. Park fires are capricious and ruled by the forces of nature. All the planning in the world cannot guarantee a good outcome, nor always save property and more importantly save lives. Sometimes humans are simply not in control, and in such turbulent times we can only stand back and watch, in awe and wonder.

WILDLIFE POLICY

If there is agreement on one subject in Jackson Hole, it is the almost universal appreciation of wildlife. It matters not if people are rich or poor, Republican or Democrat, or whether they value the national parks or not—all set great store by wildlife, from songbirds to grizzly bears. Valuing wildlife translates into a sincere concern for the habitat of the various species.

In Jackson Hole and certainly in the park, concern regarding wildlife has led to an evolving ethical view of animals' rights to life and freedom to exist and migrate across the landscape. The Muries, as well as many others, subscribed to the beliefs of their friend Aldo Leopold, the path-breaking naturalist and founder (with Olaus and others) of the Wilderness Society. Leopold is mostly remembered for his lyrical treatise *A Sand County Almanac,* published posthumously in 1949.[29] In this classic work Leopold proclaimed that ethics should not be limited to the relationship of one human to another but rather enlarged "to include soils, water, plants, and animals, or collectively: the land." Such a land ethic, he professed, would change "the role of *Homo sapiens* from conqueror of the land-community to plain members and citizens of it." With particular relevance for national parks, he believed that "a thing is right when it tends to preserve the integrity, stability, and beauty of the biotic community. It is wrong when it tends otherwise."[30] Not many residents of Jackson Hole have read Leopold's classic, but it is fair to say that a majority subscribe to his ideas. Wildlife is valued in Jackson Hole and always has been. Residents in large numbers still shoot antelope or elk with a rifle, but an increasing number do their shooting with a camera. Leopold would welcome both, with reverence and understanding.

Jackson Hole Wildlife Park

Leopold would also agree that to maintain stability, most of the valley's wildlife inhabitants need space. With just 310,000 acres, Grand Teton National Park lacks enough space for sizeable wildlife populations such as elk and bison, wolves, and grizzly bears. At first view, the park is expansive, far larger than its 310,000 acres. Driving north from Jackson, the visitor encounters the open space of the National Elk Refuge, and then vast lands to the north and east. The park gives the illusion of space, but is really quite confined, surrounded by land under different jurisdictions. By Park Service standards, it is instructive to note that Glacier National Park (1,013,572 acres) and Olympic National Park (922,654 acres) have about three times the space to manage wildlife.[31] The undersized acreage of Grand Teton spawns competition between human wants and wildlife needs. It also urges creative, though not always wise, solutions. For example, in the late 1940s Laurance Rockefeller and his friend and mentor Fairfield Osborn decided that the national park and national monument needed a wildlife commons within their borders.[32] The Rockefeller family's good works in the park need no introduction. Fairfield Osborn is less well known, yet he was nationally known as the director of the New York Zoological Society and as the author of the well-received *Plundered Planet*, one of the first modern environmental books. The two wildlife advocates had little trouble convincing themselves that megafauna under fence, such as buffalo, antelope, moose, deer, and elk, would be useful additions to Grand Teton park. National Park Service founder, and later second director, Horace Albright, gave his blessing. With such approval, these men formed a board of directors for the Jackson Hole Wildlife Park, and then fenced a large enclosure in a meadow a mile down river from the Jackson Lake Dam near the Oxbow Bend area—land that in 1950 would become part of Grand Teton National Park. They reasoned that without the enclosure, few visitors would encounter such animals as elk and bison during their short stays. Osborn ventured that "only a pitifully small minority have the time or ability to pack off into the wilderness." Anticipating the future popularity of Grand Teton National Park, he noted that the wildlife park would be "for the many, not the few."[33]

Osborn's egalitarian—one might say leveling—arguments had a special appeal. After all, when he was Yellowstone Park superintendent, Horace Albright was particularly proud of his popular garbage pit shows, featuring the bears of Yellowstone pawing, fighting over, and eating the refuse of visitors. It was a daily summer evening entertainment, and for many visitors it was the most memorable aspect of their stay in Yellowstone. If travel plans made viewing the show impossible, you would surely encounter a few "beggar bears" on Yellowstone's roads. An American family who made the iconic trip to Yellowstone was sure to have bear stories and often a few photographs of their encounter. But did such

JACKSON HOLE WILDLIFE PARK

activities represent the values of a national park, or were they more appropriate for a zoo or an amusement park?

By the late 1940s, attitudes toward wildlife were changing within the Park Service. Many officials were skeptical about the fenced wildlife park and privately opposed it. This included NPS Director Newton Drury, who approved the project while privately voicing his objections and anticipating its failure.[34] Drury and Albright had crossed swords regarding

Yellowstone's bears. Director Drury supported Olaus Murie's study which recommended that the bear "shows" must end, and he followed Murie's advice to stop this activity. Albright warned Drury that his policy would reap a "world of trouble," but Drury favored Murie's recommendations and his own inclinations. He dismantled the visitor viewing bleachers and the bear shows ended without fanfare by 1940. But displays of wildlife did not end. If anyone but Laurance Rockefeller had made such a proposal, it would have been easily scrapped. However, there was no greater friend to the national parks than Laurance and his father, John D. Rockefeller Jr., and if Laurance fancied the idea, the NPS would not stand in the way. In the summer of 1948, the wildlife park was dedicated and opened for public viewing.

Although the NPS sanctioned the wildlife park, important naturalists were vehemently opposed. From the beginning, Olaus Murie made no secret of his opposition. His career with the U.S. Biological Survey (now the U.S. Fish and Wildlife Service) had been to observe animals in the wild. He worked for the National Elk Refuge in Jackson Hole and was perhaps the world's leading expert on elk. If Fairfield Osborn had credentials, the Murie's were equally distinguished. They were soon at loggerheads.

Murie had always seen the National Elk Refuge as an unavoidable compromise. He soundly opposed any sort of artificial restraints on wildlife. As to the argument that the wildlife park might aid scientific study, Murie scoffed that he could not "imagine naturalists, particularly ecologists, thrilling at the opportunities presented by a group of animals under fence." This "zoo," as he often mockingly called the wildlife park, should be resisted.[35]

But Murie did more than defend the rights of free-roaming wildlife. In expanding his thought, he used the wildlife park as an opportunity to question the direction of the American character, and secondarily, the role of national parks. He recognized the display as just another sign of a "national laziness" that favored pleasure with the least possible exertion. For him, catching sight of a moose after a strenuous hike was an altogether different experience than peering at it through a fence. He worried that such roadside presentations demeaned magnificent wildlife, while contributing to the increasing tendency of Americans to be spectators rather than participants.[36] The wildlife park was just one more vulgar show to be resisted, and it was doubly insulting that it was located within a national park.

Osborn and Rockefeller fell back on their egalitarian position. Murie's idealistic view of wildlife and the world, they considered to be impractical. Osborn branded Murie an elitist: one of those admirable but out-of-touch Americans. The New York naturalist certainly understood that restrained wildlife was not ideal, but the quality of a wildlife experience would be lost on most visitors, while the actual viewing would be remembered (just as garbage bears had been in Yellowstone). And he believed many visitors might become advocates for the park.

The wildlife park was doomed not only on philosophical grounds but also along practical lines. Prominent Jackson realtor Richard Winger questioned the project from its inception, noting that fencing in wildlife would not be easy. Also, he warned that their escape from the enclosure in the winter would result in their dispersal, and the challenges of finding them and driving them back to the reserve would be a nightmare. Winger had a list of practical objections to the management of the wildlife, and many of his concerns proved on the mark.[37] In a sense it was a contest pitting the values of Albright/Rockefeller/Osborn versus those of Murie/Drury/Winger.

Enclosure opponents included another advocate. Olaus Murie's half-brother, Adolph Murie, had completed a path-breaking study of coyotes in Yellowstone and concluded that—contrary to the views of park authorities—coyotes were not decimating wildlife populations. All through the naturalist fraternity, from George Wright to Joseph Dixon, Ben Thompson, and Stanley Cain, positive attitudes toward predators including wolves, mountain lions, and grizzly bears were becoming common. Ideas of ecology emerged, and they certainly did not include wild animals under fence. In the 1930s, it seems that park administrators believed that the purpose of wild animals was to entertain humans who enjoyed looking at them. By the 1950s, ecologists and others saw those same animals as having the right to be free and live on their own terms without human interference.

Olaus Murie, although deeply disturbed about Rockefeller's wildlife park, restrained his criticism, and wrote to Osborn that, "I will not allow myself to go off in a corner and pout."[38] As it turned out, there was no reason to pout, for the project was self-destructing anyway. While Osborn and James Simon, the field director in the Moran site, tried to assure Robert Enders in early 1953 that the project "has proved a great success," they were privately trying to unload the operation to any agency that would take it.

First they offered the site to the Wyoming Game and Fish Commission, which had supported the wildlife park concept but made only a minimal contribution to its upkeep. Osborn's offer met stony silence from the state organization, where officials recognized all the inherent problems.[39] The National Park Service was the presumptive inheritor of the wildlife park once the federal government accepted John D. Rockefeller, Jr.'s land gift. In the minutes of the Jackson Hole Wildlife Park board, Laurance stated that it was "appropriate that the continued maintenance and operation of the Exhibit become the responsibility of the National Park Service [since] within those boundaries the project lies." Hardly any responsible wildlife biologist would endorse such a project. I could find no correspondence indicating that the NPS might jump on board and continue what was becoming a failed operation.[40]

Nor is there evidence of serious discussion over the fate of "the Exhibit." Well-known Wyoming dude ranchers Charles Moore and Struthers Burt, both on the advisory board, wanted the wildlife park to continue. They were annoyed when Osborn dissolved the corporation and distanced himself from the whole wildlife operation, before retreating to New York. The two dude ranchers also questioned the future commitment of the National Park Service to the wildlife park, and of course, they were right.[41] Although generally favoring the end of the experiment, the park staff did maintain the fence for a time. Deer, elk, and moose wandered away during the winter, but park rangers fed the bison and dutifully gathered up a couple dozen animals each spring for visitor viewing and enjoyment. Meanwhile, in 1963 the Leopold Report reviewed natural resource management policies in the national parks. Its key conclusion was that each park should be "an illusion of primitive America," creating a "mood of wild America." Authored by A. Starker Leopold, Aldo's son, this report helped change the direction of wildlife management as it stressed scientific research based on ecological principles. Could the fenced-in bison survive this scientific salvo? They could not. By 1964, the fence had deteriorated, and Park Service workers did not repair it. The bison wandered away to become the nucleus of today's Jackson Hole bison herd.[42]

One other matter had to be resolved, and that was the wildlife research arm of the project. A half dozen small buildings just down river from the dam housed Director James Simon and a team of academic researchers. Osborn had been successful in courting the University of Wyoming to take over this research center. President Duke Humphrey thought it would be a good idea for his institution to establish a presence in the northwest corner of Wyoming. So, Grand Teton National Park and the school signed an agreement to continue research on wildlife matters related to the park, eventually moving the center to the AMK Ranch, some seven miles north. This UW-NPS partnership has worked well, and the research station (described in chapter 2) continues to flourish today,

likely one of the oldest research stations in the National Park System.

Thus ended an ill-advised project, a path poorly chosen. If you wanted to take the "wild" out of the megafauna of Jackson Hole, there was no better way than to put them under fence solely for public viewing. Olaus Murie understood the folly of this idea, as would every wildlife biologist since that time. Even if it provided some benefits to the public, it was a clear violation of the spirit and role of a national park in managing wildlife. It is noteworthy that when Osborn dissolved the wildlife park corporation, director James Simon took a position with Walt Disney Enterprises. It also seemed fitting that the wildlife park evolved into a research center dedicated to keeping park wildlife free and flourishing. At Oxbow Bend, no evidence of the wildlife park experiment remains today.

Visitors to Grand Teton will certainly see free-roaming animals, but the wildlife themselves create the terms under which they are seen or not. In the fall bugling elk and their harems are easily observed at the base of Timbered Island, and visitors may see a moose or two browsing the willows below the Snake River bridge. Bison are numerous on or near the Antelope Flats Road. Grizzly bears, now common throughout the park, can cause massive bear traffic jams along several park roads. Obviously, these animals have little fear of human beings, yet they are wild and as such, they warrant our respect as well as our awe and admiration.

ELK REDUCTION

Perhaps there is no other wildlife species more associated with the Jackson Hole valley than the abundant and impressive elk. A majestic mature bull elk represents the king of the ungulates, a much admired animal. Yet elk have a paradoxical relationship with humans in Jackson Hole. Historically, people have protected the valley's elk herd, but they also kill elk for sport or for meat. There are still some families in Jackson Hole whose red meat fare consists of nothing but wild meat. For many pioneers, cattle were for selling while elk were for eating.

Some of the earliest exploration parties came specifically to hunt elk. The Englishman William Baillie-Grohman sought to gain a trophy. Theodore Roosevelt killed "a great bull elk" in the Thorofare region of southern Yellowstone. Perhaps the most elaborate hunting party arrived in northern Jackson Hole in 1898, headed by Dr. Seward Webb, the son-in-law of Cornelius Vanderbilt. The 150 men, 113 horses, and 164 mules assured that the seven hunters would be comfortable. The famous Yellowstone photographer F. Jay Haynes photographed this expedition with images of taxidermists in the field preparing the many bull elk heads to adorn the libraries of eastern homes.[43]

Guiding hunters augmented the incomes of many early settlers, and the meat enhanced their tables. These pioneers developed an ambivalent attitude toward elk, which would continue into the national park period. There was no group more despised in Jackson Hole than lawbreakers known as "tuskers." These men often lived deep in the woods of northern Jackson Hole in rudimentary log shacks. They made their despicable livelihood by killing elk, preferably bulls, and removing just their top two canine teeth— or tusks—with pliers, leaving the rest of the dead animal's body as carrion for the coyotes. This form of market hunting just to make money from Elks Club members, who prized a pair of tusks, was unacceptable to local people. Local resident were understandably appalled at the waste and brutality. Unfortunately, affluent Elks Club members seemed unaware that their obsession fostered such a cruel and wasteful business.

Through these practices, elk entered the political world and remain a dominant issue to this day. In 1882, General Philip Sheridan expressed concern regarding the condition of Wyoming's wildlife, recommending conservation of a "greater Yellowstone area" that would extend to the northern tip of Jackson Lake. Acting Yellowstone Superintendent Colonel S. B. M Young, in 1897, deplored the poaching of elk outside his jurisdiction and proposed that Yellowstone National Park be extended into Jackson Hole. The next year, Charles D. Walcott, director of the U.S. Geological Survey, suggested an expansion of Yellowstone, or "a separate park, to be known as the Teton National Park." Walcott thought it totally incongruous that the government would protect elk in their summer Yellowstone range while exposing them to be slaughtered on their winter range. He had no confidence that either the U.S. Forest Service or the state of Wyoming would offer protection.[44] Remarkably, Sherman, Young, and Walcott all favored a national park in Jackson Hole as a way to protect the elk. Yet nothing came of their idea.

Perhaps Walcott was needlessly mistrustful of the local populace, for many were sympathetic to the elk's winter plight. When ranchers' roads and fences cut off the traditional migration patterns, the starving elk pilfered ranch haystacks. Local rancher Stephen Leek was there to record the tragedy. This guide, photographer, and wilderness lodge owner, shot the weakened elk with his camera rather than a rifle. Carcasses littered the valley, and they appeared in his photographs in the May 1911 edition of *Outdoor Life,* stirring the nation's conscience. The state and the federal government responded with small grants for grain and hay. A year later, in 1912, Congress passed legislation establishing a 1,760-acre National Elk Refuge. In the years to follow, donations by the Izaak Walton League and John D. Rockefeller, Jr., augmented by federal withdrawals of public land from private entry, all contributed to the expansion of today's 23,000-acre refuge.[45]

Once the refuge was established, questions of jurisdiction and management arose. Who was responsible for management of the herd—the federal government or the state of Wyoming? And which federal agency should have ultimate jurisdiction—the Biological Survey, Forest Service, or National Park

"Heater hunters" wait and watch for an opportunity.

Service? How many elk were on the winter refuge, and how many should there be? How many acres should be reserved for their use? Should the elk be given artificial feeding of hay or pellets in winter months? And, perhaps most important to the park, what should be the annual harvest number through hunting, and how should that reduction of elk be carried out? In an attempt to resolve these issues, President Calvin Coolidge created an Elk Commission in early 1927, an *ad hoc* group with members representing the National Park Service, Forest Service, and Biological Survey, the governor of Wyoming and Wyoming Game and Fish Commission, and various local and conservation interests. It sounded like an unwieldy group, but they successfully created a prudent elk management policy. Their primary accomplishment was to have President Coolidge sign an executive order on April 15, 1927, to withdraw lands near or adjacent to the reserve from public entry. This enlargement of habitat is one reason the majestic elk have thrived in Jackson Hole. Having accomplished their main task, the Elk Commission disbanded in 1934.[46]

ELK AND THE VAGARIES OF MANAGEMENT

Not surprisingly, elk were at the heart of the 1950 Act that established present-day Grand Teton National Park. There were, of course, issues concerning property taxes and grazing rights, but by word count, the management of elk received the greatest attention. Unlike stationary property or cows, which could be controlled, elk were free-roaming, indifferent to human-defined boundaries. The 1950 Act mainly reflected management compromises between the Wyoming Game and Fish Commission and the National Park Service. Jurisdiction was an issue because inside the park an elk is federal property, but outside it would be the property of the State of Wyoming. A wandering elk could come under the authority of the National Park Service, the state of Wyoming, or the National Elk Refuge, all within a 24-hour period! To assist in resolving this conundrum, the 1950 Act instructed the state of Wyoming and the NPS to submit jointly to the Secretary of the Interior and the Governor of Wyoming a program to ensure "the permanent conservation of the elk within the Grand Teton National Park." The program would include "the controlled reduction of elk in such park," to be accomplished by hunters licensed by the state and "deputized as rangers by the Secretary of the Interior."[47] This cumbersome provision was unique. In other national park areas where there has been a need for herd reduction, park rangers have taken on the disagreeable task of "culling" over abundant wildlife, not hunters licensed by the state.

Compromise is often the result of seemingly irreconcilable differences. Both Grand Teton National Park and the Wyoming Game and Fish Commission have missions, but they are distinctive and sometimes antithetical. Park officials prefer no hunting within the park's borders and certainly have wished to avoid deputizing hunters as rangers for the purpose of killing elk. On the other side, in 1950 Wyoming Game and Fish Commissioner Lester Bagley feared that the state was losing control of its wildlife property. The commissioner insisted on hunting within the park with licensed hunters. He would not budge. If Grand Teton National Park sought to become a reality in 1950, it had to accept the contradiction of being a national park dedicated to the welfare of wildlife while simultaneously agreeing to kill them.[48]

In the years to follow, the contradiction at the heart of the compromise only grew worse. Although many fair chase hunters worked the park on foot or horseback, others took the easy way. The "deputized rangers" would set up shop in their trucks on the Gros Ventre Road that separates the park from the elk refuge. Animals seeking the safety of the refuge had to cross what amounted to a "firing line." It was an ugly scene, for a downed bull elk or cow was often the object of fierce dispute among hunters over who killed it.[49] To make matters worse, these "heater hunters," as park wildlife biologist Steve Cain

ELK HERD ON THE NATIONAL ELK REFUGE

described them, attracted unwanted local and national publicity for an unsavory practices.

Among the din of criticisms has come talk of ending this so-called hunt. There does seem to be an appropriate loophole in the 1950 Act, which states the hunt will take place "when it is found necessary for the purpose of proper management and protection of the elk."[50] However, the park and the state of Wyoming have agreed on the necessity of the hunt for all but two seasons in nearly 65 years. Could this change? Superintendent Mary Gibson Scott has been asked to end the hunt, but she rightly stated that she has no authority to do so alone. Elk reduction is the responsibility of both the park and the state. She rightly maintains that she cannot end it unilaterally. Might the Wyoming Game and Fish Commission agree to end the hunt? The answer is no, unless there is a National Elk Refuge change of policy regarding feeding, along with the state's ending the winter feed grounds on USFS land nearby. Superintendent Scott admits that meetings with Game and Fish representatives are "sometimes tense," for while the commission supports conservation measures for big game, it also represents hunters' interests. Moreover, the

Wyoming Game and Fish budget is supported by hunting license fees, and the commission's purpose is to enhance hunting opportunities both for state residents and for out-of-state hunters. Restrictions on elk hunting would be anathema to its purpose, which has not changed during the 60 years in question.

But in the last few years, the role of science has taken on greater importance. Experts who have spent their lives studying elk may be poised to move the Wyoming Game and Fish Commission in new directions. Bruce L. Smith, a wildlife biologist who helped manage the National Elk Refuge for 32 years and retired in 2004, argues that elk crowded into feed grounds are at risk "from diseases that might spread among the elk like colds in a daycare center. Chronic wasting disease (CWD), a brain disorder that is fatal to elk and other deer species, is marching ever closer to thousands of northwestern Wyoming elk."[51] This dedicated scientist strongly recommends that the herd be pared back to 6,500 animals and that the practice of winter feeding end. In other words, Smith argues that the present "Wapiti Welfare" should end, and the herd should become free-roaming wild animals. He advocates a "natural regulatory system," as opposed to artificial (feeding) control of the population.[52] In many respects, Bruce Smith's reservations on winter feeding on the refuge are reminiscent of Olaus Murie's objections to the Jackson Hole Wildlife Park program.

Neither Smith nor Murie represented the general public opinion. In 1994, an Idaho survey revealed that 79 percent of the population supported their state gov-ernment funding the feeding of big game animals.[53] In Wyoming, the Game and Fish Commission is one of the most respected and powerful state agencies. They have plenty of support from people who see little danger from wildlife diseases, and they point to the successful management of the elk for 100 years. Why change a successful operation, cutting down the elk numbers and, correspondingly, hunting opportunities? This position enjoys the support of the hunting community and outfitters who have political influence in Cheyenne. On the other hand, Grand Teton has no mandate to provide recreational hunting opportunities, insisting that the yearly hunt is only a wildlife management program, specifically titled the "elk reduction program." Contrary to the wishes of many hunters, the park has discontinued the "any elk" permits, commonly termed "bull tags," reasoning that reduction of cow elk is the best method to reduce the size of the herd.

A major complication rests with the elk themselves. They are prolific and intelligent. They have adapted to their valley habitat and changing conditions, where they suffer little population loss from predators other than human hunters. Their rather privileged status, however, has been cut down. Wolves (discussed later) have found elk susceptible prey, particularly because when wolves first appeared on the National Elk Refuge, the elk "were truly naïve." However, they have quickly become conditioned to this change, and Smith states that "wolves may have killed [only] about sixty elk during winter 1998–99" on the refuge. Most agree that for management purposes and to keep some semblance of balance with other park wildlife, the herd must be culled. According to Superintendent Mary Gibson Scott, the only way to end the park hunt is for the National Elk Refuge to reduce its artificial feeding program to get the numbers down. But the state of Wyoming must also close its winter feed grounds adjacent to the park and refuge. Bruce Smith asks whether "hunting in a national park and wildlife refuge [can] be justified to afford economic rewards to local communities?" This rhetorical question is answered in the negative throughout his book. Is the solution advocated by Superintendent Scott and biologist Smith—and many others—possible? The original mission of the refuge was to sustain the elk herd through the winter, allowing for an approximate four-percent mortality rate; the founding mission did not intend to shrink elk numbers through starvation. Furthermore, ending the feeding program could result in both local and national protests. Elk dying in full view of visitors driving Highway 89/191 would cause public outrage as well as run counter to the refuge's original purpose, although the traveling public has outgrown the "peaceable kingdom" view of wildlife.

The likelihood of visitors witnessing starvation scenes is not large, because the feed program would be phased out gradually, and if absolutely necessary, emergency feeding could take place. Nevertheless, the mission in 1912 was to maintain the herd. This mission must now be modified to manage the herd.

Reducing wildlife numbers through the allowance of hunting is practiced on virtually every wildlife refuge in the nation, but it will take some education for the public to understand the concept. Meanwhile, as of this writing, the elk reduction program in Grand Teton National Park continues, exasperating as it is.[54]

An Ecological Park

As the number of cattle in the park has diminished, there has been a corresponding increase in wildlife. Bison, black bears, moose, and more recently grizzlies and wolves have become common denizens of the park. Not only have the numbers increased, but there is mounting recognition of the rightful claim of all species to inhabit park lands. Wildlife in Grand Teton National Park is prized by those who must manage the animals. Many wildlife biologists prefer not to manage through human intervention and manipulation, but rather depend on the processes of natural regulation. In Grand Teton, natural regulation would be largely determined by winter food availability and the presence of predators. However, in an area where the original web of life has been disrupted, the relationship of prey and predator needs to be balanced through intervention. For the wildlife biologist, the animals are the rightful occupants of park lands, and humans are visitors with rights secondary to those of the fauna and flora.[55] When visitors observe the many regulatory signs limiting activity, they should understand that while the signs are limiting human freedoms, they are, as Aldo Leopold would say, extending ethical rights to the land and its inhabitants. Human needs are paramount throughout most of the land, but in a national park this hierarchy is reversed.

WOLVES RETURN AND MOOSE DECLINE

The expanding ranges of bison, bears, and wolves have further complicated the relationship between people and wildlife. Wolves are the most recent addition to the panoply of megafauna in Jackson Hole. One hundred years ago they were present in significant numbers. There is a photograph of "Gram" Shrive, who lived near Buffalo Fork with her husband John Shrive, holding two wolf pups secured with a chain. They appear to be pets, but in time the pets would have matured and no doubt faced the fate of an animal not beloved in Jackson Hole in 1900.[56] Wolves in both Yellowstone and Jackson Hole were systematically hunted, and by 1926 park rangers killed two wolf pups near Soda Butte Creek, the last survivors in Yellowstone Park. By 1943, wolves were extinct in the Greater Yellowstone Area.[57] At the time most wildlife experts applauded this annihilation policy, insisting on a value difference between unloved predators and their privileged prey.

Scientists such as George Wright, a brilliant Park Service wildlife biologist whose life was cut short in his thirties, questioned such unrealistic distinctions.

The equally accomplished Aldo Leopold in Wisconsin and the hardworking team of Adolph and Olaus Murie in Alaska and Jackson Hole also challenged such traditional thinking.[58] Earlier in his life, Olaus had conducted studies of the numbers and movements of caribou, while Adolph focused his talents on the wolves of Mt. McKinley National Park (now Denali). Both did path-breaking studies on the coyotes of Yellowstone, documenting that they were not the spiteful killers they were purported to be. The essence of their work proved that predators were necessary and normal, an essential element of biodiversity. Adolph in particular realized that Americans had made a serious error in eliminating the wolf.

Not only did scientists want the wolf's return, but so did philosophers and thoughtful people exploring the human condition. Environmental writer Barry Lopez suggests we need wolves not only for biodiversity, but also for what they reveal about us. As he put it, "the wolf exerts a powerful influence on the human imagination. It takes your stare and turns it back on you." Few of us will ever have that experience, but Lopez believes wolves enhance our fears, our hatreds, our respect, and our curiosity.[59] These are emotions that we need, and the national parks ought to help perpetuate them through the possibility of seeing the "green fire" in a wolf's eye, to paraphrase Aldo Leopold. Aside from human gains, more and more American's wanted the species returned simply for itself.

The decision to reintroduce wolves into Yellowstone came about after a fierce decade-long debate. After all, Westerners had supported federal efforts, particularly that of the Department of Agriculture, in a determined effort to eliminate the wolf from the land—all of it. While the fur trapper might be the romantic figure of the early nineteenth century, the "wolfer" gained that heroic role in the early twentieth century. These wolf hunters were assisted by a generous federal bounty for every pelt. They were also supported by the populace. It was a war of hatred, in which the wolf was characterized as cruel, calculating, criminal, and conniving.

Such a strong bias would not be easy to overcome, but the Park Service and the U.S. Fish and Wildlife Service took on the task, leading the charge. Jackson Hole resident John Turner, then Director of the Fish and Wildlife Service, fought hard for introduction and showed his skills as a diplomat in dealing with opponents. He had the Endangered Species Act and committed environmentalists on his side, but ranchers, and many Wyoming residents bitterly opposed the idea. Finally Canadian trappers captured fourteen wolves and transported them to Yellowstone National Park in January 1995. Following a three-month "acclimatization" period, rangers released them. Eventually, as expected, they enlarged their range, drifting into the Pacific Creek drainage of Grand Teton National Park. In 1998, two groups of wolves, respectfully named the Jackson Trio and the Teton Duo, arrived in the northern section of the park. The Teton Duo remained in the park and evolved into the Teton Pack.[60] In 1999, they produced

a litter of pups, the first born in Grand Teton in 70 years. Since that year, the wolves have successfully expanded their range and numbers. In 2013, wildlife biologists estimate that a minimum of 59 wolves frequented the park in six packs, although these numbers are very fluid. Although their numbers decreased in 2010, they are firmly established from a biological perspective.[61] From a visitor perspective, the wolves give an added dimension of excitement to the park. Around 2006, many locals, myself included, climbed Uhl Hill with spotting scopes to watch the Buffalo Pack and their young cavort and occasionally howl. While rafting on the river north of Deadmans Bar, my wife and I witnessed a bison stampede on the west side of the river. We assumed the bison's agitation might have been caused by wolves of the Huckleberry Pack seeking a vulnerable calf, but I have since realized that this is not the bison's normal reaction to the presence of this predator. Two years ago south of park headquarters at Moose, my jogging son-in-law ran into a gray wolf face to face. He and the wolf both went their separate way. Wolves near Jackson and on the National Elk Refuge have become common in the winter. Most locals and rangers have sighted one or more wolves. In years past, park visitors who believed they had seen a wolf were routinely informed that they had no doubt mistaken a bulky coyote for a wolf. No more, for there is no question that this top predator has returned to Grand Teton National Park and has been hospitably treated, at least by biologists.

While welcoming the changes, park biologists must now manage the wildlife population more closely, for the wolf is a predator that has changed, and will continue to change, the natural equilibrium within the park. Already wolves have been accused by "coffee shop biologists" of causing a decline in the moose population in the Jackson Hole region. However, the facts suggest a different explanation. Park moose and their young declined in numbers from 400 in 1986 to fewer than 100 in 2013. Park biologist, Steve Cain, attributes the loss in numbers to a deficiency in forage. Since wolves arrived in 1998, they have perhaps witnessed the downward slope and contributed somewhat to it. But they are not responsible for the drastic decline.

If food is the problem, why do the moose lack nutrition? Cain notes that the moose decline is even more pronounced in the "herd wide" figures for the whole region (down from 1,000 to 100), a result of space limitations. The moose population decline is much greater in the wider community. Inevitably the problem leads back to us. No matter how sensitive Jackson Hole residents are regarding space and habitat, they continue to replace habitat with homes and other structures. Furthermore, many moose have been struck and killed by vehicles on valley and park roads. What will happen? If we could ask the wildlife what they need, the answer would be more space. At 310,000 acres Grand Teton is a small, long and narrow park, incredibly compressed and crowded from the perspective of wildlife habitat. A decline this serious may force officials to reconsider park policy.

How this may all play out will be settled in the future. There will also be questions regarding wolf behavior and travel outside park boundaries. Wolves do not, after all, simply coexist peacefully with other park species, nor do they observe park boundaries or respect private property, such as cattle. The Wyoming Game and Fish Department initiated a wolf hunt in 2012, which has led to differences of opinion regarding wolf management in the John D. Rockefeller, Jr. Memorial Parkway. Wolves are an emotional subject. Many people still regard them as vicious, bloody, and wanton killers. Others celebrate the return of a top predator for its potential role to trim the elk population and maintain a more complete and healthy ecosystem. Some herald their return to the region because they create a natural regulatory system, featuring wildlife balance.

Compared to Yellowstone, Grand Teton is a small park in which wolf encounters with deer and elk may be viewed from a road, a drama some will not find easy to watch. If the Huckleberry or Buffalo pack takes down an elk calf in plain view of tourists, there could be a negative reaction. One can envision the Pinnacle Peak pack hunting and killing on the National Elk Refuge, a spectacle that some may find fascinating and natural, while others will protest that they and their children should be spared from such harsh realities. From a park wildlife specialist's view, such encounters are a teaching opportunity. Yet some visitors prefer their parks free of disturbing scenes. In the past, Grand Teton National Park has presented the public with opportunities to see small and relatively docile animals or grand and imposing ungulates. Fluid wolf packs will modify management formulas, bringing in a new challenge to the goal of abundant but stable wildlife populations.

GRIZZLY BEARS

While wolves have been a recent addition in Grand Teton wildlife, bears have been present long before the original 1929 park was established. In Yellowstone, black bears have been an attraction ever since tourists plied them with food, and the National Park Service featured them in its nightly garbage-feeding spectacle. But as the parks have turned from an emphasis on entertainment to embracing more natural experiences, gone are the "shows" in Yellowstone and Yosemite. Grand Teton, blessedly, avoided any bear spectacles; but this should not suggest that bears have not been active in the park. Biologist Steve Cain's files contain many bear-human incidents in the 1990s and into the 21st century. Unfortunately, they also contain records of a number of black bears addicted to human food, bears that consequently lost their fear of humans and had to be euthanized. The loss of these bears, often the result of visitor carelessness or ignorance, occurs in spite of rangers' best efforts to remind visitors that bears are wild and not to be approached within less than 100 yards. It is not likely that people will ever be completely convinced to avoid these bear encounters.

Photo by Thomas D. Mangelsen

What has changed dramatically in Grand Teton is the presence of grizzly bears, particularly in this century. Relevant here is the fact that within Grand Teton National Park lived four of the most accomplished wildlife experts in the world. Olaus and Adolph Murie lived just south of Moose. Olaus worked for the Biological Survey as head of the National Elk Refuge, while Adolph was Grand Teton's only biologist throughout the 1950s. He spent 32 years with the National Park Service. He was best known for his work on wolves and grizzlies at McKinley (now Denali) National Park, publishing sci-

entific reports on *The Mammals of Mount McKinley*). He also studied the habits and lives of Alaska's Dall sheep and grey wolves.[62] While most of his work focused on Alaska, Adolph did advance his opinions on bears in Grand Teton, particularly on their habitat, natural areas, and management strategies. Both brothers and their wives were outspoken in their advocacy of wildness, and if there was a center of naturalist knowledge in Jackson Hole, it was at the Murie Ranch. When Adolph differed with the park, he was not shy about voicing his opinions, whether to advise the young ranger Bernard Shanks or offer thoughts on bear poli-

cy, or in his vigorous advocacy of a pesticide-free landscape in Grand Teton. The two brothers constantly advocated for all species and for a natural park free of human intrusions and spectacles. They were activist naturalists with a profound knowledge of science, proven not in a laboratory but in the field.[63]

The other two bear experts in Grand Teton were John and Frank Craighead. These brothers were independent wildlife biologists who owned property within Grand Teton (see chapter 3) and contracted with Yellowstone to do grizzly bear studies starting in 1959 and ending in 1971. They pioneered radio collar technology, gathering for the first time specific information on populations and movements of the bears in Yellowstone. By 1971, however, park administrators and the Craighead brothers disagreed over grizzly bear policy. The Yellowstone superintendent wished to end immediately the garbage dumps that artificially sustained the bears, while the Craigheads wanted gradual weaning away from human garbage. The park policy prevailed, and for a time the bear population plummeted. Fortunately, the animals adjusted and have survived, even prospered. This Yellowstone issue was controversial indeed, although beyond the scope of this study. However, it is important to note that Grand Teton benefited significantly from its association with four top naturalists who were also bear experts.[64]

Until the last decade grizzlies normally ranged only in the northern reaches of the park, finding habitat in such seldom visited areas such as the Pilgrim Creek or Arizona Creek drainages. Occasionally, visitors or kayakers might spot a grizzly in the Two Ocean Lake or the Oxbow Bend of the Snake River areas of the park, and there have been at least two maulings of hikers or runners in these and other semi-wilderness locations, responses typical of a bear protecting its food source or a female grizzly with cubs. There is no animal more committed to her young than a female grizzly, which will charge without hesitation, especially if surprised.

Because the grizzlies, like all other animals, are not good at recognizing political boundaries, coordina-tion between agencies is paramount. The Interagency Grizzly Bear Study Team is responsible for research. The Yellowstone Ecosystem Managers Subcommittee (forest supervisors, two park superintendents, and the managers of fish and game departments for Idaho, Montana and Wyoming) is responsible for management decisions. Under its interagency umbrella, the bears have done well. The Greater Yellowstone Ecosystem estimate for 2010 was 602 bears, twice the number estimated 20 years ago. With these increased numbers, a couple of females in the park have been grabbing headlines. Bears #399 and #610 and their cubs have stayed within sight of main roads, providing unusual opportunities for visitors to observe them. Bear #399 seemed to have no reluctance to roam close to the road, with her cubs romping close by. Of course all bears command tourist fascination, and these grizzly cubs captivated visitors with their amusing behavior and play. As a result, the park has a new attraction in May, June, and early July, and sometimes as late as October. "Bear jams" on park roads can infuriate drivers in a hurry, but for most family visitors, such a jam can be the highlight of their trip. For park administrators, the daily viewing of mother bears and cubs brings smiles, for they know a bear sighting will be remembered. Yet the chaotic situation on park roads can be worrisome, inviting accidents and risky encounters. Rangers and park volunteers organized as the "Wildlife Brigade" do their best to separate potential problems and encourage a safe and memorable experience. We should not forget that the first obligation is the welfare and protection of the bears. How long this exciting performance by #399 and #610 and their cubs will last remains to be seen, but for now Grand Teton National Park's visible grizzlies have captured the hearts of visitors, and the spotlight now focuses not just on Yellowstone's bears but on Teton's grizzlies too.

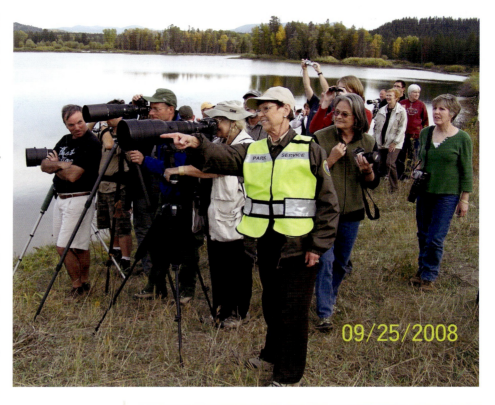

In the past few years, grizzlies have completely reoccupied all of Grand Teton park, expanding their range south toward the town of Jackson, as well as the Wyoming and Wind River Mountain Ranges. Park administrators are extremely solicitous of the bears' needs for food and privacy. They recognize that occasionally the bears' needs may take priority over those of humans. In late August 2012, Superintendent Scott took the unprecedented action of closing the Moose-Wilson Road for five days to accommodate Bear #399 and her cubs, who munched on abundant berries and other forage. This is not a main thoroughfare, but the closure certainly inconvenienced both tourists and locals. And yet there was little public protest. Everyone seemed to acknowledge that the bears' needs have primacy. It is not likely that such a thing could have happened 60 years ago.

"WILDLIFE BRIGADE"

Indirectly the bears have acquired other rights. If Superintendent Scott determines that a new building or cabin is to be built, she must take into account bear habitat. Simply put, if she authorizes construction of a 5,000-square foot building, she must find 5,000 square feet of grizzly bear habitat elsewhere.[65] Wildlife habitat is constantly shrinking, but the Park Service is minimizing the effect it is having on that precious resource.

The spread of the grizzly to the southern reaches of the park is welcome, but it does bring new issues into focus. As noted, the Grand Teton elk reduction has been going on for 60 years. Now there is a new wrinkle. Successful hunters may leave a gut pile of up to 70 pounds of biomass, attracting eagles, coyotes, wolves, and of course, grizzly bears—a kind of natural food but an artificial delivery method. The wisdom of an elk hunt on park property aside, this situation poses the possibility of confrontation between hunter and grizzly. In the 2011 fall elk reduction program, a hunter inadvertently met with a grizzly protecting a gut pile. The grizzly charged, mauling the hunter, delivering relatively minor injury. Local and regional criticism of the Park Service, the hunt, and the National Elk Refuge was unconcealed. At the very least, some suggested that hunters could clean up the gut piles.[66] In November 2012, three elk hunters surprised a grizzly protecting an elk carcass in a forested area near Schwabacher's Landing along the Snake River. The grizzly charged toward the men and was, according one of the hunters, undeterred by bear spray. One of the group shot and killed the adult male bear, the first grizzly to be killed by a hunter in Grand Teton National Park.[67]

The incident ignited severe censure, with one critic calling the elk reduction program "an anachronistic relic of a bygone eras," while another castigated the Park Service: "It's no longer 1950…The time has come" to end the hunt.[68]

The relationships among humans, bears, wolves, elk, and moose are complicated. Recently I sat down with Tom Mangelsen, a world-class wildlife photographer, to talk about park policy. Manglesen has

Photo by Thomas D. Mangelsen

made his home in Jackson Hole for many years and no one pays closer attention to the grizzlies, often up at dawn to search for the famous bear #399 and her cubs. He has often questioned the park's bear policy. He believes Grand Teton wildlife managers have over-managed the grizzly by unnecessarily trapping and collaring them. For visitors and residents alike, a collared grizzly seems the antithesis of a wild bear, and observers often express their disappointment at seeing an "experimental bear." Mangelsen would like wildlife biologists to make sure that their research (and handling) is in the best interest of the bears, not the minute, inconsequential details of science. He is not alone in that wish.

He believes the park staff should be more pro-active in protecting the grizzlies in the park and out-side as well. He would like the park to "stand up and be counted" in the grizzly delisting issue and with the policies of the Wyoming Game and Fish Commission. Both Mangelsen and NPS wildlife manager Steve Cain want the grizzly bears to prosper, but just how to accomplish that objective is sometimes difficult to achieve given the limited habitat available and the competing needs of visitors and local residents.

Respecting wildlife while protecting the public has and will always challenge the Grand Teton National Park staff.

Bison

Bison hardly have the standing of grizzly bears, but these hulking beasts draw plenty of attention in Grand Teton National Park. The current herd are the descendents of bison who wandered down from Yellowstone National Park, but also from the gene pool of the Jackson Hole Wildlife Park bison. When park workers removed the fence in 1964, the bison spread out and they have not looked back. The preponderance of the herd grazes on the forage of Antelope Flats, but they can also be seen on the vast grasslands of the old Elk Ranch near the eastern boundary of the park. As cattle grazing permits have been retired, the bison have spread out onto these former cattle ranges, becoming more prolific. In years past, some of the herd would cross the Snake River to the west side, but recently this mini-migration has not occurred.

Currently about 800 bison call Grand Teton home. Their numbers threaten to overwhelm the carrying capacity of the land. A bison consumes about two and a half times more grass than an elk. Harsh winters aside, bison have few natural threats. Some bison calves have fallen victim to wolves, but not in numbers sufficient to reduce the herds. The adjacent National Elk Refuge has initiated yearly bison hunts to cull the herd. As any wildlife expert will attest, it is necessary to kill to save. Left to their own devices, the bison herd will proliferate, bringing into question the "carrying capacity" of the park lands.

Grand Teton National Park does not have abundant land to accommodate large and numerous animals. Because of crowding and conflict, there will always be wildlife problems requiring management. One wishes that the park had the space of Yellowstone but it does not. Suitable habitat is at a premium, and in recent years, wildlife has achieved more "standing" in park circles. But at times, the wildlife habitat needs conflict with visitors' needs and desires. We cannot forget that parks are for people, and yet when conflict with wildlife arises, the park administrators today believe the desires of people must give way.

The temporary closing of Moose-Wilson Road to accommodate wildlife may be repeated and mirrored by more such actions in the future. Outside Grand Teton National Park, land continues to be appropriated for private use. Inside the park, biologists like Steve

Cain insist that both habitat and wildlife must be protected. Grand Teton National Park is bound under NPS policy directives, and a clear mandate that the park must protect "as parts of the natural ecosystem…all plants and animals native to park ecosystem."[69]

[1] Grand Teton National Park archives (hereafter cited as GTNP), Fire Management, box 1, folder 35, clipping files.

[2] Hal K. Rothman, *Blazing Heritage: A History of Wildland Fire in the National Parks* (New York: Oxford University Press, 2007), 5.

[3] William A. Baillie-Grohman, "Camps in the Teton Basin," in Robert W. Righter, ed., *A Teton Country Anthology* (Boulder, Colo.: Roberts Rinehart, 1990), 38. Excerpted from William A. Baillie-Grohman, *Camps in the Rockies* (New York: Charles Scriber's Sons, 1882). Baillie-Grohman states that he was within 1,000 to 1,100 feet from the summit, but the light was fading. He turned back. He was an experienced climber and believed he would have had no trouble: "Many a second class peak in the Dolomites . . . presents much graver obstacles than those I saw on the uppermost portion of the Teton—the very formation of rock speaking for an easy ascent." Baillie-Grohman's account reflects a slight arrogance, but depending on your view of the Langford climb, this cocky Englishman's climb might have made the first ascent of the mountain, had it not been for fire.

[4] See Stephen J. Pyne, *Fire in America: A Cultural History of Wildland and Rural Fire* (Princeton, N.J.: Princeton University Press, 1982), 162, 22.

[5] Timothy Egan, *The Big Burn* (New York: Houghton, Mifflin, and Harcourt, 2009); Pyne, *Fire in America,* 239.

[6] GTNP, Fire Management, box 1, folder 30.

[7] "Analysis of Individual Fire Report Summary, 1929–1938." GTNP, Fire Management, box 1, folder 2. "Corral time" was how many minutes it took to extinguish a blaze.

[8] "Fire Control Plan for Grand Teton National Park, 1939," GTNP, Fire Incident Management, box 1, folder 3.

[9] Rothman, *Blazing Heritage,* 78, 80. Also see Richard W. Sellers, *Preserving Nature in the National Parks* (New Haven: Yale University Press, 1997), 82-83.

[10] Sellers, *Preserving Nature,* 101.

[11] "Environmental Assessment of Proposed Fire-Vegetation Management Plan, November, 1974," GTNP, Fire Incident Management, box 1, folder 25, 1, 17.

[12] Sellers, *Preserving Nature,* 255–56, 258.

[13] Ibid., 17–22. The plan was given final approval by the Rocky Mountain Regional Office on November 7, 1974.

[14] GTNP, Fire Management, box 1, folder 29.

[15] George B. Hartzog Jr., Director, NPS, to Edward P. Cliff, Chief, U.S. Forest Service, January 31, 1972, in GTNP, Fire Management, box 1, folder 29.

[16] Sellers, *Preserving Nature,* 257. Stanley Hathaway, Governor of Wyoming, to Gary Everhardt, Superintendent, September 20, 1973, GTNP, Fire Management, box 1, folder 35.

[17] "Fire Assessment Document, 1974"; Margaret Murie to Gary Everhardt, Superintendent, July 18, 1974; Louise Murie to Gary Everhardt, Superintendent, July 18, 1974, all in GTNP, Fire Incident Management, box 1, folder 25.

[18] GTNP, Fire Management, box 1, folder 35.

[19] Ibid.

[20] Ibid. This folder contains a number of newspaper clippings that were useful.

[21] Ibid.

[22] Rothman, *Blazing Heritage,* 136

[23] GTNP, Fire Management, box 2, folder 18.

[24] Ibid., 177.

25 1988 Fire Reports, "Grand Teton National Park: 1988 Wildland Fire Summary," 9 pages, GTNP, Fire Management, box 2, folder 26. Also comments of NPS fire chief Chip Collins.

26 Ibid., 6.

27 Chip Collins, Fire Manager, interview by author, August 3, 2012. Also see Rothman, *Blazing Heritage,* 189–90.

28 Chip Collins interview, August 3, 2012.

29 Aldo Leopold, *A Sand County Almanac* (New York: Oxford University Press, 1949).

30 Ibid., 204, 224–25; also see Roderick Nash, *The Rights of Nature: A History of Environmental Ethics* (Madison: University of Wisconsin Press, 1989), 63–86.

31 Acreages from *The National Parks: Index 1991* (Washington D. C.: Department of the Interior, 1991).

32 Laurance's biographer believes that both Fairfield Osborn and Horace Albright acted as mentors to LSR, shaping his conservation ethic and often shaping his projects. See Robin Winks, *Laurance S. Rockefeller: Catalyst for Conservation* (Covelo, California: Island Press, 1997), 41-7.

33 Fairfield Osborn to Emmet T. Hooper, undated, in "Grand Teton Park" folder, box 17, Horace Albright Papers, UCLA.

34 Andrew Kendrew to Kenneth Chorley, February 7, 1946, "Jackson Hole Preserve," box 101, Cultural Interests, RG2, Private Archives of Messrs. Rockefeller. In this letter Rockefeller's landscape architect related his off-the-record talk with Drury: also see Sellers, *Preserving Nature,* 160–61.

35 Olaus Murie, "Improving Jackson Hole," *National Parks Magazine* 46 (January–March 1946).

36 Murie's arguments have such a contemporary ring. I revisit the topic in chapter 9.

37 Dick Winger to Laurance Rockefeller, July 10, 1946, Jackson Hole Wildlife Project (hereafter cited as JHWP), box 1, series 2, folder 5.

38 Olaus Murie to Fairfield Osborn, October 21, 1949, JHWP, box 4, series 4, folder 1.

39 Minutes for August 23, 1952, JHWP, Box 5, Series 14, Folder 3.

40 Minutes for August 23, 1952, JHWP, box 5, series 14, folder 3.

41 The minutes for September 27, 1952, show that the resolution to dissolve passed the board 9 to 0. Only Simon and Harold Fabian were present. The rest voted by proxy. The minutes also reflected the fact that "Mr. Rockefeller and the NY Zoological Society will discontinue support."

42 "Jackson Bison Herd: Long Term Management Plan and Environmental Assessment," Grand Teton National Park, National Elk Refuge, September, 1996, 5-6; Steve Cain, wildlife biologist, interview by author, September 17, 2012; Sellers, *Preserving Nature,* 214–15.

43 See Major Sir Rose Lambert Price, "A Summer in the Rockies," excerpt in Righter, *Teton Country Anthology,* 95–106.

44 Robert W. Righter, *Crucible for Conservation: The Struggle for Grand Teton National Park* Park (Boulder: Colorado University Press, 1982; repr., Moose: Grand Teton Association, 2000), 22-3.

45 See Stephen N. Leek, "The Starving Elk of Wyoming," *Outdoor Life* 27 (May 1911): 441–52.

46 Righter, *Crucible for Conservation, 52–54.*

47 *An Act to Establish a New Grand Teton National Park, Public Law 81-787, 64 Statute 849 (1950), Sec. 6 (a), (b).*

48 GTNP officials never use the word "kill," but rather "elk reduction."

49 These disputes were modified when the park initiated ¼ mile hunting setbacks from the roadway.

50 Ibid., Sec. 6 (a).

51 Bruce L. Smith, *Where Elk Roam: Conservation and Biopolitics of Our National Elk Herd* (Guilford, Conn.: Lyons Press, 2012), v.

52 See Sellers, *Preserving Nature,* 248.

53 Smith, *Where Elk Roam,* 50.

54 Smith, *Where Elk Roam,* vi. Superintendent Mary Gibson Scott, interview by author, December 11, 2011; Angus M. Thuermer, "Park Hunt Dangerous, Should be Stopped, Critics Say," *Jackson Hole News and Guide,* September 28, 2011; Steve Cain, chief wildlife biologist, interview by author, September 17, 2012.

55 Interview with GT wildlife biologist Steve Cain by author, September 17, 2012

56 See photograph of "Gram" Shrive and her two wolf pups in Righter, *Teton Country Anthology,* 155.

57 The last wolf survivor is a matter of mild dispute. I took my evidence from Wikipedia.org/wiki/history_of_wolves_in Yellowstone.

58 Aldo Leopold is nationally known, the Murie brothers are regionally respected, but George Wright, perhaps had the most potential of all for shaping long-range change in attitudes and practices involving wildlife. He is little known, perhaps because he died at the age of thirty-two in an automobile accident. Today the George Wright Society, devoted to wildlife research, honors his memory.

59 Barry Holstun Lopez, *Of Wolves and Men* (1978; New York: Simon and Schuster, 1995), 4.

60 The literature on reintroduction is extensive. Two articles I found particularly useful are in Robert B. Keiter and Mark S. Boyce, eds., *The Greater Yellowstone Ecosystem* (New Haven: Yale University Press, 1991). They are L. David Mech, "Returning the Wolf to Yellowstone," 309–22, and Alistair J. Bath, "Public Attitudes about Wolf Restoration in Yellowstone National Park," 367–76.

61 See "Wildlife: Conservation, Management, and Research," Grand Teton National Park, 2010, 39–40; also www.jhalliance.org/Librar/Alerts/wolvesintetons.8-08.pdf.

62 Adoph certainly changed attitudes toward wolves with his, *The Wolves of Mt. McKinley.*

63 Michael Frome, *Regreening the National Parks* (Tucson: University of Arizona Press, 1992), 162–63.

64 Ibid., 167–68.

65 Steve Cain interview, September 17, 2012.

66 See *Jackson Hole News and Guide,* September 28, 2011, October 19, 2011.

67 Mike Koshmrl, "Griz Shooting Sparks Hunt Protests," *Jackson Hole News and Guide,* November 28, 2012.

68 Ibid.

69 National Park Service, *Management Policies, 2006* (Washington, D. C.: Government Printing Office, 2006).

Peaks, Politics, and Passion: Grand Teton National Park Comes of Age

Chapter 6

Preserving the Human Heritage

IF IN THE 1990s, you drove five miles along a rough gravel road that slants eastward off the main road at Cottonwood Creek, you would eventually come to the Snake River and a cluster of old cabins. You might wonder what had happened here and if the old cabins had a story. They do, of course, and a very interesting one. But does the story of the old historic Bar BC dude ranch warrant telling? And should some of the old cabins be saved, or should they be removed, burned, or left in a state of moldering ruins?

These are hard questions to answer. What if a homestead site is situated in elk habitat? What should happen if a cabin sits on a flood plain? And what of the cost of maintenance? What of the dollars necessary to bring a structure up to code, particularly current electrical codes? Can an old building be "recycled," given a new use that is compatible with other park goals? Should the park have any "living history" exhibits, since they can be costly? What if people consider a refuse dump or a dilapidated cabin an eyesore? On that subject, some may remember the Joe Pfeifer homestead, sitting on the vast expanse of Antelope Flats. To many it was just a crumbling pile of window frames, sagging two by fours, and a roof that had seen too many hard winters: a blemish to be removed. To others it was a treasure that evoked an earlier era and enhanced the sublime view across the sagebrush flats to the mountains beyond. These competing visions underscore the difficulties at the heart of historic preservation. Beauty may be in the eye of the beholder, but historical and cultural significance is more than opinion, resting upon the considered judgment of professionals.

The challenge of whether to preserve historical structures, and if so, which ones, is magnified by the hefty number of buildings and sites in Grand Teton National Park. Also, not to be ignored are the basketful of laws to which a park administrator must adhere. The park's cultural resources program has a current inventory of 542 historic buildings that are either in the National Register of Historic Places or eligible for inclusion. The cultural resource staff has listed about 75 percent on the National Register of Historic Places. If you examine these buildings, you find that many are contained within designated historic districts, of which there are 14. The staff identified another dozen districts as eligible but unlisted. Finally, another 15 individual structures are enrolled on the National Register. Being eligible, however, does not guarantee the distinction of being registered. The park superintendent and staff have the option of submitting a nomination to the "Keeper of the Register" in Washington, D.C., or withholding it. However, strange as it may seem, it does not matter whether a building is listed on the register or not. The NPS is obligated to treat an eligible structure as though it was listed on the register. One must then ask: "What is the point of being listed?" Cultural Resources Specialist Katherine Wonson states that, "the only difference between a listed and an eligible site is the honorary distinction of being actually listed."[1] So there is an honor, but also a time factor. An eligible structure has greater protection, whereas those without such status could be more easily and quickly removed.

Many of these 542 structures the public would not consider individually significant—dog houses and sheds, for instance. Yet they are considered "contributing structures" adding to the total ambiance of the district site.[2] If a district is enrolled there is, however, no obligation to maintain the structures. Keeping up all these structures can be expensive, and given park budget constraints, various interest groups must contend for their share of a vanishing pie.

Whereas the larger Yellowstone National Park to the north contains double the historic structures and sites as Grand Teton, it contains approximately seven times the land area (2.2 million acres versus 310 thousand acres). Thus, diminutive Grand Teton has a much greater concentration of historic structures and sites to deal with since settlement preceded park status by many years. This means a richness of cultural resources, but on the other hand, it poses management challenges.

Grand Teton administrators have struggled with these challenges for over 60 years. Settlers built hundreds of cabins and barns before the National Park Service entered the picture as property owner. When people sold out and moved away, they did not take their buildings with them. Some Park Service superintendents wanted to rid the landscape of all evidence of human occupation. Others wanted to save representative samples from different times and different occupations. Clearly, park leaders had various sensibilities and options. In the 1950s and early 1960s, superintendents simply decided, without guidelines, which buildings and sites they believed were worth saving or selling. Consequently, they removed or destroyed the majority of cabins. When Congress passed the 1966 National Historic Preservation Act, this document finally provided some guidelines for future decision making. But even so, the question of whether to manage a "natural park" versus one that also interprets the park's human history as well, continues to challenge park administrators into the 21st century. Debates about the maintenance of historic structures among individual preservation advocates, the NPS regional office and/or Grand Teton administrators, the Wyoming State Historic Preservation Office (SHPO) and private, non-profit interest groups spawned contentious conversations and fierce differences of opinion. These debates are the focus of this chapter. We will see that changes in park personnel, new laws, and the determined work of historic preservation advocates and volunteer labor, have all led to a gradual yet fundamental alteration in Grand Teton National Park's cultural resource policy.[3]

The Cultural Mission

On the face of it, one might assume there would be little debate about Grand Teton National Park's human heritage. After all, it is the responsibility of all national parks to "identify, evaluate, document, register, and establish basic information about cultural sources and [their] traditionally associated peoples."[4] In Grand Teton, human history starts with Indian settlements along the shores of Jackson Lake and moves to fur trade sites. The fur trade, in particular, attracted the attention of one Grand Teton historian.[5] But no buildings and few sites represented these two themes. Early Euro-American settlement provided a more compelling candidate for interpretation, with emphasis on the popular theme of the old West and its struggling homesteaders and cattle ranchers. The advent of tourism, and the development of the

LARGE CROWD GATHERS FOR CAMPFIRE PROGRAM.

Jackson Hole dude ranching business, are worthy topics, as is the fight to create the park and expand it to its full potential.

Preserving and interpreting this vital heritage has not been easy for several reasons. Over the years many park leaders considered the park's primary mission to be the preservation of its natural resources, and consequently, they neglected historical interpretation. Most visitors, they believed, come for the stunning mountain scenery and the wildlife. Some guests come to climb the Grand Teton or fly fish on the Snake River. Administrators assumed tourists come to escape the urban world, so any human artifacts, including homesteads, houses, and barns detracted from that goal. Further, some park managers believed structures disturbed wildlife and appropriated their habitat. Others worried about the significant cost of maintaining structures. Yet others saw the Jackson Hole history as so recent, that it qualified among current events, not history. Particularly NPS personnel who served in the East tend to believe that you must *have* a history before you try to preserve it, and that to qualify, historic items, you must reach back at least a century. For archeologists, 10,000 years might be the baseline qualification.

THE EARLY YEARS

Because the determining features of Grand Teton were the mountains and wildlife, for many years there was little value placed on cultural resources. The park was intent on building new structures (Mission 66), not conserving old. In regard to older structures, both the Snake River Land Company and National Park personnel made all the determinations on the historic importance of structures. A 1957 letter from Acting Superintendent W. Ward Yeager to the regional director revealed both the policy and the methodology in force. Yeager informed the regional office that since November 1956 the park had been busy in "restoration of acquired lands" and that 33 old buildings on eight tracts had been offered for sale. As a result, the park sold ten buildings to the highest bidder; gave away 14 buildings on a "first come, first serve" basis; and burned the remaining structures.[6] With few exceptions, the park considered only two options: removal or burning. Ironically, the "remaining buildings" may have been the most historically significant. But the overwhelming sentiment at the time, called for returning the land, as much as possible, to a pre-settlement state in which few signs of human activity would be evident. The park largely succeeded in that objective. Although no count existed at that time, NPS Cultural Resources Specialist Michael Johnson later estimated that some 70 percent of all buildings within the park boundaries had been removed or destroyed by 1990.[7] Admittedly, many of these structures represented the worst examples of "cowboy carpentry." They probably deserved their fate. Yet in Johnson's opinion, it was time to end the carnage. A change in policy would not be easy.

Even at the time of the establishment of the first Teton park in 1929, there was ambivalence about its mission with respect to history. When the group who spearheaded the park's founding met at Maud Noble's cabin in 1923, most shared a particular vision. Dude rancher Struthers Burt expressed the majority opinion when he called for northern Jackson Hole to be "a museum on a hoof." Burt did not explain exactly what he meant, although certainly increased populations of indigenous wild animals were part of it. The group hankered for a park (or a recreational area) featuring awe-inspiring mountains, a fast-flowing river bisecting the valley, abundant wildlife, and vast vistas. They did *not* wish for a wilderness area, nor did they want to eliminate man's presence. They favored log houses and gravel roads, but also limits on home development. They wanted zoning to restrict new development. They desired protection against what they considered unsightly expansion but were hesitant to suggest restrictions on property rights. How to achieve their ideal, or just what that ideal designation might be, was not clear. Horace Albright, then superintendent of Yellowstone National Park, was in attendance. We cannot divine what Albright was thinking, except that he was doubtless delighted there was movement toward limitations on growth.[8]

The meeting at the Noble cabin laid out some broad ideas for safeguarding the valley, but it did not suggest any clearly defined course for meaningful action. Struthers Burt and Horace Albright agreed that the beauty of Jackson Hole must be preserved. It was a special land that must be set apart. Neither had a precise plan until, in 1926, John D. Rockefeller, Jr., his wife, and their three sons arrived in Yellowstone for a visit guided by Superintendent Albright. He soon had them motoring on the old wagon road to Jackson Hole. In spite of the rough ride, the family's initial view of Jackson and Jenny Lakes, the valley, and the Teton mountains worked their magic, as they have for millions of Americans since. Albright showed the valley to its greatest advantage. In the Jenny Lake region, Rockefeller and his wife winced at the cheap commercial structures and telephone lines punctuating the mountain view. With just a little imagination, the sensitive millionaire could envision the proliferation of these unattractive commercial ventures. His concerns almost paralleled those of the participants at the meeting in Maud Noble's cabin three years earlier. They all feared what might become of the valley they loved if such commercialism continued to run rampant. They wanted to avoid a theme park and/or a commercial vacation resort. They shared a similar vision of limited development. The difference was that Rockefeller had the resources to make the visualization real.

These attitudes had implications for the future park's treatment of historic structures. Albright and Rockefeller would eliminate many of the buildings that marred the views, but they did not want to sweep the region completely clear of houses and ranches. They did *not* envision Jackson Hole as wilderness. They merely wanted to excise the unsightly elements of human development, a kind of restorative stance. We might identify their mindset as the creation of a "windshield wilderness," in which the human presence would be apparent but neither dominant nor in bad taste. A dance hall near Jenny Lake would have to go, but the Bar BC dude ranch would be welcome.[9] Initially, the decisions about what stayed and what went fell to the privately owned Snake River Land Company, which bought land both east and west of the Snake River. Winter fires cleared away some unwanted buildings, but the company was more concerned about freeing the land of people rather than from buildings. If a building could be converted, recycled, or used in other ways, it survived. Part of the motivation for this policy was practical. The company needed to preserve buildings for employee housing, but also for tourists, who were already coming in increasing numbers.

NAVIGATING BETWEEN NATURE AND CULTURE

The Snake River Land Company team, headed by Harold Fabian, Kenneth Chorley, Richard Winger, and others, preserved ranches and outbuildings partly because they were unsure what kind of park Grand Teton would finally become. Would it be a park for nature or would it feature recreational activities associated with the historic American West? Should it become what Burt described as "a museum on a hoof"? Would it welcome visitors in the Stephen Mather tradition of entertainment and leisure activities?

AN "OLD WEST" IDEA

One Park Service professional thought hard on these issues. In July 1939, NPS Regional Landscape Architect Sanford Hill submitted a plan to incorporate the old West theme and save a lake. He was deeply concerned that park visitors were impacting the Jenny Lake area by overuse and that "the small lakes and the narrow strip of land at the base of the mountains are gradually being ruined."[10] As he put it, "each year public demand for further improvements and concessions comes pouring in." Pressure was on the park to sanction such development. In more modern terms, the Jenny Lake area was being "loved to death." Ironically, he favored entertaining tourists through history to preserve nature. His solution was to lessen the impact by restricting visitation. He favored "de-motoriz[ing] our visitors."[11] So he proposed a plan that would establish two transportation zones: the automobile zone and the stagecoach zone.

In the 1930s, all automobile traffic came to the Jenny Lake area. The highway on the east side of the Snake River was nothing more than a wagon road, rough enough to shake fillings from the teeth of unsuspecting tourists. Highway engineers planned to change that with the Jackson Hole Highway, but they did not begin construction of Highway 89 until 1947–48. Hill anticipated that the new highway would partially relieve the crowded Jenny Lake region. Driving tourists would be directed east of the Snake River, where a new park headquarters and visitor center at Moose would attract their attention. As they drove north to Yellowstone via automobile, they would enjoy the "sunset trip" with glorious mountain views and perhaps a boat trip on Jackson Lake.

The stagecoach zone would include all the land west of the river, south of Jackson Lake, and up to the "foothills of the Teton Range." Within this region, all automobile parkways would be torn up and replaced by gravel roads suitable only for stagecoach travel. Staging areas would be at the Moran Junction near the Jackson Lake Ranger Station and at the Moose area on the south end. Hill envisioned that most visitors would spend about five hours on the stagecoach ride. They might stop for a swim at Leigh Lake or String Lake or perhaps a meal at the Square G Ranch or one of the other dude ranches.[12]

To his credit, the landscape architect squarely addressed a pressing issue that would become increasingly problematic in many national parks. At Yellowstone's Old Faithful, in the Yosemite Valley, and along the south rim of the Grand Canyon, visitors with limited time crowd to the most scenic spots. Planners ever since Hill have struggled for solutions (an overpass at Old Faithful, a one-way free bus system in Yosemite and Zion, and a train at Grand

Canyon) so that visitors have an enjoyable experience but do not forgo park highlights or destroy the site in the process of seeing and experiencing it.

Yet Hill was suggesting more than freeing up the Jenny Lake area. His plan would change, and possibly enhance, the park experience. The stagecoach area would emphasize scenery but also the culture of the old West. Hill believed that children, who often seem almost immune to scenic mountains, would remember for a lifetime the experience of rattling along in a stagecoach. He likewise believed the proposal would not only help retain the area's western character but also increase tourism. In a sense, Hill was advocating a kind of modern-day theme park. Yet one can see Hill's plan as re-asserting an historic mode of transportation to recreate an era. As such, it could be viewed as "living history" rather than a theme park.

Was this plan seriously considered? If so, no records of the debate remain. Still Hill took the trouble to calculate the cost at one dollar per visitor. He also provided rough figures showing that the cost for stagecoaches, horses, and employees would be $316,100 per year, while the income would be $396,000.[13] We cannot know whether these estimates were anywhere close to reality. Hill's idea probably never rose beyond the early, conceptual stage. In those discussions we can assume park administrators focused on all the difficult issues the stagecoach zone would have caused. Possibly the majority viewed Hill's plan as romantic and quaint, but impractical.

Some may have argued that an emphasis on living history minimized the primary mission of the park: enjoyment of the scenery. Although history need not be suppressed, neither should it overshadow appreciation of the natural landscape. Some may have thought the park should balance natural history and human history: tell the story and protect the heritage of both. The stagecoach plan, in spite of admirable objectives, would have moved the park toward what one historian has labeled "carnivalism."[14] Already in the Yosemite Valley, promoters had established a wildlife park, Indian field days, the Bracebridge Christmas dinner pageant, and the "firefall" (a nightly dramatic cascading of embers from Inspiration Point down a 3,000-foot cliff)—all entertaining yet artificial attractions diverting attention from waterfalls, granite cliffs, and the spectacular beauty of nature. The trend placed the National Park System in danger of becoming a recreation and amusement center. The World War II years interrupted discussion of Hill's novel idea. Crowds at Jenny Lake, or anywhere in the park, were temporarily no longer an issue.

Although park officials did not embrace Sanford's idea, discussion of alternatives for the west side of the river continued. Superintendent Charles Smith (1940–43) faced no issues with crowds, but he was prescient. He and Sanford Hill put together a plan that called for leaving the west side as a scenic zone, largely undeveloped. Removal of west side structures was not mentioned, but the plan recommended that dude ranching be encouraged.[15] And it reiterated the idea that east of the river would be the side for fast traffic, automobile turnouts, and a visitor center.

Rockefeller's Architect Looks at Park Resources

Perhaps the most influential planning document for the west side of the Snake River came from Andrew E. Kendrew, John D. Rockefeller, Jr.'s landscape architect for his ambitious restoration of Williamsburg, Virginia as a colonial town. The latter project demonstrated John D. Rockefeller, Jr.'s commitment to historic preservation. Kendrew was also important because, as we must keep in mind, although the National Park Service might generate plans, until 1949, most of the west side land and structures belonged to the Snake River Land Company and, to the north, the U.S. Forest Service. Rockefeller and Vanderbilt Webb, president of the Snake River Land Company, sent Kendrew westward in 1942 to inventory the buildings of the JY Ranch and the many other holdings managed by the company. Kendrew did not recommend removal of any cabins at the JY, and he suggested taking out only a few west of the river. He saw great value in retaining features reflecting the "discovery and early settlements in this area," remarking that "in the future many millions of visitors . . . will wish to be informed." He was convinced that the public had "a strong interest in the more recent phases such as the ranch life, [and the] cattle industry." He expected that Rockefeller's effort to save the natural beauty and "several landmarks of early settlement" would be successful.[16]

The Snake River Land Company's commitment to historic preservation and a combination of natural and cultural history was significant. Arguably the most influential entity in the valley, the company carried weight in its stance on wildlife, lodging, the airport, or anything else, particularly with the National Park Service. We know Rockefeller sought removal of the trashy, poorly planned buildings near Jenny Lake, but this view was not a mandate to clear the west side entirely of structures.

As if to give further official sanction to the old West theme, in 1945 NPS Director Newton Drury issued a memorandum regarding Jackson Hole National Monument. In it Drury stressed that administrators must take into account old West themes such as the fur trade, government exploration, pioneer settlement, and more recent ones such as cattle ranching and dude ranching. These themes, he wrote, "should be continued and fitted into the over-all program of accommodation."[17] In all likelihood the memo was intended to assure cattle grazers of their rights in the monument, but in the process it confirmed that Grand Teton was not just about plants, animals, and mountains. It was also about the people who had lived within what became the monument and the park.

By 1960 then, the National Park Service extended its historical interests beyond the fur trade. National Park Service Regional Historian Russell A. Apple produced what became known as the "Apple Report." He outlined 10 themes he believed worthy of interpretation: pioneering, politics, ranching and farming, water utilization, transportation, communications, the elk herd, outlawry, vacationers, and land acquisition. Apple then attached structures to these themes, using a number of those identified by Kendrew. He agreed with the company's removal policy regarding what he termed "hot dog stands, gas stations, cafes, cheap tourist courts, dancehalls, multi-unit brothels . . . and junk heaps" (his vision apparently extended into the town of Jackson). Although Apple recommended many structures be destroyed, he too embraced the old West theme, citing NPS Director Newton Drury's 1945 statement that the park should retain the ranches to reflect its colorful past. Park leaders, seem to have received the Apple Report largely with indifference. Most believed that cultural or historic preservation must be secondary to the natural history aspects of the park.[18]

But 20th century history had its advocates. And, consequently, conflict eventually arose between the advocates of historic preservation and park leaders who eschewed it. One NPS policy change was particularly helpful. In 1950, officials classified parks as either "natural," "cultural," or "recreational." The classification determined the emphasis of a park, and Grand Teton was considered a "natural" park. Thus, the "cultural" aspects of the park could easily be dismissed. In 1978, however, the NPS reevaluated these three designations and then eliminated them in what

is known as the Redwood Act. The "act" was actually an amendment that expanded Redwood National Park. It stated that although each national park area was "distinctive in character," they were all "united through their inter-related purposes and resources into one national park system as cumulative expressions of a single national heritage . . ." Although open to interpretation, the Redwood Act signaled that the old categories of natural, cultural, or recreational would no longer represent policy. In Grand Teton the bias against cultural resources was no longer legitimate. Indeed, it was against park policy thereafter. From here on out all features of the park deserved attention and careful consideration.

EVOLVING POLICY

Another harbinger of change was the National Historic Preservation Act that Congress passed in 1966. Before 1966, cultural resource policy was left largely to the discretion of park superintendents. Their word was law within their own domain. Past Chief Historian Robert Utley noted that in the early 1960s "it would have been unthinkable for a Regional Historian or a Regional Archeologist to have been too aggressive in trying to tell a park superintendent how to run his park, even when they were doing so graciously."[19] With the passage of the National Historic Preservation Act, the status of history began to change as well as the power to incorporate cultural resources into park management.

The Act provided the nation's basic legislation on historic preservation. It established the National Register of Historic Places, a roster of buildings and sites of historic and/or architectural significance. To foster and support the register, the legislation mandated that each state create a State Historic Preservation Office (SHPO) to evaluate and monitor sites within its boundaries. The Act also established a state consulting committee responsible for reviewing nominations prior to forwarding them to the register keeper in Washington, D.C. Section 106 of the Act required that National Park officials consult with the relevant State Historic Preservation Office (SHPO) on all actions affecting historic properties under their control. In many ways, Section 106 is the heart of the preservation act. But a 1980 amendment, Section 110, strengthened the cultural resources mandate by requiring that structures and archeological artifacts on federal land must be evaluated and declared ineligible for the register before they can be removed or destroyed. In other words, federal land managers were henceforth required to evaluate and take into account the impact of all actions as they affected historic resources, known and unknown.

Many park superintendents and Forest Service supervisors resented this imposition on their power and prerogatives. Then Chief Historian Robert Utley recalled that, "the Park Service from the very beginning had to be dragged kicking and screaming into Section 106 compliance."[20] Resistance to the law in the opinion of NPS Historian Richard Sellers was "almost Service wide," particularly in the Western parks.[21] Superintendents, considered sacrosanct in their own fiefdom, were particularly resistant to the state preservation offices which, virtually overnight, could influence policy in federally managed parks. In Grand Teton, Superintendents Jack Stark (1979-1991) and Jack Neckels (1991-2001) were often at odds with the state. The problem, according to Dr. David Kathka who served as head of the Wyoming SHPO office from 1987 to 1994, is that the park refused to do the necessary surveys, or if they did do them, they were slipshod at best. The official procedure required the park to perform an inventory of the cultural resources and then submit the results to the SHPO, where as Kathka stated, "we commented."[22] But the Grand Teton staff believed it could determine what was historic and worth saving without any input from the state of Wyoming. Sections 106 and 110 not only added another layer of unwanted bureaucracy, but these regulations increased the possibility for conflict between federal and state governments. So Grand Teton National Park resisted and consequently in time, conflict with dedicated state preservationists, such as Sheila Bricher-Wade, absolutely ensued.

Nevertheless, prompting from the NPS Regional Office eventually produced the first survey List of Classified Structures. It showed that 321 structures had been acquired by 1979 through purchase. Of that number, 97 had been destroyed after Section 106 compliance, 200 were in use by parties other than the park, and 24 were in use by the park.[23]

Simultaneously preservation funding issues emerged, since the park received no extra monies for care of these buildings. If park administrators were not already hostile to cultural resources because they prioritized the park's natural resources, they certainly cooled toward historic preservation when faced with the strain that building maintenance placed on a shrinking budget. Stabilizing or restoring structures could seriously tax the budget, while managing the natural environment seemed comparatively less expensive . . . and more important.

In 1976, park personnel completed a master plan, really the first comprehensive guidelines for Grand Teton National Park. As earlier noted, the categories of natural, recreational, or cultural were about to be jettisoned at the national level—but not in the eyes of many superintendents. Whereas the Grand Teton plan acknowledged the "historical significance of the region," its main emphasis was "to protect the scenic and geological values of the Teton Range and Jackson Hole, and to perpetuate the park's indigenous plant and animal life." The plan called for interpretation at only three historic sites: Menor's Ferry, Cunningham Cabin, and the Maud Noble cabin. It confined dude ranching to the east side of the Snake River. Consequently, one could assume that the dude ranches, homesteads, and other various buildings on the west side were slated for demolition, removal, or burning.

Such a miserly commitment to cultural resources was unsatisfactory to many locals and to the NPS regional office in Denver as well. In an effort to keep cultural resources from disappearing, NPS regional historians, Kate Stevenson and Michael Schene, contracted me to provide historical context for a number of structures associated with historic themes. I consequently suggested national register nominations for some structures. The work was conducted as a Historic American Building Survey (HABS) study, but the natural park philosophy of Superintendent Jack Stark was in the ascendency. The study was not well received; it was virtually dead on arrival.[24]

TWO JACKS

Park superintendents have considerable power in their fiefdoms. They set the priorities. One park expert compared a superintendent's role to that of a ship's captain. The captain has little control at the dock over what the ship will carry, yet becomes the master once at sea. Unlike many other federal agencies, the Park Service is actually quite decentralized. Although their options and power have been weakened by budgetary constraints and national security laws, superintendents still set many of their park's priorities and agendas. Further, the relationship between the Washington office and the field superintendents has been inconsistent, according to former Park Service and Department of the Interior employee, Dwight F. Rettie. In his opinion, the Park Service has "never really resolved" the issue of roles: "Even with the existence of written guidelines and policies and

JACK STARK (LEFT)

the image of a uniformed service, the Park Service is a remarkably undisciplined career organization. Failed orders, ignored guidelines, and even overt insubordination seldom raise more than eyebrows."[25]

Superintendents Jack Stark (1979–91) and Jack Neckels (1991–2001) were both loyal and committed to Grand Teton. They worked hard to free the park of private land and return it to a natural state. On the other hand, when it came to historic preservation, they were not proactive. Sometimes they were quite antagonistic. The National Historic Preservation Act of 1966 was specific about the superintendent's responsibility with respect to historic properties. Essentially, it requires evaluation of sites and buildings before taking action, such as removal, and mitigation of any negative impacts an action might have on the historic resource. As amended in 1980 via Section 110, the act requires federal agencies to take measures to inventory, evaluate, and nominate to the National Register eligible structures that they own or control. Sections 106 and 110 are straightforward. The park cannot ignore these directives or remain passive. However, Grand Teton

National Park had its own tradition that preceded the 1966 Act, and that tradition did not adhere with the new preservation guidelines and procedures. And, as already noted, for 50 years the Snake River Land Company and the Park Service had been removing or burning buildings.

Even so, a few buildings had been nominated by the Wyoming SHPO and duly enrolled on the National Register. Yet, even that designation did not guarantee protection. Take the example of Leek's Lodge. Built by Stephen Leek, pioneer homesteader, guide, elk advocate, and photographer, it graced the northern shore of Jackson Lake.[26] It was registered in 1975, but remained unused for years. The Park Service had no interest in either interpretive activity there or adaptive reuse of the lodge, although its set-

JACK NECKELS

ting adjacent to Leek's Marina was perfect for a restaurant. A site ignored for many years inevitably deteriorates. By 1985, the lodge was almost beyond repair or recycling. In 1995 park administrators asked for bids to remove the building, but no ranch, family, or company was willing to take it. In a final act of disrespect, the Park Service burned down the lodge purposefully in a 1998 fire exercise. All that remains today is a forlorn fireplace. It was a case of demolition by neglect. Today most agree that this was not the proper way to administer a National Register site.

For Superintendents Jack Stark and Jack Neckels, the loss of Leek's Lodge was consistent with their park priorities. Stark believed there was little history in the park worth saving. He had served in the NPS North Atlantic Region headquarters in Boston, where history was deeper; buildings were 300 years old and architecturally significant. Grand Teton structures were too new. Most were barely 50 years old, the earliest possible age for National Register consideration. He preferred the park landscape returned to a pre-20th century state. In 1983, Superintendent Stark and I were part of a team evaluating the Bar BC Dude Ranch. As we walked together down the old two-track road that split the ranch, looking at the shoddy construction of the cabins, Stark leaned over to me and said: "Bob, I want to bring in a bulldozer and level this place."[27] He spoke his mind. He was transparent. This could be positive, but occasionally it could turn against him. At an early 1990s open meeting at the Antler Motel, Stark and John Daugherty, the park his-

torian, met with 67 community members to discuss the cultural resources of the park. Daugherty asked those in attendance to give priority ratings to a number of structures and historic districts in the park. During the discussion, some participants openly criticized the park's cultural resource practice of ranking buildings which, they feared, could accelerate destruction of properties given lower importance. Stark grew more and more agitated and red-faced. Never one for velvety diplomacy, he finally rose and blurted out: "Damn it. It's my park and I'll do what I want with it." After his outburst the meeting quickly ended. We filled out our priority list and left, knowing our opinions would be of little consequence. One resident expressed the feelings of most of those in attendance:

> As a 50 resident of Jackson Hole and an observer of the development of Grand Teton National Park, as well as the living history of the properties in question, I urge the *most serious* efforts to preserve these structures. The beauty of the natural landscape is in no way distracted by the fascinating structures left by the ranchers, homesteaders, and pioneers who created the history of Jackson Hole. The American public *wants* to *know* and *enjoy* this history.[28]

BAR BC

Superintendent Stark never succeeded in bringing in bulldozers, but he did attempt to eliminate the Bar

BC Dude Ranch by another method, in spite of its rich history. Struthers Burt, a Princeton graduate and writer, with his partner psychologist, Dr. Horace Carncross, took out adjoining homesteads on the bank of the Snake River in 1911 and proved up in May of 1912. With their love of the West and their social connections in New Jersey and Pennsylvania, they decided to start a dude ranch catering to their affluent friends. The Bar BC opened in 1912, but Burt and Carncross (the B and C of the ranch name) had little money and even less time to greet their first guests. No one could claim that the ranch's architecture was anything but utilitarian. True, it was an example of rustic log architecture, but close examination revealed structures thrown together in a hasty and haphazard fashion. Struthers Burt tells a memorable story in *Diary of a Dude-Wrangler* of how he was summoned by one of his "cowboy carpenters," who was putting the finishing touches on a chimney. He complimented the worker on finishing a three-day job in just a day. He then turned around to return to his tasks, only to hear a sickening thud. The river stones and mortar lay spread out on the ground.[29]

Burt and Carncross nevertheless got the job done, and soon the Bar BC attracted many eastern visitors, some of whom would play key roles in the West. While Struthers spent his time entertaining guests, his wife, Katharine, was carving out her career as a writer. Her novels took place in the West, some in Jackson Hole, and at least six became Hollywood films in the 1920s and 1930s, including one that was filmed on location at the Bar BC.

The Bar BC became a retreat for prominent Americans who found a vacation at Newport Beach or the Adirondacks too civilized and passive. They wanted an active experience in the West in open and stunning country. They did not favor wilderness adventure but rather a close yet comfortable encounter with nature. With Katharine's Los Angeles film acquaintances and the two men's Philadelphia and Princeton friends, the Bar BC was the place to experience the outdoors among sophisticated patrons. Notable guests included Mrs. Grover Cleveland, Francis and Sidney Biddle, Architect David Adler, Alfred A. Knopf, Countess Eleanor (Cissy) Medill Patterson, Ernest Hemingway, William Faulkner, Owen Wister, and John D. Rockefeller, Jr., his wife Abby, and their sons. The Bar BC was not easy to reach, but once there, guests found the ambiance worth the effort. They usually stayed from several weeks to all summer.[30]

The Bar BC enjoyed some good years in the 1920s as the social hub of the valley and its intellectual center. But Burt was well aware of the Rockefeller/Albright plan to incorporate his land and the surrounding area into an enlarged national park. With that in mind, he sold the Bar BC to the Snake River Land Company for a price of $45,000, though not without some agonizing debates with Katharine, who was very much opposed to the sale. Horace Carncross had died in 1928, but his sole heir, Irv

Corse, agreed to the sale as well. Both Burt and Carncross partners retained life leases, but Burt moved his operation to the Three Rivers Ranch near Moran.[31] Irv Corse struggled, buying out Burt's life lease in 1937, but the Bar BC's glory days had passed. With the Depression and World War II, Corse became increasingly depressed with the state of both the ranch and his own health. In 1953, he committed suicide. Did the Bar BC then revert to the Park Service? It did not. In a wise move, Corse had signed a 1937 lease with the provision that his immediate heirs could continue to run the place. Margaretta Corse, his new wife and 30 years his junior, inherited the lease and kept it until she died in the 1980s.[32]

By the late 1950s, the Bar BC had lost its sheen. The cabins were in disrepair, and wealthy eastern guests no longer appeared. For a time, Margaretta left the valley, subleasing the place to two or three families. Soon she returned and began renting the cabins out cheaply in the 1960s and 1970s to young people, including counterculture and mountaineering types who had little money, only occasional work, but a love for the mountains. She came to despise the National Park Service, which owned her land and buildings, and the feeling was mutual. She became erratic and few park personnel ventured near the Bar BC. I once arrived on the bench above the Bar BC with park historian, John Daugherty, and wanted to go into the ranch. John announced he would venture no farther because he was in uniform and he feared

Margaretta might fire her rifle at him. He had no idea whether she would aim to hit.

Her correspondence with the park was never cordial and usually volatile. She wanted neither visitors nor Park Service people to cross her land. The tone is evident in a 1969 letter to Frank Betts, acting assistant superintendent: "I am FED UP with people barging in to fish on the Bar BC and I think, most definitely, your rangers should be briefed about it and that it is PRIVATE PROPERTY."[33] With a life lease she did have rights to privacy, but her shrill tone belied the fact that she owned neither the land nor the cabins.

Perhaps the shaky relationship between Margaretta and park personnel blinded administrators to the historic importance of the Bar BC. They saw the old ranch and Margaretta primarily as a problem for the Park Service. Furthermore, occasional raucous parties and other goings on at the Bar BC raised concerns—and hackles. The Burts' substantial role in park history became lost in the concern that some investigative reporter might pick up on unsavory activities at the Bar BC, which of course was on national park land. Yet those with a sense of the past knew that without Struthers Burt and the Bar BC, the park as we know it today would probably not exist. Alongside Horace Albright, Burt was at the forefront of the park expansion movement. And beyond the part it played in park politics and history, the Bar BC Dude Ranch had literary significance. Two books focused on the place and the fascinating life there, a treasure trove of stories and observations about how

THE BAR BC RANCH

a classy dude ranch operated in the American West.[34] Katharine and Struthers Burt were both writers of national reputation. Still, the evolution of the ranch from its heyday between 1912 and 1929 to the run-down reality of the 1960s and 1970s was startling. It made administrators focus on getting rid of the place.

Negotiations between Margaretta and the NPS were never simple. She was like a badger in a barrel, angry and unpredictable. The NPS may have missed an opportunity in 1962, when she wrote to Wyoming Senator Gale McGee and Superintendent Harthon Bill, asking if her descendents might run the Bar BC as a dude ranch after her death. She admitted that it was in poor condition but claimed "my son and I are contemplating putting a good deal of money into it to put it back in first class condition as a dude ranch."[35] Given her personality and hostile relationship with the park, Superintendent Bill might have rejected this idea out of hand. But he did not, because aspects of the proposal were enticing. Park officials were committed to dude ranches and the Bar BC was of historical importance. In the end, Director George Hartzog told her that there was a possibility that the ranch could continue, but the NPS could not make such a decision until after her death.[36] So, Margaretta continued to let the structures deteriorate, spending only for the most basic repairs.

The history of the Bar BC and the state of the structures might have been quite different had the NPS pursued Margaretta's proposal. One of the problems of life-lease arrangements is precisely that lessees do not maintain the property, even though they are expected to do so. Why should they? When they pass on, the property reverts to the federal government. The lessee has no incentive to maintain it, so infrastructure work is not accomplished, and the NPS inherits not only a property but a problem. That was certainly the case when the NPS finally gained complete control of the Bar BC. Had Superintendent Bill and Director Hartzog worked out a new lease agreement, other issues might nevertheless have arisen to doom the dude ranch. Yet with proper conditions, the Bar BC might have been spared its total downfall.

In 1986, Margaretta resided in a Philadephia nursing home. Hoping to squeeze the last ounce of profit from the old place before her death in 1988, Margaretta surrendered her life lease and then authorized the Frome Auction Service of Afton, Wyoming, to dispose of the remaining Bar BC property, mainly furniture and memorabilia. Local preservationists, however, alerted by NPS Historian John Daugherty, were aware that something was amiss when Frome advertised that they would auction off not only the cabins' contents, but also the Bar BC guest cabins, main house, dining hall, and recreation hall.[37] Didn't these buildings belong to the National Park Service as a result of Rockefeller's (Jackson Hole Preserve) gift in 1949, and not to Margaretta Corse? A check with the Teton County Assessor's office revealed that county property taxes had not been collected on the buildings since 1948— indisputable evidence that the buildings belonged to the federal government.[38]

When confronted with these facts, park administrators retreated. Faced with local and state newspaper publicity and concern from the National Trust for Historic Preservation, the Advisory Council for Historic Preservation, as well as NP Regional Park Historian Rodd Wheaton's office, Grand Teton Assistant Superintendent Bill Schenk admitted that "ownership was still unclear . . . and they [the cabins] would not be offered for sale Saturday."[39]

Schenk simplified a rather baffling park correspondence between the regional office and Superintendent Stark's office focusing on whether the park could allow the auction company to sell the cabins. The regional office said no, while Stark and his staff said yes. But Stark had no answer to the query posed by Thomas Merceau, the Wyoming deputy state historic preservation officer: "We seek clarification on how a private individual [Margaretta] is in a position to sell public property." There was no acceptable answer to Merceau's question. The administrators at Grand Teton National Park had attempted to rid the park of the cabins without going through the normal steps of evaluation under the 1966 Historic Preservation Act (Sections 106 and 110). Local vigilance, the media, the Wyoming SHPO, and the help of national organizations all combined to expose these plans, thus thwarting an illegal action.

Although neither Superintendent Stark's 1983 desire to bulldoze the Bar BC nor a plan to sell off the cabins succeeded, the status of the dude ranch remained in question. In 1990, Park Historian John Daugherty successfully listed the Bar BC in the National Register. Regional Historian Rodd Wheaton

NPS Cultural Resource Specialist Mike Johnson restored cabins with little resources by many volunteers.

found over $200,000 to hire a firm to complete a historic structures report on the Bar BC. He contracted in 1991 with Roy Eugene Graham and Associates for the extensive report that went through several versions. One draft suggested that the 160-acre property be enclosed by a cyclone fence. Another recommended the dilapidated cabins be restored at a price tag estimated at near $1 million. Preposterous in cost and impractical in its recommendations, the thick report merely gave Grand Teton administrators and Jack Neckels, the new superintendent, license to do nothing.

HARRISON GOODALL (CENTER) LEADS A GROUP OF VOLUNTEERS STABILIZING A MORMAN ROW CABIN.

Later Mike Johnson, park historical architect and cultural resources head, stated that had all that money been spent in stabilizing the buildings and interpreting the site, it would have been money well spent. As it was, Superintendent Neckels cared no more than Jack Stark about the Bar BC and was annoyed that the Rocky Mountain Regional Office had funded the study without consultation with him, his staff, or his predecessor.[40]

ENTER THE VOLUNTEERS

Meanwhile, the Bar BC ranch structures continued to deteriorate until at last, in 1994, Mike Johnson, who had formerly worked for the Wyoming State Historic Preservation Office, came to work for the park. He would maneuver the fate of Bar BC in a different direction. Johnson realized that although there was little administrative money, there was plenty of latent local feeling for the disintegrating site. He called for a "Clean-Up Day at the Bar BC." By the end of that day, park staff and local volunteers had participated in the removal of four or five dump trucks of trash.

The place was looking much better, and all those who took part enjoyed the day and bonded more strongly with the Bar BC.[41] Johnson also found money for a contractor to install temporary metal roofs on some of the most vulnerable cabins before the winter of 1994–5. He also arranged for an inmate crew from the Wyoming Honor Farm to install support poles under failing purlins, nail plywood panels over open windows, and lock the doors.[42] Such activities represented a new, more realistic approach that might be called "limited preservation." Mindful that the recommendations for Bar BC restoration suggested by the Roy Eugene Graham Associates "Historic Structures Report" could never be accomplished, Johnson embarked on stabilization of the early (pre-1930) structures, using volunteer labor and drew up a plan for visitor use. In other words, he suggested a pragmatic solution for preservation and use. Johnson understood there was a local reservoir of goodwill toward the Bar BC as well as the buildings on Mormon Row and the Geraldine Lucas homestead. When he called for help, the public responded. The "Michigan Volunteers," lead by Ed Brown's school teachers, the newly-created Teton County Historic Preservation Board (another initiative Johnson recommended), the Wyoming SHPO office guided by Sheila Bricher-Wade, all rolled up their sleeves and went to work, often lead by Johnson and/or log restoration expert Harrison Goodall. They got the work done, but, just as important, they proved that the NPS often puffed-up costs for stabilization and restoration for historic structures could be reduced dramatically by creative use of volunteer labor. The expense of stabilization was not eliminated, but it was no longer such a handy excuse for deferring cultural resource projects.

Beyond stabilization, another issue at the Bar BC was access for visitors. Few tourists would brave the five-mile gravel road to the ranch, with the last mile occasionally passable only with a four-wheel-drive vehicle. Johnson proposed a horseback/hiking trail to commence at Moose (possibly the 4 Lazy F Ranch), follow the river for about three miles, and end at the Bar BC. The historic site would feature some stabilized buildings, but mainly signage for interpretation. The trail would then wind up the bench and return the riders to Moose. Besides providing a spectacular horseback ride, the trail would inform visitors of the cultural meaning of the ranch, with its emphasis on wilderness, horses, political activism, and the vibrant social life the place had once hosted.

Each year Johnson submitted his cultural resources budget reflecting his plan for stabilization and interpretation, and each year other projects co-opted his request. In spite of volunteer labor, Superintendent Neckels pleaded poverty, but he also believed that natural resource funding was his primary task. He assumed that sites such as the Bar BC were of local significance only. Furthermore, Neckels once suggested that history could be interpreted for the public without the structures! No one convinced him otherwise.

But local preservationists soon realized what even one committed cultural resources person could do. Johnson succeeded in preserving buildings on a shoestring. Without support from his superintendent or Chief of Interpretation Bill Swift, Johnson scavenged building materials from here and there and found free labor from volunteers who arrived each summer to help out with various stabilization projects. And Johnson was out there himself with the volunteers, hammering nails and lifting beams. In 1997, they enclosed many windows and repaired doors and reroofed a few cabins. It began to look as if the Bar BC might survive.

Beyond offering free labor, some preservation supporters offered financial help. In 1999, an anonymous donor offered $10,000 for stabilization of the Bar BC cabins. Johnson asked if I would head a fundraising committee to match the donation. I was pleased to take on the task, but to raise resources we needed the superintendent's commitment not only to stabilize the Bar BC but to interpret the site. The superintendent would make no pledge. I met with the donor, and we agreed that without a park commitment, it would be impossible to raise matching funds. We abandoned the idea. Such gifts were generally unwelcome. Often the offer comes with strings attached which may be objectionable to the park administration.

Johnson was more successful with another idea— an important one. He needed a cultural resources ally outside the park. The Wyoming SHPO office was encouraging counties and cities to form what they called Certified Local Governments. He urged inter-ested residents to approach the Teton County commissioners to establish a CLG, and so Jackson Hole residents Carole Hofley and Sherry L. Smith took up the challenge. They convinced the commissioners to establish a new board to encourage preservation of cultural resources in the park, contract historical surveys, and encourage and fund local programs and National Register nominations. Today the Teton County Historic Preservation Board has raised the profile of history within the county as well as in the park. Often the board meets with the superintendent and cultural resources staff. Underscoring new cooperation and indicating how much has changed, by 2011 two NPS cultural resource employees held seats on the board.

Johnson left a memorable legacy with his projects and the establishment of the county board, but in time his job wore him down. In 1997, he remarked that the "Park Service moves at a glacial pace. It's very frustrating."[43] He often remarked how exasperating it was to be passionate about a cause, but not to have the backing of your superiors. Neckels was less hostile than Stark, but at best merely tolerated rather than encouraged cultural resources projects. When in 2000 the NPS offered Johnson a position at the San Antonio Missions National Historical Park, he took it, knowing his talents would be better appreciated away from Grand Teton.

A Change in Direction

As Johnson departed for Texas, Superintendent Neckels was contemplating retirement, and he soon left too. After a brief tenure by an interim superintendent, Steve P. Martin came to Grand Teton in 2002. He had already served as superintendent of Denali National Park and Gates of the Arctic National Park. Energetic and perceptive, Martin soon became aware that within Grand Teton previous leaders had tipped the scales in favor of natural resources, to the detriment of cultural resources. He called for evenhanded management of both. With Martin came Pam Holtman, a young and enthusiastic cultural resources specialist and historian. She was still a student at the University of Colorado at Denver but soon received a master's degree and permanent status within the park. With Martin's support she continued Johnson's efforts, organizing volunteer work parties and encouraging visits by both the Michigan and Wisconsin volunteers. Martin, meanwhile turned his attention to the White Grass restoration project, without neglecting the Bar BC. With Holtman's leadership and Martin's support, the policy toward the Bar BC became one of stabilization and preservation, with interpretation through wayside signs and exhibits.[44]

STEVE P. MARTIN

I visited the Bar BC in the summer of 2012. What I found was encouraging. Several interpretive signs now describe the importance of the ranch in conservation circles and explain the dude ranch experience. I was heartened, for these simple signs, at last, indicated commitment to a site that for decades seemed only a week away from the wrecking ball. Walking into the ranch, I found preservation expert Harrison Goodall and a group of Teacher Restoration Corps volunteers stabilizing the old ranch store. Goodall is an ex-professor who is simply passionate about restoring old buildings. He is a miracle worker who loves to work on log cabins in Grand Teton, arriving with his wife, Lee, and their trailer each summer. He had already transformed many of the Murie Ranch cabins from "uninhabitable" to "comfortable." Now he was at the Bar BC, putting Humpty Dumpty cabins together again, ensuring that they could withstand anything a Wyoming winter might throw at them. Farther down the two-track road, I came to a group of University of Pennsylvania students working under the directorship of Professor Frank Matero. They were looking at what remains of the dining room and reading room, where guests assembled to socialize and dance. The roof was gone, and the walls were falling down. I saw no possibility even of stabilization. But Matero posed a provocative question: "Can you really interpret a dude ranch without having the central gathering place structure?" I thought about it, and my answer was no. He and his students have completed their assessment and continue their involvement.

In the meantime, the new cultural resources specialist, Katherine Wonson, a Columbia University M.A. in historic preservation, is building upon the information developed by Matero and others. She has recently completed a Conservation and Management Plan for the Bar BC Dude Ranch that, as she enthusiastically expresses it, features "a triage approach." The park will stabilize and interpret the pre-1930s cabins, but the post-1930s cabins will be left in their current condition. The plan has met with the approval of Superintendent Mary Gibson Scott and will soon move ahead.[45] Through all the studies and controversies one point is now clear. The Bar BC will survive in a form that allows visitors to understand the importance of dude ranching and, more significantly, the role of Struthers Burt and his friends in creating the park we know today.[46] Preserving the Bar BC structures has been a long, slow struggle. But the effort proves worthwhile indeed when the occasional tourist stumbles upon the place and discovers its story, when river guides point it out to clients as they float by, or when a new generation of historic preservation students travel from Philadelphia to see the place where other Philadelphians came to enjoy the Tetons a century ago.

This emphasis on the Bar BC saga is illustrative of the larger theme of contestation over the park resources. Changing constituencies and changing park policies influence priorities within the park's cultural resources inventory. Superintendents can wield enormous power, but they cannot ignore the directives of their own agencies, particularly whenever the public and the press pay attention. Moreover, committed park employees can make a huge difference. It is not easy to challenge one's boss, but sometimes it is the right thing to do and may ultimately lead to right results. That certainly has been the case with the Bar BC. Two other historic sites, specifically the Lucas-Fabian Homestead and the White Grass Ranch, demonstrate the value of local influence and partnering to save historic structures and maintain critical pieces of Jackson Hole history.

Photo by Carole Holley

A GROUP OF LOCAL VOLUNTEERS TAKE A BREAK WHILE CLEANING AND RESTORING THE LUCAS/FABIAN CABINS IN 1996. A NUMBER OF VOLUNTEER GROUPS HAVE BEEN INVOLVED WITH THE NPS TO ASSURE THAT THE OLD HOMESTEAD SURVIVES.

Lucas-Fabian Homestead

Permanent Park Service personnel are not necessarily permanent in one location. During a career, an employee may move to different NPS units at least a half dozen times, usually moving up the ladder one rung at a time while competing for their next position and assignment. Obviously from an administrative view, this promotion structure has advantages and disadvantages. New administrators have fresh ideas. On the other hand, those familiar with the cultural resources of the park may feel frustration with the need to re-educate new employees, when well-informed ones move on to another park. Often, a new superintendent will delay a decision by calling for a new study. It is not within the parameters of this work to pass judgment on continual studies, except to say that while studies continue, the resource deteriorates. Sometimes when the report finally points to action, natural processes of deterioration have already determined the outcome.

This seemed the likely destiny of the Lucas-Fabian Homestead. Geraldine Lucas built the cabins, hugging Cottonwood Creek and in the shadow of the

Grand Teton. This spunky and independent settler arrived in Jackson Hole in 1911 and took up a homestead along the creek, about two miles south of Jenny Lake, where she lived until her death in 1938. An eccentric woman, she was best known for her ascent of the Grand Teton in 1924, the second woman and the first local woman to complete the strenuous climb. Many stories about her oddities circulated in Jackson Hole, and Katharine Burt wrote a nasty novel about her.[47] By adroit and determined use of the land laws, Geraldine Lucas acquired 580 acres of prime scenic land. She put up a few structures, installed minimal irrigation for the homestead, and lived a quiet life. The place was known to only a smattering of people. When it was acquired by the Snake River Land Company, there was every reason to expect that her cabins would be burned or removed. After all, the general policy was to clear the west side of the Snake River of all but essential structures. The Square G Dude Ranch buildings were soon removed, as were those of the Half Moon Ranch, the latter bordering the creek and near to the Lucas-Fabian Homestead.[48] The same fate awaited the Lucas homestead but for the intervention of Harold and Josephine Fabian. Harold, as the chief attorney for the Snake River Land Company, grew to love Jackson Hole and also grew tired of the long commute from his office in Salt Lake City, Utah. Why not renovate Geraldine's place as a summer home? In short order Harold and Josephine moved into a sturdy, nicely appointed log home Geraldine had built for her son, Russell. He never lived in the cabin, but the Fabians found it perfect for their later years in Jackson Hole. It was built with straight and true lodge-pole pine logs harvested from nearby Timbered Island. In Park Service circles the old homestead was now called the Fabian vacation home.

Over the years, the Fabians' modest residence became known for hospitality and convivial dinner parties. Harold died in the early 1970s. Josephine continued to spend summers at Cottonwood Creek until her health failed, forcing her to live in Salt Lake City. For a few years Russell's cabin housed summer park employees, but when the automobile bridge across Cottonwood Creek became unsafe, Superintendent Stark marked the place for demolition. Homesteader Lucas had been forgotten and the prevailing official preference was for land free of the evidence of human settlement.

But local residents of Jackson Hole had a different view. Some believed the old homestead, with its matchless view of the mountains and its setting on Cottonwood Creek, should not suffer the fate of so many other historic structures in Grand Teton. Historian Sherry Smith took on the task of researching Geraldine Lucas's life in detail, framing the woman and the site with historical context and significance.[49] A National Register nomination followed, and the site was listed in 1998. Park Service people began to call the site the Lucas-Fabian Homestead. But what to do with the place? Lorna Miller, of the Teton County Historic Preservation Board, advocated for an artist-in-residence retreat, where two or three painters at a

MAIN CABIN FROM GALEY HOUSE 1950S

time might spend a few weeks in the summer. She organized a Lucas-Fabian Board of Directors to explore the idea and lobby the National Park Service. Other advocates thought it would be a perfect place for a mountain climbing museum, since many of the early climbers crossed Lucas' land for Teton ascents. Others favored a winter warming hut for cross-country skiers on the popular trail to Jenny Lake.

Another source of support came from Salt Lake City. The law firm Fabian and Clendenin had grown in size and stature, and to introduce new employees into the history and culture of the firm, a yearly outing to the homestead became a tradition in the 1990s. Young lawyers, their spouses, and children would spend the weekend helping with projects planned by park historians, Mike Johnson or Pam Holtman, often directed by log maintenance expert Al Williams or Harrison Goodall. In the summer months the Wisconsin or Michigan volunteers worked to stabilize structures. Finally, the Teton County Historic Preservation Board and the SHPO held clean-up days in which volunteers removed truckloads of old bed springs, broken furniture, tools, and junk from the garage, making it all presentable. Much of this activity received publicity through articles in the local newspapers: the *Jackson Hole News* and *Jackson Hole Guide*. The site has been saved, in other words, largely through the efforts of volunteer labor, supported by the Grand Teton cultural resources staff.

This volunteer support accomplished two goals. First, it demonstrated to Superintendents Stark and Neckels that significant numbers of people did not agree with park policy of eliminating all evidence of human occupation. They wanted some historic structures to remain and be showcased with interpretive displays. Second, the success of park cultural resources staff and the CLG in marshaling free volunteer labor put to lie the official huge cost projections. As suggested earlier, over the years there has been no argument against preservation more persuasive than the expense of stabilization, maintenance, and interpretation. No one would suggest that it is inexpensive to maintain the historical resources of the park, but the interest of the public—often evidenced in a day's work at a site—made a compelling case for action, restoration, and interpretation.

Today Geraldine Lucas's homestead site contains two interpretive signs explaining its historical significance. The place has been cleaned up and the cabins have been stabilized. Although the park does not draw attention to the site, skiers in winter and hikers in summer continue to enjoy the place and stop for lunch or just a pause on the porch. Although the significance of the site is no longer in question, its use still is. No clear adaptive use has emerged, although the forthcoming Historic Properties Management Plan calls for use as an interpretive site.[50] The infrastructure necessary for habitation is missing and would be costly. For preservationists, it is sufficient that this National Register site be stabilized. Yet, although the Lucas-Fabian place is now secure, the scenic homestead requires maintenance. It should find a use. Perhaps a stop along the nearby bike path could be an option for those in need of a rest or a taste of history.[51]

THE WHITE GRASS RANCH

The White Grass Ranch is a wonderful story not only about the past, but also about the future. The scenic

A WHITE GRASS CABIN IS STABILILIZED ON THE WAY TO BEING FULLY RESTORED.

spot was the third oldest dude ranch in Jackson Hole, first started by Harold Hammond and Tucker Bispham in 1917. It began taking in visitors two years later and continued to do so until the mid-1980s. Frank Galey, Jr., Hammond's stepson, and Galey's wife, Nona, ran the place for many years. In 1957, the National Park Service bought 301 acres of the ranch and gave Galey a life estate. As Galey aged, the White Grass fell into disrepair. After his death in 1985, Nona sold the horses, saddles, and furniture at auction, but she stayed on. When she asked Superintendent Stark what would happen to the place, he replied that although he would have to examine the buildings, ultimately his desire was "that the entire area revert to the natural part of the park, which would mean the buildings would be removed or allowed to fall down on their present site."[52] The cabins—property of the park—remained, but true to Stark's prediction, they continued to deteriorate. An electrical fire destroyed the Galeys' home and the park sold one of the most significant buildings—the barn—to park naturalist, Jon Gerster, for one dollar. [53] In 1989, the park completed Section 106 compliance for removal of 14 cabins, determining that the remaining 13 cabins were eligible for the National Register.

Over the course of the 1990s, the remaining 13 cabins deteriorated to the point where restoration seemed hopeless. Like the Bar BC cabins, they had been of questionable construction quality to begin with and some had add-on bathrooms and storage sheds that compromised their architectural integrity.

Yet the White Grass Ranch had a dedicated "alumni," individuals and families who had stayed in the summers, year after year. They were a loyal group, who organized reunions to celebrate the old place. They represented a constituency for preservation. But they were not hopeful. Supported by the views of Superintendent Jack Neckels, the Jackson Hole Conservation Alliance maintained that the area was important to wildlife, especially elk. Beyond that, Neckels claimed he simply did not have the funds to repair and maintain the cabins, or what might be best described as shacks. Later he admitted that the official intention was to remove the ranch buildings.[54]

Removing cabins eligible for the National Register of Historic Places, probably by burning, was not a popular option, of course—so the buildings continued to deteriorate. However, Al Williams, a Park Service carpenter responsible for maintenance of the park's log cabins, took on the task of unofficial or "rogue" preservationist. On his own time, he kept the roofs from falling in, even though his superiors wanted just the opposite. In spite of Williams' effort, the White Grass structures seemed doomed until the arrival of a more sympathetic boss.

In 2002, Superintendent Stephen Martin took over the reins of the park and began a change in direction. Martin regarded every park as having both natural and cultural resources that must be protected. At the regional level, Director Karen Wade of the NPS Intermountain Region agreed with him. The long-suffering Wyoming State Historic Preservation Office,

THE WHITE GRASS RANCH, READY FOR RESTORATION

so often at odds with Superintendents Stark and Neckels, eagerly awaited any positive action that Martin would make. It did not take long.

In 2003 Richard Moe, executive director of the National Trust for Historic Preservation, arrived in Jackson Hole for a tour of the park's historic structures. He had been forewarned of the neglect of cultural resources by Barbara Pahl, director of the National Trust's Mountain/Plains Regional Office in Denver. Thus on a beautiful August day, Martin and Moe spent time together visiting historic sites in the park, including among them Mormon Row, the

Lucas-Fabian Homestead, the Murie Ranch, the Bar BC, and the White Grass Ranch. Karen Wade, Barbara Pahl, and the new park historian, Pam Holtman, joined them.[55] At the Bar BC Dude Ranch, the group began to discuss the future. They agreed that the Bar BC should be stabilized as a site representative of the park's dude ranch era.

The last site they visited was the White Grass Ranch. It seemed beyond repair, let alone restoration. It featured cracked windows, rotting window frames, decomposing logs, sagging purlins, and serious foundation problems. It looked hopeless. But Karen Wade had an idea. She suggested that the cabins be restored for use as a preservation training center for the NPS and other agencies to help remedy the deferred maintenance of the nation's log buildings. Thousands of historic cabins were deteriorating throughout the West, not only on national park lands but also on U.S. Forest Service, Bureau of Land Management, and state and private lands as well. The center could identify such structures throughout the West and then help restore them. As Pahl later put it, the goal of the center would be "to preserve, through adaptive use, the historic buildings at White Grass but also to create a work force of trainees who can tackle other buildings in the park in need of stabilization, maintenance, and preservation."[56]

In short order Grand Teton National Park and the National Trust signed an agreement to restore the White Grass Ranch. Funding would be on a 60-40 basis, with Grand Teton providing the 60 percent. The National Trust pledged to raise $950,000 for the project, while the park moved quickly to establish the Western Center for Historic Preservation, bringing in preservation specialist, Craig Struble, from Yosemite National Park as director and the experienced Al Williams as construction chief. Struble, Williams, and others took on a big job, since entirely new plumbing and electrical infrastructure had to be installed before workers could renovate cabins.[57] By 2012 a series of cabins had been restored or rebuilt. In August 2012, the National Trust and the park hosted a festive lunch for all who had contributed to this remarkable project, one that will aid historic preservation throughout the West. This major project's expected date of completion is 2016, the hundredth anniversary of the National Park Service.[58]

There are many projects in Grand Teton awaiting the expertise of the Western Center for Historic Preservation (WCHP) Already the center has led preservation efforts at Mormon Row, the Bar BC, the Lucas/Fabian Homestead, the 4 Lazy F Ranch, and has even assisted in launching the historic Menor's Ferry, the only living history display in the park. A skilled team from the center heads these projects, but it also relies on volunteers who come from as far as Massachusetts, Tennessee, Wisconsin, and Florida. It is effortless to entice volunteers living in the hot and humid Midwest, East, and South to spend a few weeks in Grand Teton National Park and work on historic preservation projects. But while volunteers come to the park, the center team is also reaching out. With a skilled staff, and a state-of-the-art woodworking shop, the Center has contracted with Bryce Canyon National Park and Capitol Reef National Park to help in their restoration efforts. Also, in Santa Fe, the WCHP team undertook the task of preservation of the "Old Santa Fe Trail Building."[59] The work of restoring the White Grass Ranch has yet to be fully completed, but already the Center's work is gaining a regional reputation.

MANY DECISIONS REMAIN to be made with the park's 2014 Historic Properties Management Plan. In the inevitable debates that will arise over its implementation different interest groups (both in and outside of Grand Teton) may be pleased or disappointed. But no one can dispute that the park has come far since the turn of the 21st century in preserving some of Jackson Hole's most important historic sites. Yet, we should not forget NPS past Chief Historian Robert Utley's recollections of earlier transgressions. At the conclusion of a very long 1985 interview with Richard Sellers and Melody Webb, Utley's interview included "Appendix A, Examples of NPS Deficiencies." This document listed 40 parks and monuments, often with very minor cultural resource infractions. When it came to Grand Teton, however, the evaluation was harsh:

> Systematic destruction, without professional evaluation and over professional protest, of dozens of historic structures associated with ranching, homesteads, and early tourist periods. Menors Ferry and Cunningham Cabin survived only because of expressed interest of Rockefeller.[60]

OF ALL THE CRITICISM OF GRAND TETON POLICIES from 1950 to 2000, the neglect of cultural resources and the lack of cooperation with the preservation laws may be the park's greatest failing.

It is evident, however, that attitudes toward cultural resources and historic preservation have changed enormously. From an era when the park policy was to remove old structures, whether significant or otherwise, we have moved into the age of evaluating, sometimes restoring, and even using historic cabins and sites. The park has come, in short, a long way since the days when an administrator could approve the destruction of a National Register site, such as Leek's Lodge, for a fire-fighting exercise.

Yet successes such as the Bar BC, the Lucas-Fabian Homestead, and the White Grass Ranch should not obscure the hard reality that many other structures remain, and their future continues to be problematic. The root of the problem remains money. Park budgets are perennially stretched, and valuable historic sites remain in limbo, awaiting leaders' decisions on their fate. Historic preservation and cultural resources now have representation and agency within the park, but that does not make the decisions regarding these resources any easier to resolve. Furthermore, planning efforts have been frustrated by a Congress willing to shut down the national parks, and generally force Grand Teton to continually adjust to budget crises.

We will have answers for some of these properties with the completion of the Historic Properties Management Plan (2014). In the debates over its implementation, the public will be engaged through written comments and hearings. At present the HPMP preferred alternative is to continue preservation treatment on 29 historic properties and continue work on the White Grass Ranch until it is fully operational as the Western Center for Historic Preservation. The latter has been an expensive job, but fortunately the National Trust continues to partner with the Park Service. Other historic structures such as the old Snake River Land Company building or Buffalo Dorm, Beaver Creek #10, and the Four

Lazy F Ranch may receive infrastructure improvement to the point they can be "adaptively reused." Improvements at the Bar BC Ranch and the Lucas/Fabian Homestead may allow them to be opened and appreciated by visitors interested in the history of the park. The commitment of Grand Teton to these two sites has been in question for many years, thus this is good news, indeed. Finally, under the "preferred alternative" the park intends to use or continue to use the Upper Granite Patrol Cabin, the Manges Cabin, and the Hunter Hereford Ranch for park operations.

The HPMP recommends, however, that the Paul McCollister complex, the Sky Ranch, and the Wolff Ranch all be removed by sale or demolition.[61] Their fate will be questioned by some as the management plan undergoes public comment.

Whatever the outcome, all can be grateful that an open, spirited, free debate and discussion will characterize the process.

[1] Katherine Wonson, Cultural Resourses Specialist, GTNP, comments on January 16, 2013.

[2] See "Historic Properties in Grand Teton National Park," 2012 list, and "Main Historic Properties, updated October, 2011," both available in the Cultural Resources Office, Grand Teton National Park.

[3] I have been involved in some of the issues this chapter describes. At times I was a participant and a partisan. I hope that the issues have been presented fairly, although I am sure some will disagree with my view.

[4] National Park Service, *Management Policies, 2006* (Washington, D. C.: Government Printing Office, 2006), 60.

[5] Historian Merrill Mattes led the research into fur trade history and its association with the park. The display in the old Moose visitor center represented much of his work. It was eventually donated to the Jackson Hole Historical Society and Museum. Mattes was a dedicated NPS historian, but one who felt that in his era historians had little status and were often denied promotion or advantageous transfers. Mattes' treatment demonstrates the relatively low esteem given to both history and historians in many parks not specifically deemed as historic sites.

[6] Grand Teton National Park archives (hereafter cited as GTNP), Grazing Records, box 1, series 003.1, folder 006. On Mission 66 see *http://www.mission66.com/mission.html*.

[7] The park has no list of the original structures that the Jackson Hole Preserve or the National Park Service removed or destroyed, but from conversations with Johnson I believe this is a reasonable estimate.

[8] Robert W. Righter, *Crucible for Conservation: The Struggle for Grand Teton National Park* (Boulder: Colorado University Press, 1982; reprint, 2000), 33–34.

[9] The term "windshield wilderness" comes from David Louter's *Windshield Wilderness: Cars, Roads, and Nature in Washington's National Parks* (Seattle: University of Washington Press, 2006). Louter is a National Park Service historian working out of Seattle. His concept fits the interpretive objectives of many western parks.

[10] "A Plan for Teton Incorporating the Land Extension," submitted by Sanford Hill, Resident Landscape Architect, July 1939, GTNP, Land Records, box 4, Series 002.2, folder 002GTNP.

[11] Ibid.

[12] Ibid. Hill did not specify the other two ranches; Kimmel's place at the Geraldine Lucas homestead or the White Grass Ranch were possibilities. The Bar BC is not mentioned, because it is far off the main wagon road, while the Rockefeller-owned JY Ranch would probably not be available. Just which ranch facilities would be chosen is a matter of speculation.

[13] Hill, "A Plan for Teton," 3.

[14] Alfred Runte, *National Parks: The American Experience* (Lincoln: University of Nebraska Press, 1979), 163.

15 Charles J. Smith, Superintendent, "A Preliminary Plan for Grand Teton National Park and the Jackson Hole Country," July 28, 1941, RG 79, box 1054, National Archives. Found in Sara Elizabeth Scott [Adamson], "Balancing History and Nature in the National Parks: The Management of the Bar BC Ranch in Grand Teton National Park," M.A. Thesis, Interdisciplinary Studies Program, 2005, 56.

16 A. E. Kendrew, "Report on OWNED Structures of a Historic Character, Jackson Hole, Wyoming," July and August, 1942. The manuscript contains reports on other structures owned by the Snake River Land Company. Copy in possession of the author.

17 For Drury's memo see Scott, "Balancing History and Nature," 53.

18 Ibid., 56–58

19 "An Interview with Robert Utley on the History of Historic Preservation in the National Park Service, 1947–1980" by Richard Sellers and Melody Webb, September 24, 1985, December 27, 1985, Reel 2. See www.nps.gov/history/history/on_line books/utley/utley.htm

20 Ibid., Reel #8.

21 Phone interview with Dr. Richard Sellers by author, February 18, 2013.

22 Phone interview with Dr. David Kathka by author, February 18, 2013.

23 Ibid., 59.

24 National Park Service, Grand Teton National Park Master Plan, Department of the Interior, 1976; Robert W. Righter, "Historic American Building Survey for Grand Teton National Park," GTNP, Cultural Resources, HABS Study file. Schene could find funding for the study only as a HABS report, but insisted that it would be in name only, and I could tie buildings to themes and offer recommendations. Unfortunately, those opposing emphasis on cultural resources rejected the study on the grounds that it was not a HABS study.

25 Dwight F. Rettie, Our National Park System (Urbana: University of Illinois Press, 1995), 137. For a recent critique of the National Park Service as an agency, see Paul D. Berkowitz, The Case of the Indians Trader: Billy Malone and the National Park Service Investigation at Hubbell Trading Post (Albuquerque: University of New Mexico Press, 2011), particularly pp. 58-82.

26 Stephen Leek's photographic essays of starving elk (Outdoor Life, May 1911) contributed to the establishment of the National Elk Refuge.

27 I was a member of the Wyoming National Register Review Board at the time.

28 Report in "Correspondence between SHPO and GTNP, 1990s, 2004 2005" (folder), GTNP, Cultural Resources. Stark's outburst was not recorded in this report but comes from my vivid remembrance.

29 See Maxwell Struthers Burt, The Diary of a Dude-Wrangler (1924; New York: Charles Scribner's Sons, 1938), 140. Burt's entertaining book contains a number of stories of the first days at the Bar BC and the numerous problems of construction in isolated country.

30 Scott, "Balancing History and Nature," 42–43.

31 Burt also sold the Three Rivers Ranch to the Snake River Land Company with a fifty-year lease. When Burt's son Nathaniel attempted to renew the lease in 1980, the NPS turned him down. Nathaniel sold the buildings and today there is no evidence of the retreat.

32 For details see John Daugherty, A Place Called Jackson Hole (Moose, Wyo.: Grand Teton Association, 1999), 235–36. For a day by day account of the management of the Bar BC between 1922 and 1942 see Renee Howard Smelker, The Bar BC Chronicle (Sioux Falls, South Dakota: Pine Hill Press, 2009).

33 See Scott, "Balancing History and Nature," 114.

34 Besides Struthers Burt's book, his son Nathaniel—born on the Bar BC kitchen table in 1913—wrote Jackson Hole Journal (Norman: University of Oklahoma Press, 1983), largely the story of his boyhood in Jackson Hole and on the Bar BC.

35 Margaretta Corse to Harthon L. Bill, Superintendent, and Margaretta Corse to Senator Gale McGee, June 12, 1962, in Scott, "Balancing History and Nature," 112–13.

36 George B. Hartzog Jr. to Mrs. Irving R. Corse, June 1966, in Scott, "Balancing History and Nature," 113.

37 *Jackson Hole News*, July 30, 1986, 1.

38 Once in a while historians get to play detective. My wife, Sherry Smith and I visited the Teton County assessor's office, discovered the damning evidence, and shared that important information with Angus Thuermer of the *Jackson Hole News*. Soon the *Casper Star-Tribune* got wind of the story and published it, as well.

39 *Casper Star-Tribune*, August 16, 1986, B1.

40 Mike Johnson, Cultural Resources Specialist, interview by author, March 5, 1999; Roy Eugene Graham Associates, "Bar BC Ranch Grand Teton National Park, Wyoming, Historic Structures Report," July 1, 1994, Archives, National Park Service, Denver, Colorado.

41 "Clean-up Day at the Bar BC" (flyer), GTNP, Cultural Resources, Bar BC files. See Scott, "Balancing History and Nature," 140.

42 Ibid., 141.

43 Melanie Harrice, "Park ranks historic sites for restoration and repair," *Jackson Hole News*, October 22, 1997.

44 Ibid., 150–52.

45 Katherine Wonson, GTNP Cultural Resources Specialist, e-mail to author, March 8, 2012.

46 Although the Bar BC is surely saved, it is not readily accessible to the public—an issue yet to be addressed. The ranch is not easily reached by raft or boat, by horse or hiking, or by driving. Public use is a factor in historic preservation, under the axiom: "If you don't use it, you lose it."

47 The novel was Katharine Burt's *Hidden Creek* (1920; repr., New York: Signet Classics, 1979).

48 Happily some of the cabins from the Square G and Half Moon Ranch were not destroyed but rather moved to the Colter Bay Lodge, where many old log cabins have been renovated and are rented out to guests. Cultural resources experts dislike the idea of moving a cabin from its original setting, but this is certainly better than destruction. There are 186 cabins gathered from throughout the park. See Mary McKinney, "The Cabins at Colter Bay" (leaflet).

49 Sherry L. Smith, "A Woman's Life in the Teton Country: Geraldine L. Lucas," *Montana: The Magazine of Western History* 44 (Summer 1994): Also Bonnie Kreps, *Windows to the Past: Early Settlers in Jackson Hole* (Jackson: Teton County Historical Society and Museum, 2006). 122-42.

50 Information from Cultural Resources Specialist, Katherine Wonson.

51 Articles on the clean-up and volunteer efforts at Mormon Row and the Lucas-Fabian place can be found in the *Jackson Hole News*, July 26, 1995, October 11, 1995, July 3, 1996.

52 GTNP, Land Records, box 10, folder 10, Frank and Nona Galey.

53 *www.nps.gov./grte/whitegrass*; Scott, "Balancing History and Nature," 95. Gerster dismantled the barn and stored it in Pinedale. However, Carole and Norm Hofley purchased it, returned it to Jackson, and reconstructed it on their Fish Creek Road property.

54 Jack Neckels, interview, March 6, 2005, in Scott, "Balancing History and Nature," 96.

55 Barbara Pahl, "Changing the Culture at Grand Teton National Park," *Forum Journal*, Summer 2008, 21–29.

56 *Jackson Hole News and Guide*, October 8, 2003: "Time Share," Preservation, (January–February 2004, 21; also see Kate Siber, "Rebuilding the Past," *National Parks*, Fall 2012), 12–14.

57 I can't speak to the electrical system of the cabins, but for plumbing many cabins used a septic system of an old car, its top cut off, and filled with rocks.

58 *www.nps.gov./grte/whitegrass*.

59 *www.wchpgrte.blogspot.com*.

60 "Interview with Robert Utley . . .," September 24, 1985, see Appendix A *www.nps.gov/history/history/onlinebooks/utley/utley.htm*.

61 These recommendations may all be found in the "Historic Properties Management Plan Environmental Assessment – Project completion 2013." Copy available through Cultural Resources Management, GTNP.

Chapter 7.

Airport Paradox and Other Intrusions

JIM STANFORD, A RIVER GUIDE FOR BARKER-EWING, regales his rafting clients with colorful stories of the natural and human history of Grand Teton National Park. Clients love the scenic float trip between Deadmans Bar and Moose, a spectacular 10-mile stretch of river featuring swift, clear water and unmatched scenery. No roads or bridges encroach on the Snake River, and rafters enjoy a near wilderness adventure. Yet they do not enjoy solitude. A Boeing 757 often intrudes from above, and Jim must pause for this interruption of jet noise. In fact, over the course of his float trip his narration must allow for a number of such interruptions.[1] As Jim and his guests enjoy the river's soothing sounds, they must also cope with airplanes, of all things. Commercial aircraft, numerous private jets, and prop planes all share the glide path over the Snake River into Jackson Hole Airport, the busiest airport in Wyoming.

If the wind dictates a northern takeoff, the noise increases with the jet engines' accelerating thrust. This is the only commercial airport in the nation situated within a national park. Today its intrusion on the serenity of the park has been perhaps the most invasive and contentious issue confronting park officials day in and day out.

How could this happen? How could a park dedicated to the natural setting and relief from the stresses of urban life accept a noisy airport in its midst? Who could have anticipated the effects of new technologies or the increased demands the traveling public would place on Jackson Hole? Who would have predicted a booming winter economy; one where flying skiers is much more profitable than herding cows? Add to that, the arrival of the super wealthy, people who live in Jackson Hole, but work elsewhere, and depend on air transportation for both. Per capita income in Teton County is among the highest in the nation. Wealthy people insist on having an airport that can quickly get them wherever they want to go. The pressure was great, and neither the park nor the community had the conviction to say no. There are no simple answers to the growth of the airport. A look at the park's beginnings helps explain how the park/airport anomaly developed.

EARLY DAYS

In a sense, the park and the airplane grew up together. The first pilots to enter Jackson Hole were those romantic, daring men known as barnstormers. They flew Curtiss JN series biplanes dubbed "Jennys." When the Great War ended, a surplus Jenny could often be purchased for a few hundred dollars. Barnstormers bought them and created a new and risky business. They loved to set out for small towns, where they landed in a field or on a gravel road and then advertised plane rides to the locals. They were a pretty crazy bunch, for whom life insurance was no doubt impossible to obtain. From photographs, we know that they landed in Jackson Hole, but who they were and what they did is lost to history. [2]

The airborne pioneers came and went, but a pilot named A. A. Bennett was less transient. His first flight to Jackson Hole came in the dead of winter in the 1920s. Landing on the outskirts of town, near what is now the end of West Kelly Road, he set down in an alfalfa field 700 feet long, located between irrigation ditches. He was on a mercy mission. A woman in Victor had suffered a stroke. Bennett picked up Dr. Charles Huff and nurse Virginia Kaffelin, turned around, and gunned his engine to fly them over Teton Pass. The plane lifted off so smoothly on its 10-foot skis that, 300 feet into the air, Kaffelin reportedly asked, "How soon does the airplane leave the ground?" [3]

Soon other primitive landing strips appeared in the valley. One was at Struthers Burt's Bar BC Dude

THE WORT BROTHERS GREET A DC-3 AT THEIR LANDING STRIP JUST SOUTH OF SIGNAL MOUNTAIN.

Ranch. Harold Turner relates that a couple of United Airlines pilots had a strip constructed near the wagon road above the Triangle X Ranch. South of Moose and just west of the Moose/Wilson Road, aviator Howard Bellew graded a 2,200 dirt airstrip for his Piper Cub with which he informally gave tours around the mountains. He shared the strip with David Lowe, another "bush" pilot who often flew from and to Driggs, Idaho transporting passengers and also occasionally supplying hunting camps. He and his brother, Richard Lowe, were best known as world-class mountain climbers who in the 1960s and 1970s, pioneered routes and made a number of first ascents in the Teton Range.[4]

Constructing a landing strip was quite easy to do. Although Jackson Hole is known for its mountains, much of the land is level and covered with sagebrush. Local ranchers and homesteaders knew how to "chain away" sagebrush. Using such a land-clearing method, they could create a landing strip in a matter of days.

The most captivating airstrip—and potentially the one with the most intrusion to the future park—was scraped clean by John and Jess Wort. In the 1930s, the enterprising brothers planned the landing site just southwest of Signal Mountain to service the Wort Lodge and Fishing Camp on Jackson Lake (today's Signal Mountain Lodge). They intended the strip to be open year round and "capable of accommodating the large planes."[5] Fortunately, the brothers' ambitious plans never materialized. A major airport in that location would have made the present airport problems pale in comparison.[6]

Although nothing came of the Wort brothers' landing strip in the long term, its brief life was recorded on film. One photo features a DC3 plane that paused on the strip, being greeted by the Wort brothers on horseback. From what we know, the plane landed in support of a Wallace Beery film, *Bad Bascomb,* featuring the venerable actor with child star Margaret O'Brien. Filming took place in the RKO area of the Snake River, resulting in an entertaining, but less than classic production.[7]

Harold Clissold was surely aware of the activity at Signal Mountain. However, an airport so far removed from the town where he served as mayor for 30 years was unacceptable. It would have to be closer. As early as 1934, the Jackson mayor asked National Elk Refuge managers to give up 160 acres of pasture land in the southeast corner of the reserve for a landing strip. They refused. He then looked eight miles north to land controlled by the Bureau of Land Management, the state of Wyoming, and the Snake River Land Company. On the sagebrush flats, he found his place for an airport.

We are obviously treading the path of mythology here, but one story is that in 1939, Clissold diverted a team of men who were oiling the town square. Rain delayed the process, so the mayor persuaded the crew to come out to the airport site. Along with a bulldozer and local hands, they all helped rid the runway of sagebrush. Presumably, Clissold had obtained oral permission from Harold Fabian of the Snake River Land Company, but there was no written contract or agreement.[8] Years later Bob LaLonde, longtime local and politician, explained how the enterprising Clissold located the runway. "He used the very scientific method of putting his finger in his mouth, holding it up and checking to see which side cooled." He then allegedly paced off a mile—nearly due north-south, according to his "study"—and that became the runway.[9]

But a dirt runway inhabited by cows, antelope, and sage grouse attracted nothing more than a few small airplanes. Local politicians and business leaders such as Felix Buchenroth, William Simpson, and Clissold attempted to entice a commercial carrier, but the travel limitations of World War II precluded that. When the war ended, however, Harold Fabian, a Salt Lake City native and attorney for the Snake River Land Company, joined the effort. He convinced Western Airlines to schedule DC3 flights from Salt Lake City to the growing town in northwest Wyoming. The airline insisted on a terminal structure on the barren flats, so Clissold and his town friends dragged a glorified shed to the site when the Jackson Hole National Monument superintendent was out of town. On August 14, 1946, the first Western Airlines plane landed. Clissold, George Lamb, other dignitaries, and even the well-known actor of the day, Wallace Beery, who came down from his cabin on Jackson Lake, greeted it. To add gaiety to the occasion, "Johnny Walker's orchestra played and sang cowboy tunes, and a barbeque was served to the passengers and onlookers." Lest Western Airlines executives in Los Angeles felt neglected, local citizens donated a quarter of an elk, some moose and venison steaks, and a quarter of bear, which arrived at the coast in the remarkable time of seven hours. Whether they appreciated the gift went unrecorded, but it no doubt enhanced Jackson Hole's reputation as a wild and wooly frontier town.[10]

While the townspeople of Jackson celebrated their connection to the wider world, what did NPS personnel say or do regarding this intrusion into Jackson Hole National Monument?[11] The answer is nothing. The reasons for inaction are understandable. Title to most of the land in question still resided with the Snake River Land Company, and Harold Fabian, chief among the boosters, believed the airport would be beneficial to the business interests of the valley. Not only did he convince Western Airlines to begin service, he secured grants to improve the runway and the primitive facilities. Grand Teton National Park Superintendent John McLaughlin endorsed the landing strip. He praised the enterprise of the community and noted that an airport would be convenient for park personnel to attend meetings and for business that might otherwise be impossible.[12] He did not see the new runway as a contradiction to the park's purpose and values as stated in the 1916 Organic Act. Why should he? The whole operation seemed so simple and innocent. Here was a dirt runway on the southern edge of the national monument that attracted no more than a few planes each day.

There was, however, an important restraint on Superintendent McLaughlin. The agency's effort to expand the park had been bitterly opposed by local interests and when President Franklin Roosevelt established the national monument in 1943, most locals would have agreed with Wyoming Senator Edward Robinson who stated that it was "a sneak attack surpassed only by that of the Japanese at Pearl Harbor."[13] In this context, to question construction of an airstrip that would serve local business and political interests would have represented rare courage—

or stupidity. Superintendent McLaughlin was almost bound to support the new addition to the monument. In a different time, in a different atmosphere, the airport intrusion in Jackson Hole would quickly have been squelched at the local, regional, or national level. But in 1946, the Park Service had to tread lightly. More important, no one recognized the long-term danger. Against the backdrop of the acrimony created by the expansion of the park, the airport's arrival could actually help Superintendent McLaughlin and others as they tried to close the chasm of local loathing.

Although park officials' options were somewhat limited by bitter local animosity, one might think that the National Parks and Conservation Association would have weighed in as the defender of primitive parks. However, the NPCA had not served Grand Teton well. During the 1930s park fight, the NPCA had opposed park expansion because of the presence of the Jackson Lake dam and too much mundane sagebrush. Both, it seemed to the organization's representatives, compromised the park's wild and scenic value. The NPCA had few friends, even in the Park Service. As historian John Miles put it, the NPCA "unwittingly aided the anti-park movement against Grand Teton National Park expansion in the 1930s by too strictly adhering to standards."[14] When it came to the airport then, the association remained on the sidelines.

On a national level, park personnel did deliberate about airplanes, airports, and their effect on the parks.

For park people, airplanes represented just one of the problems of mechanization that plague the Park Service to this day. The trouble started in Yosemite with the automobile. John Muir, the original arbiter of national park values, sanctioned entry by motorized buggies in 1912. Perhaps he capitulated to the inevitable. Mechanization seems clearly at odds with a place committed to serenity and calm, whether the machine is an automobile, propeller-driven snow plane, modern snowmobile, jet boat, or outboard motor. As we have seen, in 1939 park architect Sanford Hill believed it a wonderful idea to ban "steel cocoons" (cars) west of the Snake River, allowing guests to board only horse-drawn stagecoaches at Moose for a scenic and historic ride into the Jenny Lake area (see chapter 6). The park administration rejected the idea as too impractical and quaint.[15]

The airplane was not quaint. This transportation method, the very antithesis of the old West, soon spawned debate within the Park Service. Some rangers believed airplanes should be utilized in firefighting, communications, and killing predators in Alaska. They also believed that some scenery might best be seen from the air, and it was thus desirable for the general public to be able to experience parklands that way. Helicopters should be used for game counts and mountain rescues. Furthermore, their rival agency, the Forest Service, noted that in 1957, their use of airplanes in fighting fires was up 1,000 percent in five years.[16]

As it evolved, the debate in Washington resulted in a February 1947 policy directive from Director Drury that forbade planes to land in parks except in an emergency. However, in 1950 Congress passed the Department of the Interior Airport Act, authorizing development of airfields "in or in close proximity" to national parks, monuments, and recreational areas. The airport at West Yellowstone was the first built to carry out that policy.[17] Certainly the idea was to enhance tourism, particularly by attracting people with more money than time.

During NPS Director Newton Drury's era (1940–51), the agency generally opposed the use of airplanes in the parks. Of course Grand Teton National Park was exempted from any anti-aviation rule, with grandfather clauses and plenty of local clout in place. The Park Service attempted to keep touring planes from flying below a 2,000-foot AGL (above ground level) in the parks, but again, such rules did not apply in Jackson Hole.[18]

As air traffic continued to increase in the 1960s, it did so with the park's blessing. There was little official concern. When Superintendent Harthon Bill released the park master plan in 1962, the airport did not make the list of problems. It was not even mentioned.[19] Some local environmentalists and park personnel, however, noticed the increasing intrusions on the park experience—particularly the noise. They became more and more vexed. Still, in 1971, when Congress appropriated $2.2 million to improve the airport

mainly through runway extension, the Grand Teton administration officially supported the idea. The grant was to support the safety and efficiency of the landing strip to accommodate the turbo-prop Convair 580. But anyone with an ounce of foresight knew that the Boeing 737 was coming. Soon Frontier Airlines made it official.

THE CRUCIAL DECADE

The idea of a jet port, as boosters called it, represented the last straw for many people of Jackson Hole and the nation. They believed that the proposed jet port was the absolute antithesis of a national park. Park lovers had witnessed the continual encroachment of larger and more numerous planes, encouraged by a new Jackson Hole Airport Board established in 1967 and backed by a growth-oriented business community. For park personnel, so passive in the 1960s, suddenly the airport became the key issue of the 1970s. This apprehension transcended the Jackson Hole airport. Across the country, communities protested the deeply disturbing, dish-rattling jet planes which seemed to signal the end of quiet. Increases in aircraft numbers and associated noise galvanized many of the locals. They were assisted by new environmental laws, particularly the National Environmental Policy Act of 1970 (NEPA), often called the Magna Carta of environmental law.[20] A new acronym, the EIS (Environmental Impact Statement) entered the American lexicon, forcing builders and developers to justify their plans and actions. For the Jackson Hole airport, the airline companies (Frontier and Western) and the public agencies (Departments of the Interior and Transportation) would now have to write a full EIS. This would take time, and bring to the foreground issues of the compatibility of airports and national parks.

Grand Teton National Park officials and personnel of the Federal Aviation Administration (FAA) took the lead in writing the Draft Environmental Impact Statement (DEIS), which became available for public comment in early 1973. It was a perfect opportunity for the National Park Service to say, *Enough! No more incursions on the sanctity and silence of the park*. But the leadership seemed to lack the courage to call a halt to expansion. Instead of supporting a "no action" (meaning no change) alternative, or arguing for removal of the airport, the park supported growth. The Grand Teton National Park's "preferred alternative" recommended expansion of the 6,305-foot paved runway to 8,000 feet (1,400 feet to the south and 300 feet to the

north). The runway would be widened from 100 feet to 150 feet, strengthened to accommodate Boeing 737s, and complemented with an 8,000-foot parallel taxiway. Modern equipment would include an instrument landing system, a runway lighting system, and an air traffic control tower.[21]

The draft EIS presented eight other alternatives, ranging from no action to expanding south or north to a length of 8,300 feet. Finally, the document provided the more interesting option, Alternative H, to "move the airport to an alternative site outside the park." The draft EIS explored six locations: the Snake River Valley (southwest of the airport but not on park land), South Park, Alpine, Palisades, Swan Valley, and Driggs, Idaho. Of these possibilities, the most feasible was Alpine. Within an easy drive from Jackson and within the state of Wyoming, Alpine had appeal. Furthermore, the long glide path over the Palisades Reservoir was acceptable for large jet planes. However, the approach from the south was more problematic. The FAA declared that the Alpine site did not meet its "navigable airspace" requirements.[22]

For similar reasons, the FAA deemed airport sites at Palisades and Swan Valley as also unacceptable. The only alternative site the agency considered acceptable was Idaho's Driggs airport, but this was out of the question for interests representing Jackson Hole and the state of Wyoming. There was no chance that the airport could be moved out of state without a huge political fight. There was one unmentioned final alternative—no airport at all. But that, as well, would be nearly impossible to achieve. Too many stakeholders depended on the airport for it to be eliminated altogether.

The outpouring of opposition to the proposed runway extension was truly remarkable. Letters arrived from throughout the country. Many writers had experienced jet plane noise in their own communities, and they were quick to point out that the rumble of jets was incompatible with a national treasure. Another national debate was absorbing the interest of the country at the time. Kevin Collins, of Pleasant Valley, California, took the opportunity to write to President

MARGARET (MARDY) MURIE

Richard M. Nixon that he was "greatly concerned over [Watergate]." However, even more troubling to him was "the proposed Jet airport expansion in Teton National Park. I am against it with all my heart." Alfred A. Knopf, the well-known publisher and friend of the national parks, took the occasion to fire off a message to Secretary of the Interior Rogers Morton saying he was surprised that "you have not taken the present occasion to force that dreadful airport out of Grand Teton National Park...Perhaps you should consult your intuition."[23]

On September 11, 1973, Judge John Rampton held a public hearing on the DEIS in Jackson. It convened at 10:00 a.m. and lasted until 5:50 p.m. Although the judge asked that "there be no display of emotions" during the hearing, it was clear that this was an adversarial inquiry replete with talking, hissing, and sarcastic laughing. Of the 47 individuals testifying, 29 were for expansion, 18 against. Dick Oberreit of the Teton Village Resort Association presumed to speak for national park values when he proclaimed that the "self-styled ecology elitists [forget] that the National Parks are owned, and their maintenance paid for, by the people of this country, 200 million of them, and that the Charter of the National Parks provides that they be preserved for the enjoyment of the people of this and future generations, not that they be preserved for the sake of preservation." We should not "close the gates." Margaret (Mardy) Murie followed Oberreit's statement. The esteemed environmentalist's opening sentence bears quoting: "A jetport facili-

ty within Grand Teton National Park, or any national park, would violate the purpose for which parks have been established, as well as the Park Service's obligation to protect these national landmarks 'unimpaired for the enjoyment of future generations.'" Murie elaborated on this theme for 15 pages.

At the conclusion of her prepared statement, Mardy asked the judge for permission to make a few more comments based on her residency of 46 years in Jackson Hole. The judge consented. In all her environmental contests, she seldom engaged in negative analysis, but she felt that "many people because of the business or personal connections do not feel free to express their own opinions." Furthermore, over her long tenure in the valley, she had watched "the national parks, so desperately opposed by many residents [become] a gold mine in which they have been busily digging ever since. I have seen the whole county business grow; I have seen the unbelievable lack of foresight, lack of town or county planning. I have seen the greed grow too; until it now seems that the beauty and peace of the most enchanting valley in the world is a thing to be exploited so that a few may profit financially; profit from a treasure which belongs to the whole nation." Her peroration brought the issue back to the airport: "In America growth seems to be god; one compromise follows another and it seems there is little control over what happens on this airport."

Tom Mangelsen, a young wildlife photographer, put the matter a little differently. Even though his studio depended on tourists coming to Jackson Hole, he testified: "I'll be damned if I will prostitute this beautiful valley for another dollar that jet service or snow machines will bring me." He mentioned that he traveled a great deal and had come to realize that Jackson Hole is a special place. He did not want it to change.[24] No matter how eloquent and determined Murie's and Mangelsen's arguments, they did not represent a clear majority of the locals, who favored the runway expansion that Murie chastised. Their livelihoods depended on it, as well as their personal needs for air travel. A resolution from the Wyoming Jaycees reflected the opinions of those focused on growth. They favored expansion, stating that: (1) the economic health of Jackson Hole depended on tourism, (2) the airport contributed to healthy tourism, (3) a 1,700-foot extension would have no adverse effect on Grand Teton National Park, (4) there was no suitable alternative site for the airport, and (5) environmental groups were spreading misinformation. The Jaycees' position mirrored the view of Wyoming's congressional delegation. Governor Stan Hathaway, Senators Gale McGee and Cliff Hansen, and Congressman Teno Roncalio were all in favor of the airport expansion. Hansen, twisting the tail of the Park Service, remarked that it defied comprehension that the NPS had not made a decision regarding the future of the airport. The senator admonished the agency for its snail-like progress: "One of the foremost reasons for public disenchantment with the federal government is the bureaucratic practice of continual postponement of decisions on grounds that additional studies are required."[25] Of course, he fully expected that the final EIS would endorse the expansion alternative.

Secretary Morton and Grand Teton Superintendent Gary Everhardt, however, were required to consider more than the opinions of Wyoming politicians and local boosters' economic interests. The park had received some 5,200 letters, almost all of them deeply opposed to a jet port in a national park.[26] These letters had to be weighed against local opinion and the values of the National Park System. In the early phases of the debate it seemed that Morton and Superintendent Everhardt, who publically professed neutrality, were inclined to allow the expansion of the airport runway to 8,000 feet. That path certainly represented the politically easy one, at least at the state and local level. However, they could not ignore the outpouring of opposition to expansion. In the end, the National Park Service abandoned its preferred alternative and the final EIS decision recommended "no change," with a promise to continue to study the problem. The park position did not represent a victory for either side. For the minimalist faction, the airport would remain, but the runway would be strengthened and made suitable for the Boeing 737, which soon arrived at the Jackson Hole Airport. The maximalist faction did not get expansion of the airport, however, in spite of the short runway, the jets arrived. Thus Hansen's criticism proved prescient, as the jet port's future remained unclear.

The National Park Service went further in defense of park values than anyone expected. Not only would the record of decision recommend "no change," but then came the shocker: further continuation of the airport's special use permit *would be denied*. In August 1979, NPS Director William Whalen explained that "the existing airport is in direct conflict with the purpose for which Grand Teton National Park was created and the presence of the associated aircraft degrades the opportunity of visitors to use and enjoy the pristine environment of the park." He declared that there were "feasible and prudent alternate locations" and that the airport was "not essential to carrying out the functions of the Department of the Interior." In April 1980, the National Park Advisory Board informed the Airport Board that "only complete elimination of the airport from its present site would solve the essential problems involved: Noise, overflights, excessive traffic, and general incompatibility with park values." The two statements represented an astonishing turn of events. As if to second these actions, Bob Herbst, assistant secretary of the Interior, informed Isaac Hoover, deputy regional director of the FAA, that the Park Service would not sanction improvements to the airport since it is "our intention not to renew the airport special use permit in 1995."[27] It seemed, briefly, that the park might actually rid itself of the airport afterall. On the national front, ever since Earth Day 1970, Americans looked with watery eyes and wounded ears at the impacted world that surrounded them. Their more critical view of modern America caused them to question the direction of "progress" in aviation. It reached, perhaps, its pinnacle when the House of Representatives killed the American Supersonic plane (SST–Boeing 2707) funding on May 20, 1971.[28] In retrospect, it was a defeat for American technology, but a victory for the environment and common sense.

Here in Jackson Hole, Secretary of the Interior Cecil Andrus addressed the Western Governors' Conference. No doubt he had been involved in the decision to end the airport special use permit in 1995. As if to put another nail in the airport coffin, Secretary Andrus proclaimed that the airport was not controlled by the whims of local politicians. Peter Jorgensen, former state representative from Jackson, remembered his excitement when Andrus announced that the airport was not a local or county airport, but a national one.[29]

POLITICS MATTER

These were powerful declarations and, to park officials who understood the mission of the Park Service, very welcome. But they were not the final word. People who believe national elections do not affect local or regional issues should reconsider, for Ronald Reagan's election to the presidency in 1980 spelled the end of any hope that Grand Teton National Park could ever rid itself of the airport. Reagan appointed James Watt as his Secretary of the Interior. The Denver-based attorney had made a reputation and a successful career fighting federal regulations, particularly regarding environmental protection. Soon, he reversed many decisions that the Jimmy Carter administration had made, including Director Whalen's announcement on the airport. Watt wrote to Roy Jensen, president of the Airport Board that, "I find there is no basis for the Department's past position that it, rather than the Airport Board, is the proprietor of the

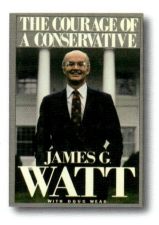

Jackson Hole Airport. . . It is abundantly clear that the operation, management, utilization, and maintenance of the airport is the sole responsibility and privilege of the Board." In what can only be considered an abrogation of his authority as well as his responsibility, Watt declared that his department "retains only the barest authority to approve or disapprove those actions proposed by the Board." To Senators Simpson and Wallop, and Representative Dick Cheney, interior secretary Watt admitted that he had some "statutory obligations to protect the park," but he assured them that he would "consult with, and consider the needs of, the local committee before taking any action." The message was clear—the board could do as they pleased. Jurisdiction over airport policy should rest at the state and local level. In November 1982, Watt signed a statement that "the Jackson Hole Airport is necessary for the proper performance of the functions

of the Department of the Interior." No further explanation of this critical policy turn-around was forthcoming.[30]

The capitulation was complete when Secretary of the Interior James Watt and the Airport Board signed the 1983 agreement still in force today. It spelled out that the board would operate the airport, although they must consult with park administrators. It said nothing about relocation; clearly that possibility was no longer viable. The airport would stay where it was.[31] As far as park standards were concerned, the emphasis henceforth would be on noise reduction. "Acoustical energy" would be monitored, and acceptable noise levels would be set. These measurements are difficult to establish, for we each have our own definitions of what constitutes "acceptable" noise. However, the agreement offered its definition that "no aircraft will be permitted to operate at the Jackson Hole Airport which has a single event noise level which exceeds 92 on the dBA scale on approach." Such standards would be enforced, and the "failure to enforce this noise standard shall be a material breach of the agreement."[32]

While Grand Teton now focused its energy on noise levels, the Sierra Club did not concede that the entrance of commercial jets was a *fait accompli*. The club filed suit against the FAA and argued before the United States Court of Appeals on May 7, 1984, that the FAA erred in finding that commercial jets would have "no significant impact," and that the FAA had not taken a "hard look" at airport alternatives to minimize harm to the park.[33] Judge Robert Bork, who later gained fame as President Reagan's unsuccessful nomination to the Supreme Court, sided with the FAA. He cited a study by the University of Wyoming engineer Sam D. Hakes that in terms of noise, the C-580 and the B-737 were "relatively interchangeable as long as landing and takeoffs were made to the south." He concluded that little was to be gained or lost if either aircraft was used for commercial operations. Judge Bork noted that "since the B-737 has almost twice the seating capacity of the C-580, any increase in noise intrusion attributable to the B-737 "could be more than overcome by the smaller number of flights needed to accommodate the same number of passengers."[34] In regard to the Sierra Club's second concern, the court simply stated that a new EIS was not necessary and that "we find that the FAA did take a hard look at the problem."[35] Redress through the courts was over.

In 1985, the park and the airport board revised the noise abatement plan, basically regulating *cumulative* noise standards for airport operations, with measuring (by park personnel) of daytime and nighttime averages. With the increased number of landings and take-offs, measurements regarding the cumulative standards had become necessary. Quieter engines on the Boeing 737 and Boeing 757 allowed the airlines to meet these standards. The agreement also stressed good behavior. Letters of thanks would go out to the airlines and individual pilots and crews who made an extra effort to abide by the noise abatement procedures. On the other side of the coin, the procedures encouraged individuals to complain when aircraft deviated from the normal pattern. Such complaints would then be investigated by the airport staff and judged as (1) a justified procedure, (2) an unjustified procedure, or (3) an unfounded report. No matter how a complaint was determined, the person who complained was entitled to a written response. If the complaint proved justified, the pilot (or airline) would be warned and on the second (or any additional) violation, a Town of Jackson Summons and Complaint would be issued.[36]

What was the consequence of these procedures on the park experience? Do procedures lessen the assault on quiet? Certainly more modern planes featuring quieter engines have made a considerable difference. Furthermore, when one Boeing 757 carries five times the number of passengers that the smaller turbo-prop planes brought, the cumulative noise impact diminishes. Yet with pages of procedures in place, whether noise is mitigated usually comes down to the commitment or lack of it in the pilot and crew. For instance, landing from the north, pilots are asked to maintain a course to the east of Highway 89 and at a distance from the Snake River. Some do follow such a path, often circling around Blacktail Butte. But many ignore the recommended route, entering the park as far north as Moran, following a glide path directly over the Snake River, and providing their passengers with impressive views of the Tetons. These commercial flights combined with numerous private jets have a decidedly detrimental effect on those rafting the Snake River or hiking in the Tetons.[37]

In terms of effects to the south, "aircraft operators are asked to plan their arrival and departure routing from the south of the Airport, avoiding the noise-sensitive areas of the Park."[38] The 2010 EIS Record of Decision reconfirms the 1983 statement that runway 01 (from the south) "is the preferred arrival runway" and runway 19 (to the south) is the "preferred departure runway."[39] (It should be noted that there is only one runway!) The question remains, does the control tower and do the pilots follow the recommended procedure? The answer is seldom, because the prevailing wind is usually out of the south, requiring a northern landing over the park. Departures are often to the south, again to take advantage of the wind. On calm mornings, however, aircraft often depart to the north over the park, leaving the airport in a cacophony of noise and reminding the many park employees living at Moose that they are not living in a perfect park. How do these early morning northern direction take-offs happen? There are different theories, but one thing is clear: they should end. They are not necessary. They violate written procedure, and they disregard the sanctity of the park.

Refusing to honor the 2010 Record of Decision reminds us that aircraft people and park people do not necessarily share the same values. Some pilots do not understand or care that they are drowning out the natural sounds park visitors have come to experience

and expect. They do not worry that a park ranger must interrupt a talk in mid-sentence to accommodate incoming or outgoing aircraft noise, or that the Murie Center—dedicated to nature, solitude and wilderness—is often inundated with jet noise. Certainly not all pilots are insensitive to the park, but they are paid by their airline company. Traffic tower employees as well are hired under private contract, but ultimately they draw their salaries from the FAA.

The Controversial Runway

A number of planes, both commercial and private have overshot the runway. Perhaps the most dangerous and dramatic came in 1994 when two Boeing 737 jets landed too far down the runway and could not make the turn into the taxiway. The first, a Delta flight from Salt Lake City, ended its flight burrowed in the snow. It had to be towed back to the terminal. The 96 passengers, understandably nervous, applauded when the plane finally stopped. There were no injuries or damage to the plane.[40] The second 737 overshot the pavement by 61 feet in late July, 1994. The pilot, perhaps embarrassed, simply backed out of the safety area, blowing "quite a bit" of rock and debris over the runway. Airport Manager George Larson commented, "I don't know what he was thinking."[41] Amazingly, former Secretary of the Interior James Watt was one of the passengers, who took the occasion to remark: "The runway is too short. Period, paragraph. We're lucky no one's been killed there, but eventually somebody will be."[42]

Watt's remark simply added to what has been, perhaps, the longest debate in Grand Teton National Park recent history—the length of the runway. According to Manager Larson, by the end of 2000, 19 aircraft had run off the end of the airstrip. Each time it happens, there is a call for extension of the 6,300 foot runway. The Federal Aviation Administration has consistently certified the runway as safe, but clearly favored a longer runway. Usually the proposal is to expand to the north where sagebrush flats are inviting. There is little land for southern expansion, and in many proposals the removal of private homes would be required. In the period 1970 to 2000, competing interests were at loggerheads. The FAA, the Jackson Hole Airport Board, and the town commercial interests, and the Jackson Hole Mountain Resort ski interests, favored expansion. The NPS, the Jackson Hole Conservation Alliance, and other environmental groups consistently argued against it. In 1990, Interior Secretary Manuel Lujan and Grand Teton Superintendent Jack Stark issued a brief statement opposed to a longer runway, stating that "at this time it appears that economic advantage to the airlines and some local businesses is the only valid and assured rea-

JACK STARK (RIGHT) VISITS WITH DR. DAVID LOVE

son for the proposed runway extension." From their point of view "decreased noise levels are not guaranteed by a longer runway and indeed, a northern extension is more likely to increase noise in the Park."[43] The NPS has not changed its stance since 1979.

But the runway expansion issue is more than simply a question of the park values and passenger safety. Two sacrosanct agencies (NPS and FAA) butted heads and neither would give up easily. As Superintendent Stark put it in 1991, "what the FAA calls insignificant, we regard as intolerable." Author and climber Ted Kerasote offered a view from the mountains: "Now from many belay ledges and from all peaks we are assailed by the sound of landing or taking-off planes." In a broader sense, businessman Alan Hirschfield put the whole issue in perspective: "The issue of extending the runway has become a metaphor for growth. I believe a sense of hysteria has been created."[44]

Fortunately, some of the hysteria has abated. In 2000, the Airport Board approved construction of two 300-foot runway safety areas at each end of the runway. In 2012, workers constructed an additional 700-foot safety area to the south. These special safety areas may not be used for normal take offs or landings, and are simply an insurance against pilots overshooting the runway. Thus the useable runway is still only 6,300 feet, but there is an additional 1,000 feet to the south, if needed.

The issue of the airport runway continues to be argued and debated. Whenever an aircraft skids off the landing field, the proponents of a longer runway come out of the woodwork. Safety is their argument, and it is a potent one. No one, least of all the National Park Service, would condone an unsafe jet base. But those groups in opposition to further runway expansion, particularly the Jackson Hole Conservation Alliance, claim that the ski industry and the business community raise false alarms on this topic. And even if people agreed on the need, where would an extension go? The Park Service opposes a runway extension to the north, for it would take more land, further encroaching into the heart of the park, and mandating an even lower approach over the Moose headquarters. Extension to the south is not palatable to the Airport Board, since it entails rerouting Spring Gulch Road and would require the removal or destruction of about 15 homes. In 1992, James Ridenour, director of the NPS, visited Jackson Hole and proclaimed that new technology would provide the answer. To a degree, technology has proven his case. Jet aircraft engines have become more powerful and thus able to contend with shorter runways. At the same time, technology is producing quieter aircraft.[45]

Yet, acknowledging that in the future Grand Teton National Park must live with the airport, what are park officials to do? The problem of noise in a space committed to natural quiet is vexing to the park. Is quiet possible? The obvious answer is no. Even in the alpine mountains, or in the northern part of the park at the Oxbow Bend of the Snake River, one is never free of airplane noise intrusion. There are numerous places in the park that lend themselves to a quiet, reverent, and worshipful frame of mind, but attaining such a mood is difficult. This is true of historic as well as natural sites, for part of the pleasure of slipping back in time at an old homestead site is not only the structure and the landscape, but also the "soundscape."[46] Nothing can jolt you from a contemplative mood more quickly than a jet passing overhead.

Grand Teton National Park has tried to limit the noise. When the Airport Board and the park signed a new agreement, the park insisted on strict noise testing. Under contract with the Jackson Hole Airport Board, Bridgenet International Company now monitors different sites for airplane noise levels over the park. The noise intrusion of individual airplanes has decreased and yet the likelihood that one will hear a plane overhead or within sound range has increased. NPS Sound Ecologist Shan Burson explains that while individual plane noise has lessened the cumulative noise of *more* aircraft offsets the gain.[47] Thus the aircraft noise intrusion continues.

If it appears there is nothing good to say of the airport, it is only because this work is based on a foundation of national park principles. The Jackson Hole airstrip violates them. However, many locals and park personnel, as well, use and appreciate the convenience of the airport and how it connects them to the larger world. It is a regional airport that allows many residents to live successfully in this special place. Most people in Jackson Hole realize that the airport does not belong in a national park, but they are quite willing to live with the paradox.

HISTORICALLY, TWO FUNDAMENTAL attitudes toward the airport emerged during the decades from 1960 to 1990. William Whalen, NPS director in the late 1970s, believed there was no place for an airport within Grand Teton National Park. He made his views known, and he announced that when the lease expired in 1995, the airport must go. His decision was premature and short-lived. By 1981, Secretary of the Interior James Watt reversed the Whalen decision, turned over authority to the Airport Board, and extended its lease to 2013. The question becomes: Who was right—Whalen or Watt? Obviously people disagree vehemently, and the Watt faction carried the day. From the viewpoint of the National Park Service's 1916 charge to protect the public's use and enjoyment for future generations, the airport cannot be justified.

Justified or not, the airport is a reality. Since the Watt faction's victory, there has been no end of fighting. Two antithetical cultures have been thrown together. In the last decade the "players" in the airport saga have learned to live with each other, or at least found an uneasy truce. According to NPS Management Assistant Gary Pollock, who is also liaison to the Airport Board, relations are dominated by cooperation, rather than confrontation. Agreements, such as the nightly air traffic curfew, are not enforced by penalties and fines, but rather by voluntary compliance. The system is working reasonably well. Furthermore, according to Pollock, the Airport Board and Grand Teton are in general agreement. He is particularly encouraged by the turn around of the FAA, once a barrier, now a team player that acknowledges the special circumstances of the Jackson Hole Airport. Now if such harmony could only translate into a quiet park, people and nature would all benefit.

ACCIDENTS, IN AND OUT OF THE AIRPORT

Perhaps it is inevitable that an airport located in a mountain valley would be the location of tragic events. The first notable loss of life took place in January of 1950. A Christian missionary group from Chico, California, headed for Billings, Montana in a DC-8, slammed into Mount Moran. All 21 crew and passengers on board the DC-8 died, including several children.[48] Notably, the plane neither landed nor took off from the Jackson Hole Airport. Other plane crashes occurred in 1983, 1995, 1996, and 2002. Perhaps the most publicized crash came in December, 2000 when actress Sandra Bullock's jet approached the airport at night and missed the runway, digging a furrow in the snow. Amazingly, she walked away from the severely damaged aircraft, but not from national media attention. More serious, a deadly and spectacular boom occurred on the night of August 20, 2002. President Bill Clinton and family had left the valley the day before, concluding their second year of enjoying Jackson Hole for their summer vacation. His support plane, described by one reporter as a "slow, fat, reliable workhorse" C-130 cargo plane lifted off from the Jackson Hole Airport to the south loaded with cars, equipment, and some 18 tons of fuel. It circled to the left, but then slammed into Sleeping Indian Mountain, exploding in a huge ball of orange flame seen throughout the valley. Eight members of the crew and one secret service agent died instantly. Of course

Sleeping Indian Mountain is within the Bridger-Teton National Forest, but most people would view the crash from the point-of-view of the airport and the park.[49] Given all these crashes and mishaps, it should be noted that no fatalities have been a result of the location of the airport or the size of its runway.

HELICOPTER CAPERS

Perhaps as detrimental to the park's serenity from airport noise was the threat of scenic helicopter tours over the Teton Range. Of course helicopters were not strangers to Grand Teton National Park because their use in mountain rescues was a matter of life and death. No one opposed that aerial activity. In the spring of 2000, however, Gary Kaufmann, owner of Vortex Aviation, announced his intention to offer scenic helicopter flights in Grand Teton National Park, providing a service for tourists and a profit for himself. From the beginning, Kaufmann, an interloper, faced a skeptical community and the NPS. The Park Service had regretted the increasing loss of solitude at Grand Canyon National Park, and now faced the same incursion at Grand Teton. The Airport Board lacked the authority to ban Kaufmann's business, since the FAA did not oppose the idea. On this issue, however, the local community united in opposition. There were no local economic interests to gain from scenic helicopter rides, and there was plenty to lose in terms of a livable valley. The Jackson Hole Conservation Alliance, supported by the Greater Yellowstone

Coalition, the Natural Resources Defense Council and Wilderness Watch, rallied the community as "HELI NO" bumper stickers appeared throughout Jackson Hole. Furthermore, the Alliance gathered roughly 6,000 signatures (in a community of approximately 12,000 people) opposing the helicopter tours. They presented the petitions to the FAA.[50]

Those who believed that the overwhelming sentiment of the community along with the recently passed National Parks Air Tour Management Act of 2000 (severely limiting air tours) would sway the FAA, were sadly mistaken. The FAA was certainly respected for its focus on safety, but in Jackson Hole many equated the agency as a lobbyist for the unlimited rights of pilots and aircraft. After all, the opening sentence on the air tour management act states, "Congress finds that the Federal Aviation Administration has sole authority to control airspace over the United States."[51] The FAA essentially overruled the community opinion when it informed the Jackson Hole Airport Board that it "has no authority…to prohibit scenic operations from taking off or landing at Jackson Hole Airport."

With no help evident from the FAA, Franz Camenzind, Director of the Jackson Hole Conservation Alliance, turned to Wyoming's U.S. Senator Craig Thomas to introduce legislation that would ban any scenic helicopter flights over Grand Teton and Yellowstone, as well as adjacent wilderness areas and wildlife refuges. As I have noted before, the Wyoming national politicians frequently sided against positions favored by the NPS. In this case, Senator Thomas did not hesitate to support the community's wishes and that of the NPS. He was also aided by Kaufmann's belligerent, alienating attitude of entitlement. His acidic personality did not help his case. The die was certainly cast, when Governor Jim Geringer, responding to a plea by locals Marcia Kunstel and Joe Albright, backed Senator Thomas' position. An amendment to the Air Tour Management Act of 2000 prohibiting air tours in Grand Teton and Yellowstone parks ended the threat of scenic tours, presumably forever.[52]

SNOWMOBILES

National parks capitulated to the automobile long ago. As earlier noted, John Muir agreed to the invasion of the noisy, smoky machines in Yosemite Valley by 1912. The appearance of "over snow" vehicles did not come until later. Snow planes had some popularity in Jackson Hole in the 1930s, mainly because they were handy for ice fishermen to get around on Jackson Lake or to get to town on a wintry day. It was not until after WWII, that engineers built commercial vehicles for more general recreation. In the 1960s, the powerful two-stroke engine offered new possibilities for recreation. Soon snowmobile advocates penetrated the winter silence of Grand Teton National Park.

Snowmobilers found the park's Potholes region to their liking, and soon they cavorted over these hilly,

sagebrush-covered 20,000 acres each winter. This concession to allow snowmobile use in the park proved controversial, and in August 1979, Superintendent Robert Kerr announced that the Potholes area would be closed to snowmobiles. In the future, the machines would be confined to roads and frozen lakes. This did not sit well with the Jackson Chamber of Commerce and various other recreational interest groups. The issue soon reopened, and after meeting with the Wyoming congressional delegation, NPS Director William Whalen reversed Kerr's decision. The Jackson Hole Snow Devils club celebrated, while distressed Park Service employees wrote memos of protest.[53] Whalen's decision was another reminder that parks do not exist apart from a community and often must bow down to local desires.

Of course Grand Teton National Park was not the only destination for snowmobilers. To the north they found the deep snow of Yellowstone inviting, setting off a controversy that continues to this day. By the mid-1960s, these mechanized snow sleds became popular as well as increasingly powerful and loud, with the Old Faithful region proving the preferred destination. Wyoming Senator Gale McGee held a hearing in Casper, August 1967 to gather information on whether to keep Yellowstone roads plowed for automobiles or limit winter travel to snowmobiles and/or snow coaches. For reasons of cost, wildlife entrapment in deep snow cuts, and the fear that Yellowstone would become a highway thoroughfare, Senators McGee and Cliff Hansen rejected the plowing alternative. However, Senator Hansen and others, looking out for the snowmobile interests, argued successfully to plow the 17 miles of road from Colter Bay to Flagg Ranch. In a spirit of compromise, NPS Director George Hartzog agreed that Grand Teton would assume the cost of plowing the road. Flagg Ranch has been the southerly jumping-off point for Yellowstone snowmobile traffic ever since. Meanwhile, Grand Teton park officials continued to wrestle with what to do about this new recreational toy. Under pressure, they reopened the Potholes region. In retrospect they should not have allowed off-road snowmobiling, but it was only on the condition that an average of three feet of snow lay on the ground, protecting the vegetation.

Winter quiet disappeared in 1973–74 when some 35,000 snowmobiles arrived, mainly in Yellowstone but also in Grand Teton. The distant hum of a snowmobile seemed to be everywhere. Non-snowmobilers complained not only about the noise, but also about the bad behavior of heartless operators, chasing down and exhausting coyotes and sometimes running over them.[54] By 1979, the Jackson Lake Lodge offered snowmobile tours of the park. Participants met near the Moose Visitor Center, where guides provided suits, boots, and helmets. Once on their individual machines, participants were off to the northern section of the park, exploring various bays on frozen Jackson Lake and racing up the snow-covered road to Signal Mountain summit. All this came to a halt on the evening of January 30, 1985. Five lodge guests and their guide became stranded on Jackson Lake on their snowmobiles in slushy ice. The temperature hovered at zero, with no moon or stars for visual reference. Guests had to crawl to shore in the icy waters. Fortunately there were no fatalities, but that was the end of the snowmobile tours. Grand Teton Lodge Company historian Mary McKinney notes that the lodge manager made the decision, but no doubt park administrators concurred, terminating a venture they never liked.[55]

A CONTINENTAL DIVIDE SNOWMOBILE TRAIL

As activity at the airport was intensifying, so was the snowmobile frenzy. An entrepreneurial woman in Lander, Wyoming, had an inspiration. Why not create a world-class snowmobile trail? In June 1988, the promoters formed the Wyoming Continental Divide Snowmobile Trail Association and produced a booklet describing in glowing terms the 340-mile trail, beginning at Lander, crossing Togwotee Pass, dropping into Jackson Hole and Grand Teton National Park, continuing to Flagg Ranch, then on to Yellowstone and Old Faithful, and terminating at the town of West Yellowstone. She presented this epic journey as the ultimate recreational adventure, as well as an unprecedented opportunity for the state. "What downhill skiing is to the states of Colorado and Utah," she proclaimed, "snowmobiling will be for Wyoming." Superintendent Jack Stark received the idea in booklet fashion and was asked to approve or disapprove the concept. Caught in that common trap set by commercial interests to ensnare the park for its own aggrandizement, Superintendent Stark vacillated. He asked for time, neither approving nor disapproving the idea, explaining that before he offered an opinion, "we must finish the Winter Use Plan."[56]

This plea, however, was unacceptable to Senator Alan Simpson, who was on board with the trail idea. Well liked by his Wyoming constituents as well as his colleagues in the Senate, Simpson decided to exercise some of the power that goodwill earned him. He shot off a letter to National Park Service Director James Ridenour on the subject of the trail, stating that the staff at Grand Teton "are pleasant and sincere—but they are stalling and really not doing a damn thing." He attributed such inaction to the "many purists" in the Park Service who would prefer no winter use. Simpson would have none of it. In a bombastic statement, he announced that "if I do not determine that adequate and vigorous progress is being made in the next few weeks, I will introduce and work for legislation requiring the Park Service to allow the snowmobile trail to be completed through Teton National Park. I don't know if I will succeed, but I'll sure give it my best shot."[57]

Was this an idle threat? Hardly, for numerous towns throughout the state supported the idea, as did Governor Stan Hathaway and members of the Wyoming congressional delegation. The only evident obstacle was the National Park Service and the concern of environmental groups. Moreover, Simpson had many friends in the Senate who would be more than willing to sign on to the idea, thus doing their Wyoming colleague a small favor. The outcome was not surprising. Regional Director Lorraine Mintzmeyer replied that the winter use plan would be accelerated and given top priority. Grand Teton National Park soon finished the plan, agreeing to construct the trail from its east boundary at Buffalo Fork to the southern entrance to Yellowstone (Flagg Ranch). Sleds were zipping over the trail by 1993, but with the compromise that the Potholes region would once again be closed to snowmobiles.

The new trail was never popular, and by the year 2000, trail usage shrank to only 20 to 25 snowmobiles a day. When the park instituted new requirements in 2004 that sleds must be equipped with the "best available technology," usage dropped to about 15 sleds all winter. With a maintenance cost of $100,000 for the season, even Senator Simpson could not justify that ratio. The park closed the Continental Divide Snowmobile Trail in 2008. There was little opposition, although snowmobiling in Yellowstone National Park continues.

To some snowmobiling is contradictory to the mission of national parks. As *The Snowmobiler's Companion* explained it, snowmobiling "brought back some of that edge-of-danger excitement, those feelings of man-against-the-elements adventure and man-over-machinery mastery that have been lost in every other form of modern transportation."[58] Given this embrace of danger and the nuisance effects of noise, bad behavior, pollution, and damage to vegetation, snowmobiling strikes many as not a good fit in national parks. Today in Grand Teton, snowmobiling is allowed only on the frozen surface of Jackson Lake to accommodate access to ice fishing, and on the Grassy Lake Road in the John D. Rockefeller, Jr. Memorial Parkway, which is managed by the superintendent of Grand Teton National Park.

THE AIRPORT AND SNOWMOBILE TRAIL sagas remind us that Grand Teton National Park has more than one master. Park Service administrators have considerable power, from the director on down to superintendents in the field, but they must always look over their shoulders at politicians, particularly the state's congressional delegation and local interests. Congressmen wield the "power of the purse" and thus are able to influence policy. And of course, they represent their constituents. In Jackson Hole, locals are not always in agreement, but they are very local and vocal. Historian Susan Flader chastised managers of the Ozark National Scenic Riverway because the

NPS personnel had "gone local," which translates into capitulation to local demands.[59] The problem becomes serious when the goals and values of politicians and locals are at odds with those of the Park Service. When a dominant politician like U.S. Senator Simpson gets crosswise with a park superintendent, the outcome is as plain as the nose on your face.

The skilled superintendent must be a diplomat, internalizing park values but understanding that the choices often come down to resignation or compromise. These choices usually hinge upon two big *E*'s: environment and economy. Unfortunately, although they may claim differently, Wyoming politicians give less weight to the environment than to economic development. When the two collide, economics prevail. President Theodore Roosevelt once warned famed naturalist John Muir that *his* "constituents"—the flora and fauna—did not have the vote. It is a good thought to remember. Political figures such as Senator Alan Simpson know that economic arguments are paramount with the majority of voters. In his case, harassing Grand Teton National Park qualified as a family tradition, for both his grandfather William and his father Milward opposed establishment of Grand Teton National Park and often used it as a punching bag to further their respective political careers. Like many prominent families in the state, the Simpsons love the park but believe this should not detract from Wyomingites' efforts to make a living from it. The ongoing clash between the forces for economic aggrandizement and those of preservation over resources guarantees that Grand Teton National Park will always be striving toward realizing Park Service ideals while never quite attaining them. Park-making is an ongoing process, and it is well to remember past NPS Director Arno Cammerer's belief that "an ideal is something toward which to work; it should not be something that keeps us from working."[60]

[1] Jim Stanford, interview by author, May 17, 2010. The aircraft could be one of the following airlines, all of which serve Jackson Hole: American, Delta, United, Frontier, or Continental.

[2] The Jackson Hole Historical Society and Museum has a file of aviation photographs including a half dozen images of barnstormers.

[3] See January 10, 1934, and Grand Teton, January 23, 1934.

[4] Excerpt from "Class III Cultural Resources Inventory of the Moose-Wilson Realignment Project," GTNP. September 3, 2012.

[5] The *Jackson Hole Courier* ran a brief story in August of 1939. See Jackson Hole Historical Society and Museum, aviation clipping file.

[6] In the late 1930s the Wort's landing strip would be on U. S. Forest Service land.

[7] Information from Harold Turner, Triangle X Ranch. The photo may be seen in the Jackson Hole Historical Society and Museum, aviation photo file. RKO takes its name from the company that filmed along the river.

[8] No documentation exists, but presumably he would have contacted Harold Fabian, representing the Snake River Land Company.

[9] Lorraine Bonney, "Airport Established by the Big Squat," *Jackson Hole News and Guide*, October 1, 2003; Richard Abendroth, "Airport Squabbles Dates Back to the 1930s," *Jackson Hole News and Guide*, September 15, 1993.

[10] *Jackson Hole Courier*, March 7, 1940; Abendroth, "Airport Squabbles."

[11] While the airport landing strip was within the Jackson Hole National Monument, the land was owned by the Snake River Land Company until 1949.

[12] I cannot locate the 1946 McLaughlin letter, but I remember my surprise at reading his endorsement. Now that I have explored the issue, his sentiments seem more understandable.

[13] Robert W. Righter, *Crucible for Conservation: The Struggle for Grand Teton National Park* (Boulder: Colorado University Press, 1982; repr., Moose, Wyo.: Grand Teton Association, 2000), 110. See Chapter 1 for more on this.

[14] John C. Miles, *Guardians of the Parks: A History of the National Parks and Conservation Association* (Washington, D.C.: Taylor and Francis, 1995), 323.

[15] A. E. Kendrew, "Report on OWNED Structures of a Historic Character, Jackson Hole, Wyoming," July and August, 1942. Copy in possession of the author.

[16] See John Ise, *Our National Park Policy: A Critical History* (Baltimore: Johns Hopkins University Press, 1961), 487, n. 50.

[17] Ibid., 486–87.

[18] Ibid., 487.

[19] Master Plan for the Preservation and Use of Grand Teton National Park: Objectives and Policies, April 1962.

[20] See J. William Futrell, "NEPA and the Parks: Use It or Lose It," in *Our Common Lands: Defending the National Parks,* ed. David J. Simon (Washington, D.C.: Island Press, 1988), 107. Also see "History of the Jackson Hole Airport Pertinent to Runway Related Issues," NPS typescript, 6 pp., n.d, no author.

[21] "Jackson Hole Airport, Draft Environmental Impact Statement," February 1973, GTNP, box 32, folder 14.

[22] Today a private landing strip of 5,800 feet exists in Alpine. It accommodates small jet craft. This is only 500 feet shorter

than the Jackson Airport landing strip. Rex Doornabus, pilot and resident of Alpine, interview by author, June 24, 2012.

23 Kevin Collins, Pleasant Valley, CA, to President Nixon, undated; Alfred A. Knopf to Secretary of the Interior Rogers Morton, May 28, 1974, GTNP, unnumbered box, "Airport, Prior to 1975."

24 Murie statement, in "Public Hearings on the DEIS for the Jackson Hole Airport," Jackson, September 11, 1973, 170; Tom Mangelsen to Lorraine Mintzmeyer, April 13, 1981, GTNP, box 32, folder 14.

25 Resolution from the Wyoming Jaycees, March 2, 1974; Senator Cliff Hansen to Secretary Rogers Morton, March 14, 1974; Airport Board to Secretary Rogers Morton, October 23, 1973, GTNP, unnumbered box, "Airport, Prior to 1975," folder "comments on FES, Airport, for expansion."

26 During this period Grand Teton archival records were not a high priority. Park curator Alice Hart eventually discovered a disintegrating cardboard box labeled "Airport Prior to 1975." After we had cleared away the mouse dung, we found numerous 3 x 5 cards that recorded letters received on the DEIS and also NPS responses. Many cards contained a brief extract of the letter. Giving up on counting them all, I measured the length of the card files: 52 inches. I counted the number of cards in 1 inch: 100 cards. Hence 52 x 100 provided the estimate of 5,200. The letters were from all over the United States. Most all that I examined opposed the jet port. The writers did not necessarily understand the issue, but they understood that national parks and jet ports are like oil and water—they do not mix.

27 Memo from Deputy Director to Assistant Secretary of Parks, November 2, 1982 (contains the Whalen decision of August 1979); Memo to Secretary of the Interior from Chairman, National Park System Advisory Board to Jackson Hole Airport, April 12, 1980; Bob Herbst, Assistant Secretary of Parks, to Isaac Hoover, Deputy Regional Director, FAA, May 7, 1980.

28 http://en.wikipedia.org/wiki/boeing2707

29 Interview with Peter Jorgensen, former Wyoming state senator, by author, August 31, 2013.

30 James Watt, Secretary of the Interior, to Roy Jensen, President, Jackson Hole Airport Board, April 15, 1982; James Watt to Senator Alan Simpson (copies to Senator Wallop and Representative Cheney), April 15, 1982; Secretary of the Interior Decision Sheet, dated November 3, 1982, GTNP, box 32, folder 4.

31 In an interview with James Watt by the author, July 20, 2013, Watt mentioned that Laurance Rockefeller had visited him in Washington when he was Secretary of the Interior. Rockefeller expressed his opinion that the airport should remain in GTNP, since the park could then regulate it.

   Watt also remembered that Rockefeller expressed interest in moving the airport to Daniel, Wyoming (about 15 miles north of Pinedale) and was even prepared to buy land. Watt recalled that he told Rockefeller that he could not support such an idea. They never talked of the airport again.

32 "Agreement between the United States Department of the Interior and the Jackson Hole Airport Board," April 27, 1983, 8. Typescript in possession of the author.

33 753 F2d 120 Sierra Club v. United States Department of Transportation, p. 8, paragraph 26. See http://openjurist.org/print/290281.

34 Ibid., p. 4, paragraph 14.

35 Ibid., p. 8, paragraph 27.

36 "Jackson Hole Airport Revised Noise Abatement Plan," March 14, 1985, 3–9. Typescript in possession of the author.

37 Ibid., 5.

38 Ibid.

39 2010 FEIS, Jackson Hole Airport Agreement Extension – Record of Decision, December 23, 2010.

40 "Christine Burdick,"Delta airliner slides off runway," *Jackson Hole Guide*, January 5, 1994.

41 Richard Abendroth, "Plane lands, keeps going," *Jackson Hole Guide*, July 27, 1994.

42 Ibid.

[43] Reported in Michael Sellett, "Park officially opposes airport runway extension," *Jackson Hole News*, February 4, 1990.

[44] Views expressed in the *Jackson Hole News*, June 19, 1991, 20.

[45] "Ridenour: New Aircraft Change Runway Debate," *Jackson Hole Guide*, July 1, 1992; also see "Airport Ignites Debate about Park Values," *Jackson Hole News*, June 9, 1993.

[46] See Bob Rossman, "The Importance of Soundscapes in National Park Management," in *People, Places and Parks: Proceedings of the 2005 George Wright Society Conference on Parks, Protected Areas, and Cultural Sites.*, ed. David Harmon (Hancock, Mich. George Wright Society, 2006), 335–40.

[47] Sherman (Shan) Burson III, telephone conversation with author, August 21, 2012.

[48] Stu Beitier, "Mountaineers Start Search Today for Plane Believed Downed on Rugged Peak with 21 Aboard," Associated Press, December 8, 1950.

[49] "Nine dead following C-130 Crash," *Jackson Hole Guide*, August 21, 1996: Also Tim Weiner, "9 die in Crash of C-130 Carrying Clinton Cargo," *New York Times,* August 21, 1996.

[50] *Jackson Hole Guide*, May 23, 2001

[51] 49 USC 40128, "National Parks Scenic Air Tour Management Act of 2000."

[52] Rebecca Huntington, "Governor backs ban on park heli flights," *Jackson Hole Guide*, June 27, 2001.

[53] *Jackson Hole Guide*, October 18, 1979; *Jackson Hole News*, October 17, 1979, quoted from Michael Frome, *Regreening the National Parks* (Tucson: University of Arizona Press, 1992), 200.

[54] For much of my information I rely on Michael J. Jochim, *Yellowstone and the Snowmobile* (Lawrence: University of Kansas Press, 2009), 64–76.

[55] Mary McKinney, *The View That Inspired a Vision* (Privately printed, 2010), 119.

[56] "Wyoming Continental Divide Snowmobile Trail" (booklet), GTNP, Land Records, Solicitors copies, box 13, folder 28.

[57] Letter quoted from Jochim, Yellowstone, 106.

[58] Quoted in Joseph L. Sax, *Mountains without Handrails* (Ann Arbor: University of Michigan Press, 1980), 34.

[59] Susan Flader, "A Legacy of Neglect: The Ozark National Scenic Riverways," *George Wright Forum* 28, no. 2 (June 2011): 114–26, quote at 124.

[60] Written by Cammerer in response to critics to creating GTNP, 1935. See Righter, *Crucible For Conservation*, 91.

Peaks, Politics, and Passion: Grand Teton National Park Comes of Age

Chapter 8.

Interpreting and Partnering

"HOW LONG IS THE 26 MILE DRIVE?" Such a non-sensical question hardly deserves an answer. Yet Victoria Mates, Grand Teton National Park Chief of Interpretation, believes it does. She surmises that the visitor often seeks not an answer to the question asked, but rather another, such as "How long will it take?" or "Is it worth it?" or "What will we see?" or perhaps other information not so obvious. The challenge for the ranger is to understand the person's needs, desires, and expectations, and then do his/her best to respond to them. The ranger must "read the needs of the visitor and respond" by careful listening to not only words but voice inflection. This takes a special talent, combining empathy, good listening skills, and perhaps a little psychology. According to Mates, interpretive rangers must listen to the needs of visitors and then do their best to fulfill them.

The interpretive mission of Grand Teton National Park is broad. Besides deciphering questions from visitors the interpretive ranger must help to reveal the mountains, streams, the Snake River, the vast sagebrush plains, the human history, and, of course, the wildlife that call the park home. The interpretive ranger should also foster the idea of stewardship to both the natural features of the park as well as human themes. Few visitors to Grand Teton National Park fail to appreciate the mountains and major features of the park, but if they do not, park interpreters are there to do their job. Introducing millions of visitors to the park's beauty and features is an important task, one that will enhance lives long after they have left the park. Not only will the visitor receive valuable educational information, but the hope is that the recipient may adopt new behaviors and even modify values.[1]

For many visitors, the first contact with Grand Teton National Park is through the visitor center. Grand Teton's first visitor center, actually built by the U.S. Forest Service in 1908 as a district ranger station, was modest indeed. Building #10, as it is called, located at Beaver Creek, provided a rudimentary introduction to the park. Certainly the staff answered questions, but by any standard the small log building was inadequate. The Mission 66 Visitor Center, completed in 1960, provided an immense improvement in both size and services. It also signaled the move of park headquarters from Beaver Creek to Moose. Certainly that visitor center was sufficient for a time, but as visitation figures exceeded four million the

Moose facility appeared to "shrink," especially as much of the square footage became devoted to NPS staff office space. The fur trade display seemed dated, space for the bookstore was limited, and when part of the roof collapsed in the winter of 1985–6, it seemed to signal the need for change.

It was time for not only a new structure, but as well, a different interpretive approach. Actually interpretation does not really change, but rather evolves with fresh objectives, techniques, and technologies. In the past a ranger station, such as at Beaver Creek, provided basic park information and services. While necessary, such an approach proved limiting. It stressed a one way street in which the interpretive ranger simply informed. We have all been on tours in which a guide droned on without concern for the listener's patience or interests. That would not be acceptable today at Grand Teton. The more current goal of the interpretive ranger, according to Victoria Mates, Chief of Interpretation, is "connecting people to place."[2] The staff also wishes to connect with the visitor, and that involves more than simply informing. To successfully connect the visitor to Grand Teton, the interpreter, whether in a visitor center or on the trail, must listen as well as talk. He/she must figure out why visitors come to the park, determining their expectations and their interests. [3]

At times the interpretive ranger simply cannot tell everything. He/she has a dual mission: to connect people to place but also to protect the resource. If the ranger knows the whereabouts of moose, he/she might not advertise that information to protect the moose and the general resource. These are delicate situations.[4] Of course the visitor should not be deceived, but knowledge can be tailored if it might harm the resource. Neither may the visitor be denied information for selfish reasons. As a fairly avid fly fisherman, I occasionally succumb to self-interest, providing general information on where to fish, but avoiding specifics. An interpretive ranger may do the same (but not for self-interest) providing the visitor with the general location of wolves, but denying the specific site of the pack's den. Again, it is the constant tension between the desire of the visitor to know and the need of the ranger to protect the resource.

Park planners recognize that the visitor center is often the guest's initial contact with Grand Teton. Some visitors judge their whole park experience based on interactions at the visitor center. The centers must have rangers on staff who can answer the most prosaic question without sarcasm and are also equal to handling more technical questions about mountain climbing, fishing, wildlife, cultural resources such as homesteads, or any number of other more scientific or cultural inquiries into such fields as geology, anthropology, or history. They must be prepared for questions on a wide assortment of topics, but also be able to craft an answer that is unique to the visitor's passions, interests and skill levels. Is this always possible? Probably not, but it is a challenging goal.

The center should introduce the central attractions of the park, and it must introduce caution or, in the

words of Superintendent Mary Gibson Scott, "it must teach safety." The public should be cautioned against foolish and dangerous behavior, whether with wild animals, fire, climbing, or river rafting. Yet the visitor center should not promote fear; it should be a prelude to getting outside and seeing the real thing. Thus communications professor Robert Bednar argues that there is a certain tension between "presenting to" and "protecting from" that is evident in all centers, whether their focus is sensitive landscapes, wildlife, artifacts, or significant structures.[5] For instance, the specific whereabouts of some cultural sites are not emphasized at a center nor are highway signs evident. There are no road directions to Hedrick's Point (one of the "inspiration points" of Grand Teton park), or to such cultural sites as the old Bar BC Ranch, the Lucas-Fabian Homestead, or even the Mormon Row Historic District. Why is this so? Often the visitors' enjoyment of such sites is in conflict with resource protection. I often think it unfortunate that tourists are not directed to some of my favorite spots in the park, but I also realize the conflict between the public's right to enjoy and the preservation of these resources for future generations.

THE CRAIG THOMAS DISCOVERY AND VISITOR CENTER

It was a bright, sparkling morning as some 600 people assembled to acknowledge a notable accomplishment: the completion and dedication of the Craig Thomas Discovery and Visitor Center. Assembled on the dais was a distinguished group, including Vice President Dick Cheney, Secretary of the Interior Dirk Kempthorne, NPS Director Mary Bomar, Wyoming Senator Mike Enzi, Susan Thomas (widow of the late Senator Craig Thomas), and, of course, Superintendent Mary Gibson Scott. On this day, August 7, 2007, the audience looked out on a dazzling building designed by the well-known architectural firm of Bohlin, Cywinski, and Jackson. It features rather traditional log and wood siding, but huge glass windows face to the west, showcasing the panorama of the Teton landscape. Enclosed by the U-shaped structure is a courtyard featuring granite rocks to entice children. Attached to the south wing of the structure is an auditorium, constructed later, that seats some 150 people plus four wheelchair spaces.

The theatre dwarfs what one finds at most park visitor centers and it serves the community as well as tourists. Deputy Chief of Interpretation Mike Nicklas books speakers and programs attracting a local audience. Experts on geology, history, or conservation have taken the lectern. One recent program featured Wellington "Buddy" Huffaker, Executive Director of the Aldo Leopold Foundation (Wisconsin), introducing and commenting on the exceptional film, *Green Fire: Aldo Leopold and a Land Ethic for Our Time.* Continuing on the environmental theme, the 2012 Grand Teton Film Festival brought conservation films to Jackson Hole, drawing the participation of both locals and park employees. Assistant Chief of Interpretation Mike Nicklas hopes the film series will become a yearly event.[6] In short, the auditorium gives the Park Service a facility within which to reach out to the community as well as park travelers.

The main exhibit room offers displays on wildlife, mountain climbing, settlement, and geology. These topics fall under the themes of "Place," "People," and "Preservation." Elaborating on theses themes are professionally designed, attractive displays on wildlife, geology, and mountain climbing. There is one particularly innovative feature that interests adults and enthralls children: the video river. On three separate areas of the floor screens project flowing rivers, alpine scenes, and wildlife views. They are eye-catching because they are horizontal, on the floor, rather than vertical, on a wall. In Nicklas' view they provide an "artistic expression of what we are trying to do." People enjoy watching one another's reactions. Some adults do not want to walk on this installation, fearing

THE DEDICATION OF THE THE CRAIG THOMAS DISCOVERY AND VISITOR CENTER, AUGUST 7, 2007

their weight may damage the screens and perhaps the moving scenes. Children often stomp on them, as if to test them, and the more pacific kids lie down, as if to swim on the flowing water. Reactions differ. My older brother was fascinated, remarking that he might come back to the visitor center just to view the video streams again. The thought that kept going through my head was: Is this education or entertainment? I readily acknowledge that it can be both. What was all this technology accomplishing, and did it serve the Park Service's educational mission?

Nicklas was closely involved in the decision to install them. They cost $700,000, almost half of the $1.5 million budget for interpretation.[7] However, as I was soon informed, this funding did not come from taxpayers' dollars, but rather from the funds of the

Grand Teton National Park Foundation and the Grand Teton Association. Each video stream contains three computers and three cameras, for a total of nine each. Hardly ever have all three "rivers" worked properly. However, their reliability has improved. I wondered whether they would be functioning ten years from now, but Leslie Mattson, Executive Director of the GTNP Foundation, assured me that they would, for the foundation has endowed the video streams.[8]

However, sometimes old interpretation styles win the popularity contest. Next to the video streams are patches of deer, elk, bear, and antelope hair. Nicklas informs me that the tactile experience of stroking the hair or fur on these patches is the most popular interactive display in the center for both children and adults. Second place went to a pile of elk and deer antlers and bighorn sheep horns that could provoke some creative play.[9]

The idea for this exceptional visitor center came from Superintendent Jack Neckels. By the mid-1990s he saw the need, and he was determined to raise the money. Clearly it could not be raised quickly through federal grants or the regular park budget. Private contributions would be necessary. The GT Association provided the first $100,000 to create the GTNP Foundation. The foundation, founded in 1997 by a few wealthy, committed Jackson Hole residents, was wildly successful in raising millions of dollars for the visitor center. The site for the new center, however, proved contentious. Superintendent Neckels had in mind a spot on a bluff on the east side of the Snake River, just south of the intersection of the Jackson Hole Highway and the Moose Road. It would be very visible. Local people wanted a less conspicuous location, however, and the Jackson Hole Conservation Alliance was prepared to go to court over the issue. They believed that the location should be discrete and the design traditional, in keeping with natural surroundings. The new visitor center should complement the natural environment—never overshadow it.

The project bogged down, and at his retirement in 2003, Neckels had not seen his dream started, let alone completed.[10] Meanwhile, the Foundation continued its efforts, and it was through their dedication that the project ultimately materialized. The GTNPF contributed over $12 million, while the GTA donated $1.5 million. Senator Craig Thomas shepherded legislation through Congress to make up the final $8 million to complete funding for the project.

Some have questioned whether this edifice is simply too large, elaborate, and less "green" than many would like. Of course, visitor centers will often be controversial, reflecting personal choice between "maximalist" and "minimalist" views. Speaking in general of visitor centers, retired NPS leader Dwight Rettie suggests that visitor centers "are afforded a level of significance higher than they naturally deserve." In his view, "they are also often larger than they need to be and are often sited in bad locations only because someone wants them to be more visible."[11] The Grand Teton park planners successfully

THE CRAIG THOMAS DISCOVERY AND VISITOR CENTER

resolved the site issue by placing the center on low land just west of the Snake River. However, one wonders if $8 million would have been sufficient for a visitor center to meet the needs of the park? Probably the answer is no and yet isn't the whole 310,000-acre park itself a "visitor center"? The spectacular vistas on the inner road and at Jenny Lake speak to tourists more strongly than any display at the center ever will. There is a minimalist argument to be made in scenic parks. A few interpretive displays, trails, and restorations (of historic buildings) may be all that is necessary to fully appreciate the park's features. In some parks and monuments, however, a visitor center is absolutely necessary. Some 15 years ago a friend and I visited Fossil Buttes National Monument in Southwest Wyoming. The location is unimpressive,

and the surrounding hills are easily forgotten. There is nothing that especially attracts the eye. The key aspect of interest was not immediately evident. But when we entered the visitor center, built at $5 million, we understood the significance of the place. For us, the visitor center was the attraction. How exciting to wander through the center and realize that the whole region had once been an inland sea, as was evident from the three hundred fossils on display.

At Grand Teton, one's appreciation should not begin and end indoors. The visitor center should urge and inspire the visitor to get outside—hike the trails, search for wildlife, explore an old homestead, or raft the river. There are daily programs which encourage a close encounter with nature. The interpretive staff are out in the park each day, interacting with visitors on trails, pathways, roads and the scenic overlooks, sharing nature knowledge and stories. These are the experiences visitors will remember best and from which they learn the most—the classic paradox of interpretive facilities. Being outside, at the sites, with the elements at play always surpasses the "inside virtual," because it is real. The mountains speak to us in a way no building can. Rivers, elk, bears, moose, and flora all converse in a myriad of different ways. Grand Teton National Park, from the moment a visitor crosses the boundary, educates us in so many ways if we are listening and watching. Books, lectures, and exhibits can enrich what we take in and how we understand it, and travelers who do justice to both indoor and outdoor components come away from the park with a whole new appreciation and knowledge of nature.

COLTER BAY AND JENNY LAKE

The Colter Bay Visitor Center serves the traveling needs and curiosity of those staying at such facilities as the Jackson Lake Lodge or the extensive campground at Colter Bay and Lizard Creek. Like the visitor center at Moose, the Colter Bay facility is also a Mission 66 building, one of the thousands of inexpensive structures thrown up to serve the vacationing crowds following World War II. The interior has been renovated and is less significant in square feet but in a sense the visitor center has moved outside with attractive views where rangers and visitors alike

enjoy the natural environment. The unique feature of the Colter Bay Visitor Center has been the outstanding Indian artifacts of the David T. Vernon collection. Park curators removed all 1400 of the artifacts in 2005 and 2011 for conservation treatment. Now they have returned in much better condition and 46 items are displayed in the Craig Thomas Discovery & Visitor Center at Moose, while an additional 34 items are at Colter Bay. The remaining collection is in storage awaiting a permanent home.

At the moment the downsized Colter Bay Visitor Center Visitor Services Plan stresses the advantages of the outside environment. With Jackson Lake practically washing the shores of the visitor center and with trails emanating out from it, rangers and visitors can take full advantage of nature experiences free of walls.[12]

THE HISTORIC HARRISON CRANDALL STUDIO TODAY HOUSES THE JENNY LAKE VISITOR CENTER.

At Colter Bay outside space will provide experiences and knowledge that inside space never could.

To the south is the small and charming Jenny Lake Visitor Center, once the studio of Harrison Crandall, the pioneer photographer of the Tetons. Moved twice but now perched beside the wide Jenny Lake parking lot, the diminutive cabin represents a throwback to an earlier era. It welcomes visitors and encourages visitors to participate either on a ranger-led walk or on their own, enjoying the remarkable natural beauty of the area. Close by is the Jenny Lake Ranger Station, a place for climbers to plan, get permits, and check weather conditions on the mountain.

LAURANCE S. ROCKEFELLER PRESERVE

A recent addition to the park's suite of interpretive hubs is the Laurance S. Rockefeller Preserve, featuring the "first platinum-level, LEED certified visitor center in the National Park System."[13] In November, 2007, Superintendent Mary Gibson Scott announced that the Laurance Rockefeller Preserve—likely the most valuable gift to the NPS—had been conveyed to the federal government, "a remarkable generous gift from Laurance S. Rockefeller to the citizens of the United States and the world."[14] The official dedication came in June, 2008. In the past few years the preserve has become extremely popular and is a favorite place for local people to bring guests. The stunning visitor facility is out of the way, located down the narrow, twisting Moose-Wilson Road. Its purpose is to put visitors in touch with nature in a quiet and spiritual way. This interaction is aided by interpretive rangers in the building or on the trails, which reach to Phelps Lake and on to the cliffs of Death Canyon.

The actual building, designed by Jackson architect John Carney, is quite modest. A cozy reading room offers a small library of books on the park and a few environmental classics. It is easy to spend an hour curled up on a chair. A circular second room features benches and four large vertical screens, perhaps five feet high, where projectors display nature scenes from the park—flora and fauna, summer water to winter snow. The only sounds are natural sounds—gurgling streams, birds calling, and animals declaring their presence. Only adults were attending the multi-screen displays when my brother and I watched; small children with big voices belong elsewhere. The final room, round, small and hidden away, features

Photo by Nic Lehoux Carney Architects

LAURANCE S. ROCKEFELLER PRESERVE VISITOR CENTER INTERIOR

Photo by Nic Lehoux-Carney Architects

LAURANCE S. ROCKEFELLER PRESERVE VISITOR CENTER

gentle, soothing nature sounds recorded on the preserve over time. It is a place of meditation, aimed at quieting the mind, a sound sanctuary with a special feeling, gently calling for solitude.

Outside, a nine mile trail system leads up the hillside, and if you continue to follow the trails they converge on the shores of Phelps Lake. This is the site of the old JY Ranch and more recently the Rockefeller family retreat. Small cabins formerly ringed the eastern edge of the lake. When Laurance Rockefeller deeded the last 1,106 acres of land to the National Park Service, many urged that the well-kept cabins remain to become some sort of retreat center. However, Laurance had an epiphany that his father

would want the land returned to a natural state, and that is what happened. In a "Memorandum of Understanding" signed on February 1, 2001, by Laurance and Robert Stanton, NPS Director, the Service agreed to accept the land, "including all restoration, trails, interpretive elements and capital improvements envisioned by the Plan." [15] Thus, one of the valley's most important historic sites was disassembled and the buildings moved elsewhere. Some might disagree with Laurance's choice, but all would agree that the donation—which included an endowment fund to provide for maintenance—of the JY Ranch to the park represented another wonderful gift, given some 80 years after the Rockefeller family first

PEAKS, POLITICS, AND PASSION: GRAND TETON NATIONAL PARK COMES OF AGE

embarked upon land acquisitions which has made the park what it is today.

In designing this center to focus on a meditative and spiritual experience, planners purposely kept the parking lot small, holding perhaps 50 cars. Often during the summer months there is not sufficient parking space, and people must wait for a space, come back another time, or skip the preserve. Why so little parking? The answer is simple. Unlimited parking delivering hordes of people would diminish or destroy the peaceful ambiance of the preserve: in selected places, quantity must be limited to ensure quality.

Those visitors who successfully drop in on the preserve are delighted with the experience, often leaving in a different frame of mind than when they came. I looked at a loose-leaf folder which invited the comments of visitors in the summer of 2012. Of course we would not expect that people unsatisfied with the center would comment, yet the written comments were so uniformly ardent that one has to assume that the center is accomplishing its purpose. Some visitors simply left one word impressions, such as "beautiful," "awesome," or "fabulous." Other comments had a touch of humor and irony: "Wish Detroit was more like this place!" and "Where are the lions?" There are many thoughtful, indeed religious comments. A couple of observations were meaningful to me, including: "Stunning—in a career of more than 35 years with the NPS and visits to scores and scores of visitor centers, I've never been to one so simple, direct, powerful, spiritual, and effective. Thank you, LSR." And one other

observation: "Astonishingly beautiful! One of the finest interpretive centers I have ever seen—amazing imagery, clear architecture, and a well-stocked library, all served to enhance the experience." Of course the designers hope that the interpretive themes will appeal to youth. Ranger interpreters would take heart from a teacher's comment: "Today I introduced 10 inner-city L. A. [high school] seniors—very bright, curious students of science—to the LSR, and we're spending a couple of hours here, seeing, listening, absorbing, reflecting, and writing. I wish Laurance could have met these kids. I believe they'll get the message, and hopefully share it throughout their lives."[16]

NATURE WALKS AND CAMPFIRE TALKS

Inquire at any visitor center or glance at the Grand Teton newspaper handout, and a multitude of activities led by interpretive park rangers is apparent. People who want to understand a particular aspect of the park can sign up for ranger-led walks that may focus on nature, culture, or history. Also, in an effort to meet visitors, interpreters may be found on popular trails, overlooks, and even parking lots. These outings and efforts stretch the park's budget, but a good walk or hike is worth the effort, both for the tourist and in terms of NPS educational outreach. Unfortunately, visitors taking the opportunity to do this are on the decline. Some have not apportioned time for an educational stroll; others note the limited

attention span of their children. Others prefer a self-directed learning experience. Whatever the reasons, small group interactive education through participation on ranger-led walks has decreased. Grand Teton National Park outreach increasingly relies on the visitor centers, handouts, and wayside signs, although the staff certainly offers a personal touch and specific answers to questions.

Most people whose parents took them camping in the national parks as youngsters remember the traditional campfire circle: the warming fire and a ranger perhaps leading a song or two before giving an informative talk that the whole family could enjoy. This scenario is not so common today, often modified during times of fire danger. Ranger talks usually take place with a PowerPoint presentation on fire, wildlife, climate change, history, or other topics. Talks take

place regularly at Gros Ventre, Jenny Lake, Signal Mountain, Colter Bay, Lizard Creek, and Flagg Ranch campgrounds. Some of these campgrounds are now managed by concessionaires, but the campfire talks are still organized and given by the NPS interpretive rangers. Mike Nicklas, who coordinates the programs, sees the technological bells and whistles as supplementary. The talk, somewhere between a lecture and a chat, should stand on its own, and the media should never outshine the message.[17]

In spite of efforts to modernize the campfire programs, attendance has dropped precipitously. In the 1980s and 1990s, according to Jenny Lake District Interpreter Andrew Langford, rangers could expect huge numbers with all seats taken. Ranger Langford provided recent statistics showing that between 2003 and 2012, attendance at the northern campground's evening programs had fallen from 33,659 to 18,870. Projections show a continuing downward trend.[18] There are many theories for this slide. We know that family camping numbers are declining. Langford theorizes that among those who do still camp, some spend evenings watching TV or videos in their recreational vehicle. Kids are not urging parents to get out to the park programs, and neither are parents urging kids. The information factor in the campfire talk seems to be a casualty of the electronic age.

Partnering For the Park

Earlier in this book I mentioned that Grand Teton National Park was certainly an impoverished place in the early 1960s. The park lacked facilities, but more importantly, cooperating partners. The Jackson Hole Preserve, Inc., continued to support the park in many ways, but after 1960 its commitment did not often extend to visitor services. Aside from the Grand Teton Association, created in 1937, the park had no other supporters who could assist in educational programs, visitor services, fund-raising campaigns, scientific research and a host of other activities. Consequently, beyond federal funding, the park had few other revenues.

The situation has changed. All supporting partners have certain qualities in common: love of the park, a commitment to philanthropy and a willingness to give of their time. Certainly Grand Teton had benefitted greatly from philanthropy: In fact it can be argued that without truly generous donors and supporters the park would not exist. However, by the 1960s it became apparent Grand Teton needed partner groups as well as individuals who were committed to improving the park and providing the resources to make that happen. The Service could not do it alone. It needed contemporaries who shared a common goal.

There is another class of partners, one with a closer association with the park administration. These non-profit organizations support the mission of the park in presenting educational programs and, most significantly, raising funds and accepting donations on behalf of the Service.[19] Some, such as the Grand Teton Association are housed at the main administration building in Moose. They help the park accomplish its mission and are committed to long-term stewardship. In many respects they are a main reason that Grand Teton National Park has moved from a park of outstanding scenery to one of outstanding interpretation and educational opportunity.

Grand Teton Association

The Grand Teton Association has been active in the park for over 75 years. Established in 1937, well before the 1950 Act, the association (then called the Grand Teton Natural History Association and before that the Jackson Hole Museum and Historical Association) provided the structure to disseminate educational and interpretive materials as the park's Cooperating Association: one of many throughout the National Park System and other federal agencies. The association manages the bookstores connected with the visitor centers and reaches beyond the park with educational merchandise at the Jackson Hole and Greater Yellowstone Visitor Center and a shop at the Jackson Hole Airport. The association also runs the small, quaint store associated with the historic Menor's Ferry, the only living history exhibit in the park. Underscoring its historic roots, the store features only items that could have been sold during the time period of 1890 to 1918. The Association has been a mainstay of support for the Park, and Jan Lynch is only the third director in its lengthy history.

THE ASSOCIATION'S WELL-STOCKED BOOKSTORE.

With exposure to thousands of people who want to know more about the park, or perhaps take a book or an item of remembrance home, the Grand Teton Association is a profitable enterprise. However, lest anyone suppose Executive Director Jan Lynch and her staff profit handsomely, be advised that the association is a nonprofit partner with the Park Service: "When you make a purchase from our park bookstores, you are supporting the educational, interpretive, and scientific programs in Grand Teton National Park."[20] Much of the profit is used to finance new publications or assist the National Park Service in its mission. Like the foundation, the association is a very committed partner to the park. Although the Foundation raised the lion's share of the construction costs of the Craig Thomas Discovery & Visitor Center, the Association's contribution of $1.5 is not an inconsiderable amount.

The Association board has also funded a number of scientific and conservation projects that would not otherwise become reality. The Association publishes park-related educational material. It is a key partner in interpreting and fostering the connection of art to the Park and to conservation in general. In 2012 it sponsored the first annual Plein Air for the Park gathering, bringing a number of regional artists to Grand Teton and then exhibiting and selling their art with a portion of the proceeds to go to the Park. Last year was the first, but it will surely not be the last artist get-together! Perhaps not so evident, the Association provides funding for ranger interns to staff the visitor centers during the busy summer months. Superintendent Scott is particularly fond of the Association board because when she meets with them, they ask "what do you need," and then do the best they can to provide it.[21]

Occasionally the Association sponsors other kinds of projects, such as the Boyd Evison Graduate Fellowship. Evison was a superb ranger, superintendent, Regional Director and biologist with a broad perspective.[22] When he retired, he moved to Jackson and this park visionary was soon asked to run the Association. Regrettably within two years, in 2002, he was struck down with cancer. The Association established the fellowship in his memory, providing up to a $10,000 stipend for a graduate student to conduct new research related to the greater Yellowstone ecosystem. The Evison family is still involved in the selection of the research projects.

GRAND TETON NATIONAL PARK FOUNDATION

The Grand Teton National Park Foundation is a strong financial partner for the park. One of the hundreds of foundations supporting parks, monuments, and recreational areas throughout the nation, this one is notable in being among the top fundraisers working within the NPS. Only foundations in Yellowstone, Grand Canyon, Yosemite, Gettysburg, Golden Gate, and Cuyahoga Valley can claim comparable funding achievements. Since its establishment in 1997, the Grand Teton National Park Foundation has contributed more than $25 million to a host of projects within the park. How do they do it? President Leslie Mattson points out that the park is loved not just in the valley but by people across the land. She notes that they "care deeply about Grand Teton and a trip to Wyoming is their ultimate escape, the place where they can truly catch their breath before tackling life again."[23] Leslie Mattson is a gifted fundraiser, and monetary miracles happen with such a positive, committed, and enthusiastic person at the helm. When the Foundation board chooses new members, the highest priority is a love of and commitment to the park. Second is the ability to respond when financially challenged to raise funds to support projects. Fundraising can be an onerous task, but the foundation makes it look easy.

Supported projects represent the needs and wishes of park officials combined with the resources of the Foundation. Some projects are large, such as the Craig Thomas Discovery and Visitor Center, while some are small, such as the bear box project. The Foundation has placed many bear-proof storage boxes in campsites, very likely saving foraging bears from becoming attracted to human food and possibly being removed. Only about 20 percent of established campsites feature bear boxes, but that number is rising. When a friend of mine lost his wife in 2011, another friend donated a box in her name, a satisfying and useful way to remember a woman who loved the park.

Another foundation project, still in the planning stage in 2012, focuses on the visitor experience at the

Jenny Lake area. Kim Mills, who works for the Foundation, explained that in honor of the 100th Anniversary of the NPS in 2016 the Foundation will provide the financial support for the park to transform this popular destination. The $16 million restoration of trails, bridges and interpretive exhibits will begin at the South Jenny Lake area and continue around the south shore to Hidden Falls and Inspiration Point. The intent is to improve the trails and provide wayside displays that provide visitors the tools they need to explore the area as well as explain the area's geology and importance in conservation history. The same design team that created the inviting Laurance S. Rockefeller Preserve will provide detailed plans for the Jenny Lake project.[24] In her recent visit, Secretary of the Interior Sally Jewell praised the project as well as the community and the foundation: "This community really sets a very high bar for everyone across the country for what can be done when the private community works with the public sector."[25] Further foundation-sponsored projects, particularly those encouraging young people to enjoy and understand their natural heritage, are described in chapter 9.[26]

Of course no good deed goes without criticism, especially in Grand Teton. Financial restraints limit the growth in facilities and services of all national parks and monuments. The GTNPF, by its remarkable fund raising ability, has—to a degree—offset such fiscal limitations. Critics, however, question the need to which the money is put. Some detractors doubted the need for the elaborate visitor center. Did the center's size, architecture and technological bells and whistles highlight the accomplishments of men, rather than the beauty and majesty of the park? And what of the Foundation's Jenny Lake project? It is expected to cost $16 million, of which some 80 percent will be provided by the Foundation. Will the "transformation" of the Jenny Lake area enhance the visitor's experience or just his/her convenience? One critic of the plan is historian Alfred Runte, author of a classic book on the national parks.[27] Runte criticizes the foundation and the park's inclination to over develop and enter into partnerships which leave Grand Teton "virtually run by locals."[28] Runte's conclusion is debatable, but the point is that while the GTNPF in its short life has an enviable record of park support, there will always be questions of just what is needed.

UW–NPS Research Center

The AMK Ranch, the location of the UW-NPS Research Center, has a rich history, as described in chapter 2. In 1956 the park and the University of Wyoming signed an agreement whereby the university established a field research center to study biological, physical, and social science topics related to Yellowstone and Grand Teton and the adjoining national forests. Researchers come for periods of a week to three months, living in cabins surrounding the old Johnson house. The arrangement has worked well,

AMK Ranch

according to former Director Hank Harlow, a professor of biology at the University's Laramie campus.

The UW-NPS Research Center is a particularly active place in the summer, not only for the ongoing research but because Harlow and his staff made a concerted effort to reach out to the local community. Every Thursday evening the seminar series features a speaker, often a researcher in residence, describing a particular area of knowledge or aspect under study. The talks are wide-ranging and popular. As if presentations in this delightful setting overlooking Jackson Lake were not inviting enough, the University of Wyoming staff provide a five-dollar hamburger dinner with all the trimmings. It is not quite like Dornan's, but you can expect to meet friends and interesting people at the weekly event.

One ought not assume that the AMK's hallmark is hamburgers and conversation. It performs needed scientific work for the park. In 2010 the park and the University of Wyoming signed a new 10-year agreement for the management and upkeep of the place. The way it works is that NPS Chief of Science of Resource Management Sue Consolo-Murphy submits a "needs list" of scientific projects and Director Hank Harlow does his best to fill it. The projects are wide-ranging. The 2011 Annual Report revealed that researchers came from the University of Wisconsin, University of Iowa, University of Alaska, Fairbanks, New Mexico State University, Montana State University, and, of course, the University of Wyoming. Furthermore, the AMK facilities offer a home for a number of community college and university short courses. There was a time in the 1980s and 1990s when park administrators thought of ending the UW program and turning the facility into summer employee housing, but today the research center is on a firm footing and the park values the results and the relationship. The UW-NPS partnership represents another successful wedding of interests guaranteed to thrive for many years.[29]

MURIE CENTER

The Murie Ranch is about a mile south of park headquarters at Moose. Although close by, it seems far away as one drives the washboard gravel road to the place. Originally named the STS Ranch, it was homesteaded by pioneers Buster and Frances Estes, who proved up in 1927 and established a popular dude ranch. That was the same year that Olaus and Margaret (Mardy) Murie arrived in Jackson Hole, Olaus as director of the National Elk Refuge. By 1945 Buster Estes was tired of dude ranching and sold the place to his friends Olaus and Mardy Murie and Olaus's brother Adolph Murie and his wife Louise. The ranch became the gathering place and hub of activity for many local friends as well as wildlife biologists of national stature.

The fame of the ranch increased with the Muries' reputation, particularly for their path breaking wildlife studies. As earlier mentioned (chapter 5) Olaus studied the numbers and movements of caribou while Adolph focused on the wolves of Mt. Mckinley National Park. Both the brothers studied the habits and ways of survival of coyotes in Yellowstone National Park. Their work revised, indeed revolutionized, the thinking of wildlife biologists with regard to predators and their prey.

Just as important at the ranch were the many discussions regarding wilderness legislation. Council meetings of the Wilderness Society convened at the ranch in 1949 and 1955. Ideas of the Wilderness Act of 1964 were hammered out along the ranch's meandering trails and river bank. Such well-known conservationists as Howard Zahniser, Bob Marshall, Sigurd Olson, and William O. Douglas visited the Murie place. Unfortunately, Olaus died in 1963, a year before the passage of the Wilderness Act, for which he had fought so hard. Mardy carried on, not only filling her husband's shoes but creating her own legend as a national environmental leader and proponent of the Alaska Lands Conservation Act of 1980. Her home was always open to all kinds of conservationists, students, and wilderness advocates.[30] Mardy died in 2003, after more than eighty years of service to the environment. In February 2006 the Murie Ranch was designated a National Historic Landmark, a distinct honor and one of only two such sites in Grand Teton National Park.[31]

Since 1966 Grand Teton National Park has owned the land and buildings of the Murie Ranch Historic District, partnering with the Murie Center, a nonprofit organization administered by its own board of directors. The Murie Center has sponsored a number of groups and individuals in its mission to have persons "commit to the enduring values of conserving wildlife and wild places." Perhaps the most exciting project has been hosting inner-city students from New York and other cities, exposing them to wilderness immersion in a program called Murie Kids Week. The Teton Science School works with the Murie Center, and the students have benefitted from the natural environment and interaction with the knowledgeable staff. This program is ongoing, and the hope is that participants will become ambassadors connecting other urban kids with nature.

The Murie family was legendary in the valley and in the nation for their commitment to nature and wilderness. The Murie Center reminds us of their legacy and carries on their work in partnership with Grand Teton National Park. Environmental journalist Todd Wilkinson recalls that not so long ago, local people "accused the Muries and their circle of friends of being extremists, socialists and communists, and insisted their beliefs would destroy the valley."[32] The accusers, of course, were flat wrong. The Muries and their friends were dedicated to saving northern Jackson Hole, leading the fight to establish the park we know today. The center underscores how Grand Teton National Park came into being through the thoughtful design and unending activism of the Muries and others.

THE TETON SCIENCE SCHOOLS

The traveling vans of the Teton Science Schools are often parked in curious places, but if you look closely, you can usually see kids huddled around their instructor somewhere nearby. They are learning about the natural environment and the park is their laboratory.

The school reflects the inspiration and commitment of founder Ted Major, who established it in 1967, occupying the cabins of Katie Starratt's Elbo Ranch on Ditch Creek. He had a vision of the park and the school working together to offer a unique educational experience for children and young adults.

After some rather hard times, the Teton Science Schools have emerged as a real force for nature. Children, clustered about their instructor, learn not only about the science of ecology but also something of the environmental ethics of the Muries, Aldo Leopold, John Muir, and Henry David Thoreau. These Science Schools students represent a hopeful future. Between 1988 and 2013 Jack Shea directed the many programs. A dynamic leader, Shea expanded the school's mission to general education for elementary and secondary school students.[33] The Journeys School, located just west of Jackson, complements and broadens the mission of the original Science Schools.

The Teton Science Schools offers programs for adults as well. Friends of mine enjoyed a morning of identifying and banding birds. In the fall people can sign up for "an evening with the elk." Watching bugling elk and their harems with a Teton Science Schools naturalist guide who knows elk and their habitat is a rewarding experience. Some outings incorporate Yellowstone National Park, like a trip to the Lamar Valley to view wolves. The Teton Science School also sponsors programs that train instructors. In the summer of 2012, for instance, the school hosted twenty AmeriCorps university students. The group represented 15 colleges and universities with the students majoring in a variety of science disciplines. They joined field instructors to teach courses in Jackson Hole and elsewhere in Wyoming and Idaho. Another creative program weds two Science School staff with a University of Wyoming professor to travel to state schools to review energy production, use, and conservation in their respective communities.[34] Not all these programs take place in Grand Teton National Park, but they certainly enhance its mission.

VOLUNTEERS IN THE PARK

In 2010 Grand Teton's VIP (Volunteers in Parks) program utilized 2,309 volunteers who logged 35,503 hours of work for the park.[35] These statistics are quite representative of the popular ethic of service that is sweeping the country. Americans seem particularly eager to support the cause of conservation in its many forms.[36] There are many reasons for such enthusiasm, including the willingness of Grand Teton to embrace and encourage those individual people who want to give to an organization and a place they love. Park volunteers must be given encouragement and the tools to do the job. The park has been willing to make the investment.

Volunteers have made a significant difference in maintaining the attractions of the park. Perhaps the most evident has been with cultural resources. I have

written a good deal about the crucial participation of volunteers in cleaning up, stabilizing, and even restoring historic structures in chapter 6. Without the participation of locals, teachers from Michigan and Wisconsin, and various people from around the country the park could not afford to restore and maintain buildings in Mormon Row, the Bar BC, or the Geraldine Lucas homestead. These volunteers love the park, enjoy working outdoors in cool temperatures, and are inspired by the magnificent scenery. In my experience, I also found they took great pride in cooperative accomplishments. Without their help removing junk piles, repairing roofs, and pounding nails, the park staff could not maintain and interpret the past nearly as well as they do.

Park volunteers perform many duties—too many to describe. One of the most important is the backcountry volunteers. This dedicated group (usually about 14 in an average summer) are the eyes and ears of the rangers, providing needed information. Penny Maldonado, a backcountry volunteer for a number of years, says that they "report on trail conditions, weather conditions, hazards, potential or evolving visitor issues, predator activities, and needed cache supplies which we also courier for them [the rangers]." They often spend over 20 hours a week in the mountains. Penny notes that this is a lot of time, but she has felt privileged to do it. She notes that "there are just two things that make work, whether paid or volunteer, satisfying. The first is to be doing something you believe in and the second is to have someone believe in what you do." She admires the dedication of the Jenny Lake Rangers and is proud to be an "'adjunct" to their work.[37]

She admits to two satisfactions in her volunteer work, and they are certainly ones that any Grand Teton volunteer enjoys. First is the pleasure of the place, particularly the isolation of the mountains as well as the serenity and quiet that the mountains offer. Second, the satisfaction of working in partnership with the park staff, whether resolving the chaos of the lower Cascade Canyon trail, or protecting the resource by asking visitors to do the right thing. To accomplish this goal, the volunteer must use education and persuasion rather than punitive options which might be available to a commissioned Ranger. At times it can be a thankless job, but the many satisfactions seem to dull any hardships.

There are other volunteer groups that help the park accomplish its mission. One such group with an intriguing label is the "Wildlife Brigade." The Brigade, established in 2008 and unique to GTNP, consists of volunteers who manage the crowds that quickly assemble when there is a bear siting. In a situation where near traffic chaos seems to reign, the Brigade will manage such wildlife "jams" in such a way as to protect both humans and the bruins. Besides safety the Brigade assists visitors by education about food and its proper storage. Their work no doubt prevents encounters between humans and wildlife that could be disastrous.

CONTRACTS

There are, of course, a number of companies that have concession contracts with the park. Often there is friction between the concessionaire and the park. A number of national park observers have noted the hazards involved. Dwight Rettis, a retired National Park Service official and author, fears connection of the parks with commercial interests. He notes that "businesses rarely donate money to anyone or anything without the expectation that they are getting something tangible for their money." That "something," as Rettie puts it, "need not be put in writing or even conveyed verbally." It is far more subtle, and should be seen as a "creeping menace."[38]

I found no "creeping menaces" among Grand Teton park's concessionaires. They offer legitimate services that are in line with the park's recreational and educational objectives, although they do operate for profit on park land. Some directly provide recreational services for the visitor, such as the Barker/Ewing Raft Company, or the Westbank Angler fishing guides. Dude ranches such as the Triangle X Ranch or the Moosehead Ranch (privately owned) make available needed services. The Jackson Lake Lodge and the Jenny Lake Lodge also represent concessionaires who offer food and lodging. These concessionaires represent businesses who, hopefully, will be able to make enough profit to stay in business. It is one of the tasks of the NPS (and the administrators at Grand Teton) to see that they do prosper without violating legal or ethical standards and hopefully do not "reflect adversely on the NPS mission and image."[39] It goes without saying, that the park does not accept all businesses which apply.

Perhaps the most out of the ordinary and historic concessionaire is the Exum Climbing School, created by Paul Petzoldt and Glenn Exum. Back in 1917 Horace Albright had declared mountain climbing an activity in keeping with NPS goals. Paul Petzoldt began climbing in the range in the 1920s, and soon Glenn Exum joined him. By 1925 they began to guide clients. Their first company, the Petzoldt-Exum School of American Mountaineering, evolved into the Exum Mountain Guides, which has an unmatched reputation for getting clients up and down the mountain safely. Clients must learn basic climbing skills and have the required strength before they attempt any ascents. This is surely fundamental to the school and fits well into the park's philosophy of safety and education.[40]

At the Exum school the relationship with the Park Service is spelled out in a contract. Contracts are negotiated with all the companies providing services, entertainment or education for visitors. At the Moose headquarters I spent some time with Karen Gordon Bergsma, former park concession asset manager or, as I called her, keeper of the contracts. She informed me that a typical contract is for 15 years and specifies the service, the standards expected, and the franchise fee to be paid to the park. Fees are usually set for the length of the contract but can be reconsidered if things do not go well. Some contracts are "Washington Level," meaning they are negotiated by the Washington office, while the day-to-day management is administered by park staff.[41]

A typical contract looks like that for the Lost Creek Ranch, an upscale dude ranch sandwiched between Grand Teton National Park and the Bridger-Teton National Forest. Although the Lost Creek Ranch is private property, its staff uses the park regularly for river rafting on the nearby Snake River, day fishing trips, and horseback riding. For that privilege the ranch has a ten-year contract (2010–19) and pays a franchise fee of 3 percent of gross income up to $250,000 or a flat fee of $500, whichever is greater. The contract notes how many rafts or boats Lost Creek may launch and from what location (usually Pacific Creek or Deadman's Bar). All the raft oarsmen and fishing guides must have Red Cross and CPR training. They must be trained on the river section they will guide. The operating contract goes into some detail on equipment available on the raft or boat. Visitors must pay the park entrance fee if they have not already done so. A few of the regulations seem unnecessary—for example, Lost Creek ice chests must be at 41 degrees or cooler. Karen said food regulations are set by the Public Health Service. I asked if they ever checked. She did not know.[42]

Besides contracts, the concession manager also issues permits. Permits are for a shorter duration, often with set fees determined by the Washington office. If, for instance, I embarked on a guide service for historical tours of the park, and if I advertised and

RAFTING IN RHE PARK IS POPULAR WITH VISITORS. THE DIFFERENT RAFTING COMPANIES ALL HAVE CONTRACTS WITH THE PARK.

hoped to make money on the venture, I would need a permit. This would likewise hold true for a geology or a nature tour. If the tour is regularly scheduled and is a moneymaking service, the business must have a permit to operate in the park. Karen noted that the Business Resources Office seeks to work with the concessioners, serve the visitor, and, of course, preserve the resource. As is often the case, the objective is balance.

TO JUDGE HOW WELL THE PARK SERVICE is meeting visitors' needs, each year the NPS contracts with an independent firm to survey a sample of visitors and see what they think of their stay. I glanced through an archives carton containing survey results from 1996 to 2009. Among the responses that caught my eye was one remarking that "geysers and hot springs" represent the significance of Grand Teton National Park; a comment from a slightly confused visitor. [43]

Most responses were more thoughtful. Asked the objective of the park, one person answered:

"Preserving nature as close as possible to what it was before man—should be kept for everyone to enjoy and learn." Perhaps that visitor understood that concept before visiting the park, but it is likely that the visitor centers and all the outreach in the park fortified the idea. Overall the park received high marks. The survey for 2000 was typical: a healthy 71 percent of respondents considered the overall quality of the facilities, services, and recreational experiences very good, while 28 percent rated them good. That comes to 99 percent satisfied with their stay; we might assume many visitors will return. Through the determination of the Grand Teton National Park staff and its unswerving partners, the park's interpretive mission is on course now and for the future.

1 This paragraph somewhat paraphrases the interpretive goals laid out in NPS, *Management Policies, 2006*, 7.1, p. 90.

2 Interiew with Victoria Mates, Chief of Interpretation, Grand Teton, by author, January 30, 2013.s

3 Ibid.

4 Ibid.

5 Robert M. Bednar, "Being Here, Looking There," in *Observation Points: The Visual Poetics of National Parks*, ed. Thomas Patin (Minneapolis: University of Minnesota Press: 2012), 9.

6 Ranger Mike Nicklas, Assistant Chief of Interpretation, interview by author, January 23, 2012.

7 The video rivers display as well as other interpretive exhibits were funded by the GTNP Foundation and the GT Association, thus the park budget was not used. However, one can argue that the Foundation and the Association might have funded other projects in lieu of the "rivers."

8 Leslie Mattson, Executive Director, Grand Teton National Park Foundation, interview by author, October 1, 2012.

9 Mike Nicklas, conversation on a walk-through of the Craig Thomas Discovery & Visitor Center, July 12, 2012.

10 Superintendent Neckels did have the satisfaction of attending the 2007 dedication ceremony.

11 Dwight Rettie, *Our National Park System* (Urbana: University of Illinois Press, 1995), 111.

12 Discussions with Victoria Mates, Chief of Interpretion, GTNP.

13 See message from Superintendent Mary Gibson Scott, *Teton Stewards* (Newsletter of the Grand Teton National Park Foundation), Fall–Winter 2008–9, 7.

14 Real Estate insert in the *Jackson Hole News and Guide*, December 19, 2007.

15 "Memorandum of Understanding," on the LSR, dated February 1, 2001. On file, GTNP.

16 All comments from summer, 2012, in a loose leaf binder at the LSR Reserve

17 Ranger Mike Nicklas, Assistant Chief of Interpretation, interview by author, January 23, 2012.

18 Ranger Andrew Langford, Jenny Lake District Interpreter, interview by author, August 21, 2012.

19 Ibid., 7.6.2, Cooperating Associations, p. 95.

20 For more information on the Grand Teton Association, see *www.grandtetonpark.org*.

21 Conversation with Jackie Skaggs, Public Affairs Officer, January 31, 2013. Also see 2004, 2005 Superintendent's Annual Report.

22 Boyd Evison was named the new superintendent of GTNP in 1991. However, the illness of a family member precluded him taking the position, and Jack Neckels became superintendent. Information from Jan Lynch, Director, GTA.

23 Quoted from *Teton Stewards* (Newsletter of the Grand Teton National Park Foundation), Fall–Winter 2010–11, 1. Also interview with Leslie Mattson, President, GTNPF, September 20, 2012.

24 "Inspiring Journeys: A Campaign for Jenny Lake," an advance flyer, Grand Teton National Park Foundation: Also interview with Kim Mills, Foundation manager of Communications and Corporate Relations, and Estate Planning, September 20, 2012.

25 "Jewell boosts $16M Deal," *Jackson Hole Daily*, Friday, August 9, 2013.

26 For much more information, see *www.gtnpf.org*.

27 Alfred Runte, *National Parks: The American Experience* (Lincoln: University of Nebraska Press, 1979).

28 Published in the *National Parks Traveler*, August 8, 2013, see "comments" of Alfred Runte, August 9, 2013.

29 Interview with Cultural Resources Officer Sue Consolo-Murphy, January 30, 2013; telephone interview with Director Hank Harlow, February 18, 2013. Also see "National Park Service Research Center," 34th Annual Report, University of Wyoming, 2011.

30 Twice I brought small University of Wyoming classes to visit her. She was always gracious. She never wanted to talk of herself, but always asked students of their interests.

31 The other National Historic Landmark is the Jackson Lake Lodge.

32 Todd Wilkinson, "The New West," *Jackson Hole News and Guide*, January 20, 2010.

33 In 2013 Jack Shea resigned as director of the Teton Science Schools for a position in Oregon.

34 See *info@tetonscience.org*.

35 "Superintendent's Annual Report," 2012, 14.

36 See the website of the relatively new (2003) volunteer organization—American Conservation Experience.

37 Statement on the "backcountry volunteers" by Penny Moldonado to author, April 29,2013. Penny was the postmistress at Moose for many years and has been my research assistant on this project.

38 See Dwight Rettie's Home Page, *www.clis.com/tarwathie*: also see his useful book *Our National Park System: Caring for America's Greatest Natural and Historic Treasures* (Urbana: University of Illinois Press, 1995).

39 *Management Policies, 2006*. National Park Service, 1.10, Partnerships, p.18.

40 For a fascinating climbing account of Glenn Exum and Paul Petzoldt, see Charlie Craighead, ed., *Glenn Exum*. (Moose: Grand Teton Association, 1998).

41 Karen Gordon Bergsma, Concession Asset Manager, interview by author, November 4, 2011.

42 GTNP, Contracts, Lost Creek Ranch.

43 GTNP, Surveys 1996–2009, box 1-B, Interp.-Visitor Surveys, 1998 folder.

Peaks, Politics, and Passion: Grand Teton National Park Comes of Age

Chapter 9.

Entertainment or Nature?

AMERICAN CHILDREN have moved from "loving streams to loving screens." That is the allegation made by Richard Louv in his 2008 best-selling book, *Last Child in the Woods*. Their parents watch too much television, while the kids are obsessed with video games. The result is that far too many children now suffer from what Louv calls "nature-deficit disorder." This commitment to electronics has resulted in a reversal of our historic commitment to nature and the land. The family farm is fast disappearing, and Louv suggests that "baby boomers—those born between 1946 and 1964—may constitute the last generation of Americans to share an intimate, familial attachment to the land and water."

Our rural roots have disappeared. Urban people who have a cabin in the woods or mountains are few indeed and, as Henry David Thoreau would say, lucky to enjoy "one foot in wilderness, the other in civilization." Most Americans stay firmly rooted in civilization, with any wilderness wanderings confined to vicarious or virtual experiences. Camping has fallen off in Grand Teton National Park. In the 1990s, often every park campground was jam-packed. In 2012, with the exception of Jenny Lake, most campgrounds had available spaces on most days. The Gros Ventre campground never filled that summer.[3] Moreover, much of what constitutes camping today would have been unrecognizable 60 years ago. One questions whether roughing it with four walls, electricity, television, and air conditioning qualifies as camping or is simply avoidance of the cost of motels. Pioneers such as Ernest Thompson Seton, who a century ago urged young people to learn woodcraft and was a founder of the Boy Scouts of America, would surely scoff at what passes for camping today.

Even within the recreational vehicle version, camping in the national parks is on the decline. Louv maintains that in 2001 "the number of visitors who camped in national parks dropped by nearly a third, to its lowest point in a quarter century."[4]

The same trend is evident with backpackers. Since 1979, according to newspaper columnist Nicholas Kristof, the number of backcountry campers in the national parks has fallen by nearly 30 percent.[5] Why is this so? There are many explanations, but Louv believes people avoid camping because they do not know how. Their parents never taught them, and now they are helpless to pass on such skills.

A Remembrance

Historically, the national parks have not been effective at passing on camping skills and nature experiences. As historians of the NPS have noted, founders Stephen Mather and Horace Albright wanted the parks to be fun and entertaining, and they were successful at this in the early years. They did not discourage camping, but much of their effort went into providing park guests with roofs over their heads.

For some perspective, I can draw on my own experience in Yosemite National Park. Growing up in the San Francisco Bay Area, I vacationed regularly with my parents in the park but never in Yosemite Valley, which my father avoided like some sort of plague. My family went to the Tuolumne Meadows campground in the High Sierra. Except for a few hardy souls, the meadows seemed an unpopular place. The park rangers were available, and Dad knew them by name and chatted with them. Our little trailer stayed at our campsite all summer long. In the 1950s, there were no camping time limits or fees. My father was a dry fly fisherman, and through him, my brother and I learned to appreciate cold streams and mountain water. Down in Yosemite Valley, however, crowds assembled and a smoky haze hung over the campgrounds. I often wondered why people congregated there.

During my college days I began working in Yosemite; unfortunately most of the jobs were in the valley. My first job was at the Camp Curry cafeteria, the absolute lowest rung in status and pay. But I was not there to make money. I wanted to experience the park. I soon found that my fellow workers were of two mind sets. With a day off, one group retired with a six-pack of beer to the Camp 16 beach for sun and socializing. My group was more energetic, leaving the valley for Tuolumne Meadow in the evening to hike, fish, or climb, often returning only in the morning, just before work. The two styles represented different reactions to the park amenities.

No matter what we preferred on our day off, tourist life at Camp Curry was lively. The evening's entertainment began with a stage show, often involving visiting musicians and almost always a rendition of the "Indian Love Call." Then when darkness fell, came the dramatic call to Glacier Point to "Let the Fire Fall." Off the cliff rained an impressive cascade of red hot embers. After that popular event, the crowd dispersed and younger people went to the nearby dance hall, where a live band played until 11 o'clock. On reflection, the pattern of activity was much like that of a resort.

I was right in the middle of what one historian called "carnivalism." We did not have television or video games. Instead, the concessioners provided no end of activities to amuse us. Later I worked as a bell-boy at the upscale Ahwahnee Hotel and then as a ski instructor at Badger Pass. At the Ahwahnee, guests could amuse themselves in the swimming pool, on a nine-hole golf course, or at the tennis courts. When I reluctantly left Yosemite Valley, I had had a wonderful time and earned enough money to put me through graduate school; still, the national park seemed like an amusement park in a spectacular setting. From the 1920s on, the Yosemite Valley, for all its breathtaking glacial beauty, featured a lifestyle one step removed from nature and two steps closer to commercialism.[6]

Since those halcyon days of entertainment, the Glacier Point firefall has gone, as has Camp Curry's big band sound. The golf course and tennis courts at the Ahwahnee have returned to nature, though the swimming pool remains. And Christmas revelers still enjoy the Bracebridge dinner festivities, neither of which has any connection with Yosemite's awe-inspiring natural features. Families still come to the Badger Pass ski area, one of the few located within a national park. Those who want to play golf can still swing away at Wawona (in the park) at the nine-hole course that opened in 1918. Breathtaking natural attractions were not considered enough in Yosemite. To lure tourists and their dollars, Mather, Albright, and concession leaders such as Donald Tresidder encouraged celebrations and recreational activities that had little to do with the park.[7]

THE BEGINNING OF COMMERCIALISM. THE GRANDSTAND AT THE OLD ELBO RANCH RODEO GROUNDS

HAROLD FABIAN'S PHOTOGRAPH OF THE RESTORED SITE AFTER THE BUILDINGS WERE REMOVED.

  PEAKS, POLITICS, AND PASSION: GRAND TETON NATIONAL PARK COMES OF AGE

GRAND TETON VISITATION

Grand Teton National Park was going down that same commercial path as Yosemite, but John D. Rockefeller, Jr. put a stop to it. Before he began his land purchase plan, a dance hall existed near Jenny Lake. Just south of Timbered Island, the old Elbo Ranch featured a rodeo. Various entrepreneurs, noticing the rapidly rising visitation rate, were hatching creative plans to provide entertainment. The magnificent scenery might be the initial draw, but it did not seem to be enough. A man with money, an opposite philosophy, and a deep commitment can stop such unwanted growth, and Rockefeller did. Grand Teton National Park was spared tacky structures and resort-like entertainment because Rockefeller bought them and put them out of business. Of course, if you stayed at a dude ranch such as the JY, the Bar BC, or the White Grass, you certainly were not denied a good time, for there was plenty of opportunity to experience amusements in town. In the 1920s, Jackson was famous for open gambling, raucous partying, occasional prostitution, and plenty of drunkenness, all taking place just outside the park.

But the park was a place to experience the natural world unvarnished. What better place than the Tetons to exalt in the expansive outdoors. Fannie Kemble Wister, the 11-year-old daughter of author Owen Wister, came to the JY Ranch in the summer of 1911 and later recalled her delightful encounter with a world she came to love:

Mostly we rode, I rode bareback for miles each day. Fording the Snake River, loping through the sagebrush with no trail, we went into the foothills as far as our laboring horses could climb. We were not too young to be stunned with admiration by the Tetons, and we loved the acres of wild flowers growing up their slopes—the tremulous Harebell blue and fragile, the Indian Paintbrush bright red, and the pale, elegant Columbine. We were not awed by the wilderness, feeling that the Grand Teton was our mountain and the most wonderful mountain in the world, and the Snake River, the fastest, longest river in America.

SHE WAS NOT HAPPY to leave such an idyllic world dominated by her experience: "At last we had to return East. We could not stand the thought of leaving. What—sleep in a real bed again and see trolley cars? How frightful! No more smell of sagebrush, no more rushing Snake River, no more Grand Teton. Why did we have to go back?"[8]

Here was a child with an experience imprinted on her life for as long as she lived. Could it happen today? The mountains, the river, the sagebrush are largely unchanged, but not so our attitudes. The idea of allowing a young girl to ride bareback, *not* following a trail, to ride off into the mountains and ford the Snake River at such a tender age would be unthinkable for most parents. Perhaps the best Fannie could hope for today would be a situation of "controlled risk." In this scenario, Richard Louv lets his children take risks, but one way or another he sees and follows them, intervening if necessary.[9]

The more crucial question may be: With modern conditioning, would Fannie want to ride all day in the wild? I do not mean physical conditioning, but another kind of situation. Would Fannie even have a choice? If a modern Fannie's parents were responsible, they would warn her of the dangers of a long day's riding in the wilderness. To spend so much unstructured time outdoors would be to court disaster. In all probability, Fannie's parents would forbid such unfettered freedom. As retired NPS ranger William Tweed writes: "All this reflects the culture of fear that has come to dominate America. As parents, we are afraid to allow our children out of our sight, even in nature." Tweed believes that out of such fear grows separation, and with it disinterest. He has seen children watching television in the back seat of the car as their parents tour the national park. "Apparently neither parents nor children saw any reason why the young folks should even look out the window."[10]

Photo from Owen Wister Collection, American Heritage Center, University of Wyoming

FANNIE KEMBLE WISTER

Both Louv and Tweed have lost faith in the American family's ability to appreciate nature and convey that feeling to their children. Tweed notes that "growing segments of our population have little or no connection with outdoor recreation in any form."[11] Yet it is hard to believe that television and video games can triumph over the sublime beauty of the Tetons and the sparkling, clear swift Snake River; and it is encouraging to remember that we are capable of change, especially the young. There is also a case to be made that while appreciation of nature is never-ending, our absorption with technology may, in time, ease enough for us to regain perspective about what is real and to start using technology to excellent effect. Consider the smartphone app that allows us to identify birds from their calls. Tweed's traveling children who are watching their handheld electronic devices and ignoring the beauties of the park may eventually come to realize there is no surrogate for authentic natural beauty; virtual reality is not enough.

History sometimes moves in a cyclical fashion. What thrives today, may diminish in stature tomorrow. What is fashionable today, may not appeal to the next generation. Although in Grand Teton, both visitation and camping statistics are down and attendance at evening programs is in the doldrums, we should avoid being unduly dismayed over such statistics. To put it in commodity terms: Grand Teton National Park has a superior product that will sell, year in and year out. Grand Teton is one of the half dozen most celebrated parks in the nation. We probably need not lose sleep over fluctuating visitation figures.

We live in a capitalist society that worships growth. Whether it is a business, the stock market, a city, or a nation, a healthy enterprise must demonstrate expansion. Is this a legitimate measure for a national park? We should be careful how we apply it. A better measure of success should be the preservation and enhancement of the resource and the quality of services provided. The simple idea of "bigger" flies in the face of the Organic Act of 1916, breaking the covenant and the mandate to maintain resources unimpaired for future generations. Nowhere in the *Management Policies, 2006* manual is there an imperative for parks to grow.

Yet there are other imperatives operating. National parks are funded by Congress, and congressional representatives count people. A popular park can command a larger share of available funds, and certainly the Wyoming congressional delegation pays attention to the yearly figures. The local business community also tracks visitation statistics, for the obvious reasons that a portion of their prosperity is interwoven with the park's popularity. Total visitation for Grand Teton National Park has remained steady at about 3.8 million from 1993 to 2011, while the population of Teton County has grown in 2010 to 21,294, a 17 percent increase since 2000. What does it mean that the county experienced 17 percent growth while Grand Teton National Park visitation has slightly declined? Some analysts regard the high county population statistics as indicating that people are moving to Jackson to take advantage of recreational opportunities in Yellowstone and Grand Teton. Their use of the park, however, "further suggests [that] not as many destination tourists are coming to the region as visitor numbers indicate."[12]

Although the mission of the NPS has never been to generate wealth for the local communities, it does just that by its very existence. On a national level, statistics show that in the year 2010, 281 million visitors in the 394 national park units spent $12 billion dollars.[13] On a local level, the 3.8 million visitors to Grand Teton spent $424 million dollars in the park and the gateway communities. All this revenue helps support some 6,300 jobs in northwestern Wyoming communities such as Jackson, Teton Village and Dubois. All politicians and business leaders recognize the economic value of the Grand Teton and Yellowstone national parks. Superintendent Mary Gibson Scott points out this fact as she notes that the parks "drive local and state economies in very tangible ways, and generate jobs that keep Americans employed."[14] Yet she is quick to note that economic growth is a byproduct and not the purpose for creating Grand Teton National Park.

Is this triumph of recreational tourism all good? Of course not. Like any movement, the success of one economic development is at the expense of another.

With the increased visitation to Jackson Hole, the community experienced what historian Hal Rothman called "a devil's bargain."[15] Locals lost economic and political control of their valley to "neonatives," beginning with dude ranchers such as Nathaniel Burt and continuing to Paul McCollister and the development of a "destination area" ski resort. The popularity of the park, the skiing and other attractive amenities, fueled a major economic and real estate boom in the 1980s. The argument is that these neonatives (newcomers with superior lineage, education and treasure, usually from the East) would eventually suck the lifeblood out of the local population, leaving them bitter, disillusioned, and devoid of wealth or pride. All very questionable, but I have seen individuals and/or families that did not own or purchase land in the 1970s, 1980s, or 1990s forced to leave Jackson Hole because they could not find affordable housing. They could not make it economically in a region of trophy homes where the cost of living is almost as high as the mountains. Jackson Hole has never really lived up to the oft-repeated myth of an egalitarian society, and the gap between rich and poor continues to spread. Of course we should not blame the Grand Teton National Park for this development, for the grandeur of Jackson Hole would have attracted development without the national park. I do not subscribe to historian Hal Rothman's thesis that parks and tourism can result in the loss of a community's identity and authenticity. On the other hand, I believe that a rationale for parks based on economic growth, jobs, and prosperity must always be questioned.[16]

ATTRACTING FAMILIES AND CHILDREN

Although we should not be unduly concerned with statistics alone, a lessening of interest in the park by families with children can be disturbing. Grand Teton National Park should be as inspiring to young people today as it was to Fannie Kemble Wister. As I have noted, children today have many more entertainment choices, a lot of them virtual. But children of every age, class, ethnicity, and culture also have a curiosity regarding nature that, if aroused, can set a youth on a new path. Sometimes inviting kids to partner with the park can inspire them. Grand Teton National Park interpreters extended an invitation to the fifth grade class at Schneckenburger Elementary School in Louisiana to create some podcasts on the various wildlife species they might encounter in the park. We can all listen to these podcasts produced by these children and posted on the Internet. In time the podcasts may be gone, but the children will never forget the experience or their new-found affection for Grand Teton National Park.

We might ask: Is the Grand Teton National Park staff doing all it could to attract young people to the values of nature and an active livestyle? We live in a competitive world in which there are many choices for youth. We also live in a world of advertising in which young people are bombarded daily with things to buy and how they should spend not only their money, but their time. We know that many do not spend that valuable commodity of time wisely, yet we are helpless to influence their choices. The old adapt "you can lead a horse to water, but . . . " seems to apply. We cannot make them drink, but we can make the water so attractive that it is hard to resist. In the next few pages I will present what Grand Teton and its partners are doing to try to bring young people to a greater appreciation of nature and the park. Many of the activities which the park and its partners offer visitors are not designed for children alone; they also engage adults who are open to learning about and enjoying the park as well.

TETON SCIENCE SCHOOLS

The Teton Science Schools described in the preceding chapter, plays a pivotal role in outreach to children and adults, and they so elegantly span the divide between entertainment and nature learning. What a perfect place to have a nature-based school! The park has so many interesting features and qualities—high altitude plants, abundant wildlife, clear cold streams, even glaciers. Founder Ted Majors, a man with a mis-sion and a commitment, recognized a good marriage, and he was able to forge a partnership with Grand Teton National Park.

The Science Schools also partner with many public and private schools. To give an idea of its activities, in 2011 administrators and parents from 22 states and 92 schools sent children for a stay (usually a week) at the school's campus, tucked away on Ditch Creek on the eastern edge of Grand Teton's boundary. A total of 2,938 young people participated. What did they do? At first glance, the school might appear to be a glorified summer camp, the purpose being to have fun while giving parents a needed summer break. But that would be a mistaken assessment, for the children are soon divided into small groups and introduced to uni-versity graduate students with science backgrounds who can educate, amuse and inspire young people. Two high school students later related their experi-ence: "We studied sagebrush and its amazing adapta-tion to water, practiced using a compass with topo-graphical maps, learned about aspen, [and] keyed out moose prints." The school fosters character building as well. "As we experience nature together, it brings us to a deeper understanding of ourselves and each other, thus creating life-long friendships." The week was important in their lives, and both students plan to follow an academic major related to the environment when it is time for their university education.[17]

Perhaps the most inspirational Teton Science Schools story is that of Juan Martinez. As a Latino kid from south-central Los Angeles, Juan was destined for

JUAN MARTINEZ

tional speaker and for Richard Louv's Children and Nature Network.[18]

The Teton Science Schools run a number of other programs that deserve mention. Their graduate program for master's degrees is connected with six universities, including, primarily, the University of Wyoming. Under faculty supervision, graduate students can take 32 units of science classes at the school as well as mastering teaching and leadership skills as summer school leaders. Related to the master's program is a Teaching Learning Center, which reaches out across Wyoming with programs that encourage both teacher and student to get outside.

Two more programs use the park to enrich the experiences of both adults and children. The Schools' Conservation Research Center sponsors such programs as wildlife tracking, a popular bird-banding experience, and a unique research opportunity to spend a day counting the park's pika population. Thoreau could spend a day observing ants, but for most people, pikas are more endearing and they are at risk from the effects of climate change. Finally, a popular Teton Science Schools activity is its wildlife expeditions. The school has 12 vehicles, 14 biologists on-call, and 15 different wildlife tour opportunities. In the twilight hours around the park, you may not see much wildlife, but you will probably see a cruising Science Schools or a Wildlife Expeditions van. Follow it.

All the programs at the school add immensely to the educational mission of the park. Children are stimulated by the possibilities of nature, and often

a life of gang activities and crime. Thanks to a teacher's intervention, Juan managed to graduate from California State University–Los Angeles. Nevertheless, he got into trouble with the law. Given a choice of detention in Los Angeles or seclusion—exile?—to the Teton Science Schools campus, he chose the latter. On arrival, the clear air, the multitude of stars, and the towering Teton Range gave rise to an epiphany that something good would happen to him in Jackson Hole: "I found that I had a purpose in this life." Juan has moved on to become a spokesman for nature, working for the Sierra Club as a motiva-

their parents can likewise renew their delight and appreciation of the park's wildlife with the assistance of a Teton Science Schools' instructor.

YOUTH CONSERVATION PROGRAM

On the evening of August 13, 2012, I attended a presentation in the new auditorium of the Craig Thomas Discovery and Visitor Center. Out of curiosity I had come to hear the 17 young men and women who had spent their summer with the Youth Conservation Program (YCP). It was the seventh season of this program sponsored by the Grand Teton National Park Foundation. Each participant took the stage and told the audience about their particular project, illustrated with Powerpoint images. We heard much about how they had spent their time. As an historian, I appreciated that one of the projects was to caulk the Menor's Ferry pontoons; a ferry ride was the historic way to get across the Snake River safely. Operation of the historic Menor's Ferry is the only living history exhibit in the park, and without the work of the Youth Conservation Program, the replica ferry might not have floated that summer. The YCP youngsters did much more. They also built a wooden causeway on the Emma Matilda trail, installed a boat landing at Flagg Ranch, worked on cabin reroofing projects at the old Bar BC ranch, built a couple of trail bridges for horses, cleared brush for fire prevention, and did plenty of backbreaking trail maintenance work too.[19]

On a more personal note, participants had lessons on team building and pursued their own personal growth. They learned about the park. Climbing rangers demonstrated their rescue techniques and even brought in a rescue helicopter. Biologist Jean Jorgenson taught them which plants are edible. They also learned about the crucial relationship between grizzlies and the diminishing number of whitebark pine trees.

For inspiration, these young people heard from Deputy Superintendent Kevin Schneider about his own youthful participation in the Student Conservation Association program and how it moved him toward a career in the NPS. Kim Mills of the Foundation assured the students that the organization was proud to support such a program, and would continue to do so. The park, of course, obtains considerable "hands on" work from the participants. Park supervisors appreciate their labor, knowing that their budgets would not normally stretch to cover these essential projects. From the point of view of the youths, this is not a bad job. They receive $11.08 an hour, work outside, keep in shape, learn new skills, and find themselves preparing for a possible career in the NPS. Most of the 2012 summer participants were local boys and girls, but some came from as far away as Denver, Houston, Boston, and Washington, D.C. Again, although the project is enthusiastically supported by the park, it is the Foundation funding that makes it happen.

Pura Vida

In 2010, park interpretive rangers, the Teton Science Schools' staff, and the Foundation jointly addressed a concern. Although the Latino population in Jackson Hole has been rising dramatically, few of these new-comers knew much about their neighbor, Grand Teton National Park. Why not bring the young Latino students to the park for a week? The question became the basis for Pura Vida, a program to intro-duce young Latino students to the park's recreational possibilities, its many resources, and possible careers in the NPS. The program has a perfect mentor in interpretive ranger Vanessa Torres. Raised by loving Tejano parents near San Antonio, Texas, Vanessa spent plenty of time outdoors with her nature-orient-ed mother and father. At St. Mary's College, she attended a career fair and found the Park Service booth particularly alluring. One thing led to another, and Vanessa soon embarked on a conservation career. As if to test her mettle, her first position was at Kenai Fjords National Park in Alaska. Housed in a small cabin without electricity or plumbing, Vanessa thrived. Clearly this was the career for her.[20] Today she wants to pass on her passion to young Latino stu-dents through the Pura Vida one-week spring break program, followed up by a two-week summer agenda.

What do these students do in the park? Certainly there is an emphasis on having fun. In August the group hiked to Taggart Lake, where they "snacked on homemade chicharones and fried pasta. . . . They gig-gled and chatted in Spanish between bites. Then they learned about wolf telemetry from wildlife biologist, John Stephenson."[21] They also laughed as they toured ranger Jim Dahlstrom's ambulance and played with the vehicle's microphone. But beyond the fun, there were observations like that of 12-year-old Irasis Quiroz that "it's pretty out here. I just didn't know about it." Some felt ownership. Thirteen-year-old Jamie Vargas blurted out: "It's our park too, as well as everyone else's."[22] Those are just the kind of respons-es Vanessa and Teton Science Schools educator, Rachel Schaffer, like to hear. Perhaps these students will return with friends and family.

Latino Family Days

Connected to Pura Vida, Latino Family Days is an effort by the Park Service to involve neighboring Latino families in recreational opportunities. In some cases, Jackson families have never been to the park, although it is only a dozen miles away. Vanessa Torres explained some of the reasons. National Park uniforms bear some resemblance to those of the U.S. Border Patrol, and an entrance fee may require showing identification. But perhaps most important, Latino parents are busy making a living. Vanessa points out that "they have moved to Jackson to realize the American dream." They do not allow themselves much leisure time, and when they do, it may be on the soccer field or time with family.

To break the pattern, Vanessa established the family days in conjunction with the Latino Resource Center and the Teton Literacy Center, also recruiting the Teton Science Schools for help with transportation. These special days have included hiking, visiting scenic spots, learning camping skills, understanding wildlife, and even winter snowshoeing. So far 70 participants have enjoyed the park, and all have received an annual pass, made possible through the generosity of the Foundation.

Vanessa Torres underscores an important point: "The demographics in America are changing, yet our visitors are not."[23] Programs in Grand Teton and national parks elsewhere in the nation seek to bring visitation in line with the nation's growing ethnic diversity. Perhaps some of the urban parks are gradually accomplishing that goal, but Grand Teton must continue to support programs aimed at greater diversity.

In the long run for minority ethnic groups to have input in a changing America, leadership must be developed. In Grand Teton National Park the success of Pura Vida has produced a pilot program to identify eight to ten students from Jackson Hole High School who have the interest and the skills to become leaders in conservation stewardship. The participants in the Young Stewards and Leaders program will make a one-year commitment to attend educational meetings and leadership workshops, and to volunteer at the Teton Science Schools. Those high school seniors who complete the program will be eligible to apply for the Grand Teton's National Park Service Academy program.

THE NPS ACADEMY

The NPS Academy transcends ethnicity and local programs to introduce college-age students across the country to career opportunities in the National Park Service. To the park's credit, the program is a creative pilot project instituted at Grand Teton National Park, but now the idea has spread to Great Smoky Mountains National Park, as well as the Alaska and Northeast regions of the NPS. In 2013, a third academy was added in Alaska and in 2014 a fourth academy will be conducted in Boston. Working with the Student Conservation Association (SCA), which has provided volunteers to the Forest Service and Bureau of Reclamation as well as the NPS, the SCA recruits students from "under-represented backgrounds and expose[s] them to various careers in the National Park Service." They are offered summer employment in a national park or monument. Wherever they go, the NPS Academy participants are matched up with a mentor who explores the students' interests and provides an "easy transition to careers in conservation."[24]

The NPS Academy provides talented and committed students a perfect way to set in motion a Park Service career. In 2011, the SCA gathered 29 students at Grand Teton for a week of training. At week's end 21 of them accepted summer placements. The students go out into the various parks with three themes and outcomes in mind: connections, diversity, and legacy. These themes are somewhat open-ended, but NPS Academy students are expected to connect with local cultures, study the structures and systems of national parks, and meet other passionate young leaders across the country. They focus on cultural diversity and are introduced to diverse careers in the Park Service. Finally, under the rubric of legacy, the academy students collaborate with mentors and establish long-term relationships. They are also introduced to prominent conservation leaders and especially those who understand and transmit the traditions—the legacy—of the National Park Service.

In short, these select students study the National Park Service itself: its structure, its many programs, its reach to the American public, and above all, what it stands for and why its mission matters. They also have plenty of time to assess their place in this organization with the aid of their mentor. They will evaluate whether they have the necessary dedication to make the NPS their life's work. In essence, they get

Snow desk (above); being viewed in classroom (below).

the chance to explore whether or not they have a passion for the national parks and conservation work.

The NPS Academy will not have a campus such as the military branches. While each service—the Air Force, the Navy, the Army—has a dedicated campus which instills pride and loyalty in students, the NPS Academy seeks another way. Its strong emphasis on mentoring, the summer exposures to various national parks, and the introduction of these "park pledges" to "leaders in the field of conservation current and past," will help to mold lives as well as instill a commitment to the National Park Service. [25] The program costs money, but the interest payoffs are expected to be immense.

There are other innovative programs that a creative NPS staff at Grand Teton have initiated. One is a learning program called the SnowDesk. When the weather is well below freezing, interpretive rangers compress snow and build an actual "snow desk" outside of the Craig Thomas Discovery and Visitor Center. From that frosty site, interpretive rangers broadcast live TV to schools across the country. The subject usually involves mammals and how they adapt to extreme conditions–and they can become very extreme in a Teton winter because temperatures can reach 40 below zero and snow fall can exceed 400 inches in the Teton Range. Students, particularly those living in warmer climates, ask plenty of questions and find the presentations fascinating. It is a unique program for Grand Teton and Chief of Interpretation Victoria Mates looks forward to seeing it continue each winter. [26]

TravelStorysGPS

Another fresh idea rests on the cutting edge of technology. TravelStorysGPS, which is supported by the Foundation, is the brainchild of Story Clark, a woman who for many years has been an environmental activist in Jackson Hole. She continues to be a leader in new concepts to enhance appreciation of the park. The scheme is to use a smartphone or iPad to download the TravelStorysGPS app. The visitor then has a detailed guide for traveling through the park; one that provides engaging stories about the history, the passing landscape, and local as well as national conservation themes. The cost for this audiovisual tour is free, although users are invited to make a charitable gift to one of a number of conservation organizations. [27]

What are we to make of such an innovation? For visitors with limited time, but keen interests in the park, the TravelStorysGPS app for Grand Teton will certainly be welcome. It can also engage children in the back seat who already find technology seductive and would rather be looking at an iPad than out of the window. On the other hand, the app may motivate the family to leave the car for a hike in the mountains or a stroll along the river to visit a described site. The degree to which it is passive or active depends on the user. Yet there can be little doubt about it being a clear plus for the park. In the realm of electronics, so much detracts from the actual park experience, an app that enhances our understanding must be embraced. That is the view of the Foundation and the park administration, which has adopted this new learning method to enhance education. It is also the view of Victoria Mates, Chief of Interpretation for the park. Her opinion is that Grand Teton National Park must accept technology with discretion, fashioning it to meet the park's needs and mission.[28]

Issues of technology in the parks are ongoing. After healthy debate, Grand Teton eventually allowed a cell phone tower. Some parks, such as Rocky Mountain National Park, do not have cell towers. In the Tetons, a cell phone can save lives in the case of an accident or harsh weather. However, a cell phone can give people a false sense of security. Jackie Skaggs, public affairs officer and spokesperson for Grand Teton, laments that "because of having these electronic devices, people have an expectation that they can do something risky and still be rescued." Cell phone ownership seems to bring with it a sense of entitlement. Lost hikers have called the climbing rangers for a guide, food, and even hot chocolate. Skaggs said rescue rangers can be unsympathetic and even stern with ill-equipped and unprepared climbers caught in bad weather who simply want an escort out of their unpleasant situation. Rangers must sometimes inform these climbers: "Make yourself comfortable because you are up there for the night."[29] Technology in the wilderness areas of Grand Teton will continue to be debated. It is not of paramount importance that we have cell phone service everywhere. There is a powerful argument that this technological crutch should not be available in wilderness areas. One of the reasons some people venture out is to take a moderate risk, testing themselves. It can dull your sense of adventure when that little cell phone rings. There are those who believe that parks have eliminated that sense of adventure and the unknown by an excess of technology that stifles individuality and diminishes a direct connection with nature.

LIFE SEEMS MUCH MORE COMPLEX today than in 1950, when you simply drove into the park, took a walk along the river, mounted a horse, or gazed at the mountains. Today all across the park experience, visitors are willing recruits in an educational blitz of visitor centers, program offerings at the UW-NPS Research Center, the Murie Center, the Teton Science Schools, as well as activities sponsored by the Grand Teton National Park Foundation, the Grand Teton Association, or the National Park Service itself. Have we created a hyper-park where it is impossible simply to enjoy being there? Not at all. Visitors can, of course, ignore all these activities and merely take pleasure or inspiration from the place itself, as so many have always done. What the Grand Teton National Park offers today is choice, for both adults and children. We can be as involved as we prefer. There is no quiz on departure—only the hope that we have been inspired by the unparalleled beauty we have beheld.

[1] Richard Louv, *Last Child in the Woods* (Chapel Hill, N.C.: Algonquin Books, 2008), 148.

[2] Ibid., 19.

[3] Andrew Langford, Jenny Lake District Interpreter, interview by author, August 21, 2012.

4 Louv, *Last Child in the Woods*, 149.

5 Nicholas Kristof, "Blissfully Lost in the Woods," *New York Times, Sunday Review*, July 28, 2012.

6 The "carnivalism" moniker comes from Alfred Runte, *National Parks: The American Experience* (Lincoln: University of Nebraska Press, 1979). Also see Runte's, *Yosemite: The Embattled Wilderness* (Lincoln: The University of Nebraska Press, 1990), 103-4.

7 Donald Tresidder was president of Stanford University and also headed the Yosemite Park and Curry Company, one of the first and most influential concessionaires.

8 Diary excerpts from *Owen Wister Out West,* ed. Fannie Kimble Wister (Chicago: University of Chicago Press, 1948), reprinted in Robert W. Righter, ed., *A Teton Country Anthology* (Boulder, Colo.: Roberts Rinehart, 1990), 138–40.

9 Louv, *Last Child in the Woods.*

10 William C. Tweed, *Uncertain Path: A Search for the Future of National Parks* (Berkeley: University of California Press, 2010), 174–75.

11 Ibid.

12 Statistics from *Jackson Hole Compass*, 2012, 14, 29, 45. Grand Teton Park statistics can be confusing because the park registers two numbers; Recreational visitation and Total Visitation. The total visitation number is higher. For instance in 2011, visitation was 3,866,579. In either case the visitation figures for Grand Teton do not show growth comparable to Teton County.

13 News release from GTNP, February 28, 2012, "Grand Teton National Park Benefits Regional Economy and Jobs According to 2010 Study." The news release credits Professor Daniel Stynes of Michigan State University for conducting the visitor spending analysis for the NPS.

14 Ibid.

15 Hal. K. Rothman, *Devil's Bargain: Tourism in the Twentieth-Century American West* (Lawrence, Kansas: University Press of Kansas, 1998).

16 Ibid., For materials on Jackson Hole see pages 126-140, 279-286, 341-364. I do not want to suggest that economic realities are not important. However, the park's primary purpose must be to preserve the natural resources whether natural, historic, or a mixture.

17 Ben Seaman and Laura Tully, "Blame It on the Tetons," *Telegraph Herald* (Thonline.com/Altonline), March 4, 2009.

18 When Juan Martinez is not traveling, he still spends time in Grand Teton National Park. He is the youngest member of the Sierra Club Foundation Board in the 100+ history of the organization.

19 Youth Conservation Program participant presentations given at the Craig Thomas Discovery & Visitor Center auditorium, August 13, 2012.

20 Vanessa Torres, park interpreter, interview by the author, September 11, 2012.

21 Brielle Schaeffer, "Pura Vida: Latina Kids Learn about Teton Park," *Jackson Hole News and Guide,* August 22, 2012.

22 Ibid.

23 Schaeffer, *"Pura Vida."*

24 Grand Teton National Park, flyer explaining the NPS Academy and other programs. See GTNP website or the park information center directly. Also see *http://www.thesca.org/serve/internships/special-programs/national-park-service-academy*

25 Ibid.

26 Interview with Chief of Interpretation Victoria Mates by author, September 25, 2012.

27 See www. gtnpf.org.travelstorysgps.

28 Victoria Mates, Chief of Interpretation, interview by author, September 25, 2012.

29 Leslie Kaufman, "Technology Leads More Park Visitors Into Trouble," *New York Times, Environment*, August 21, 2011.

Peaks, Politics, and Passion: Grand Teton National Park Comes of Age

Chapter 10.

Afterword

It's a sunny July day on the Snake River in Grand Teton National Park. My wife and I are floating on our little 11-foot Star raft down the river from Dead Man's Bar to Moose. We listen to the water sounds, watch for and see bald eagles, and hope to spot a moose or two or a cluster of elk. I do a little fishing while Sherry reads a novel. As we enjoy the scene, I am mindful of Wallace Stegner's description of the blessings of rivers:

> By such a river it is possible to believe that one will ever be tired or old. Every sense applauds it. Taste it, feel its chill on the teeth: it is purity absolute. Watch its racing current, its steady renewal of force: it is transient and eternal.[1]

RAFTING IS OUR FAVORITE ACTIVITY. As we float, to the right looms the great Teton Range. Billowing clouds form, then retreat. Will it rain? Probably not. We move into the river's Maze section. My attention changes from the mountains to the river, for you don't want to enter a blocked channel in this braided section. I also focus my attention on the numerous trees that obstruct our path. Sometimes I think, "Why not have a few river rangers come in here with chain saws and clean up this mess?" But then I quickly reject this idea. The river flows in its natural patterns – for its own sake, not mine.

Coming out of the Maze and now heading for Moose I reflect on how fortunate we, and all Americans, are to have this wonderful river with such a stunning mountain backdrop. It could have been so different. No development short of mining could rework the mountains, of course, but the river could have been channeled—as it is downstream—to meet human needs rather than its own. More serious, private homes, and possibly even a commercial enterprise reaching out from shore to tempt rafters with food and trinkets, could have marred the river's banks.

We are appreciative to Grand Teton National Park for policies, which protect the river, promising immersion in the sound of mountain water, to rely on Stegner's prose one more time. For over 30 years I have enjoyed the river sections from the Jackson Lake Dam to Moose, and I hope to continue as long as possible. Of course, I wish the Park Service would change a few rules. I would like to overnight camp at a number of sites, as yet undeveloped. Furthermore, I see no reason that my perfectly behaved dog cannot accompany us. He does not bark and has no interest in chasing wildlife. However, I realize that our personal behavior can, when multiplied many times over, dilute an unspoiled semi-wilderness experience. The river and its protective regulations must remain as they are. The greater good for the river must trump my selfish interests.

I am indebted to rangers who have the difficult job of protecting the resources of the park, whether it is an old cabin, a herd of elk, or visitors' safety on the river. They deserve our respect. So, too, do those who interpret the park. Visitors often return home with stories about their thrilling adventures, but just as often with a memorable experience with a sympathetic and knowledgeable ranger. Jackie Skaggs, Public Affairs Officer, believes that today's park rangers are essentially "Renaissance persons" in a modern age of specialization.[2] Deputy Chief Ranger Ira Blitzblau agrees, noting that the public does not really understand the skills that rangers must master in order to carry out the variety of tasks they confront in a given day or hour. He notes that the staff is part of a team, and that they all act as Grand Teton ambassadors, representing the park to the public.[3] John Henneberger, in a brief essay on "Rangers," concludes:

> Yet, while the focus of rangers activities might be shifting, their underlying responsibility remains the same: to safeguard America's park resources

and help assure park visitors a safe and enjoyable experience. As it strives to meet these challenges, the ranger service remains the "backbone" of the NPS.[4]

IN SEPTEMBER, 2000, Edward O. Wilson, the eminent biologist, addressed a crowd of 1500 park leaders with an uplifting message. "I don't need to tell you . . . that Americans love the national parks." He continued. "They trust you. And you have enormous credibility, probably the greatest of any part of the federal government."[5] When Horace Albright left the Park Service he implored his colleagues to "not let the service become 'just another Government bureau,' keep it youthful, vigorous, clean and strong."[6]

Of course there is some peril in taking both Wilson and Albright at their word. If the National Park Service is the crème-de-la-crème of federal land agencies, it is not perfect. Superintendents and the staff at Grand Teton make mistakes. In the preceding chapters I have drawn attention to some of them. As the NPS approaches its 100th birthday in 2016 there is cause for celebration, but also reflection and careful thought about new directions for Grand Teton and elsewhere.

In many national parks administrative errors, or well-intended policies that somehow backfire, would go unnoticed, but not in Grand Teton National Park. The articulate, educated, and opinionated residents of Teton County and national constituencies as well pay close attention, presenting a challenge and a test of diplomatic ability. A number of senior Teton Park personnel have mentioned to me that in all the parks they have served, there is no park more contentious than Grand Teton. Of course every park and monument has its issues with the surrounding community, but the local constituency of Jackson Hole seems to amplify them. Why? That is a question not easily answered. Surely the residue of the park's complicated creation story continues to spawn discord. But many of those adversaries are long gone. More likely the community's love of the mountains, the river, the vistas, and the magnificent wildlife is a major factor. People are emotionally invested.

Because so many locals have an emotional connection to the park, it is a delicate proposition for the Grand Teton staff to remind them that it is a *national park* and over 300 million other Americans, as well as citizens of the world, have a stake. This is not always an acknowledged or popular concept, but the NPS has a duty to represent all Americans. It also must abide by written policies, refined by nearly 100 years of experience. These criteria and general principles are not negotiable. Administrators base decisions on established NPS values that have stood the test of time. These policies transcend local interests, as they should.[7] Local people may be upset when Grand Teton invokes these criteria, but they are all based on what is best for the park. Every day superintendents at Grand Teton deal with the tension between local and national interests.

Superintendent Mary Gibson Scott recently noted that Grand Teton park is a plum that numerous NPS superintendents elsewhere would love to pick. It attracts not only because of the magnificent surroundings, but because of the challenges that arise everyday. Along those same lines Sue Consolo-Murphy, who worked for many years in Yellowstone, casually declared that the administrative tribulations of Grand Teton were so much more interesting, than the staid issues of the old park to the north—Yellowstone. Surely many in Yellowstone would disagree, but it is clear that Grand Teton continues to evolve, constantly progressing in handling old issues, but also facing new ones. As American society changes the NPS must respond, but again always within the parameters of its basic mission. In the near future decisions on the Moose/Wilson Road will be contentious and will surely test Grand Teton's ability to serve the various interest groups while maintaining its basic resource policy.

WHATEVER THE COMPLICATIONS of managing Grand Teton National Park, it would be difficult to question the commitment of the staff. Some friends have asked why in the world I included the word "passion" in the title of this work? I hope this book answers that question. However, in a recent meeting with Superintendent Mary Gibson Scott, Chief of Science and Resource Management Sue Consolo-Murphy, and Park Management Assistant

Gary Pollock, I pursued the passion question. I asked the three to express their feelings about their agency and what it means to them. The conversation was animated and far-ranging. Above all they share a passion for the park's mission. Why passion? Because the preservation of this magnificent place, and other places they have served, *fits* their personal values. Most of the employees I know or have interviewed did not want just any government job, they were from the beginning committed to the Park Service. As Superintendent Scott put it, "their commitment to the job is fierce." Later, I asked the same question of Victoria Mates, the Chief of Interpretation. She shares that same passion because preservation of nature and culture are such positive goals, and ones that she has held since childhood. Would she move to another federal agency if the opportunity arose? "No," she replied, "I plan to end my career in the green and gray."[8]

Grand Teton National Park has engendered intense loyalties from many other employees as well. If one were to seek an example, there could be no better example than Robert Stanton, who served as Director of the National Park Service from August 1997 until 2001. Stanton grew up in Mosier Valley, a small African-American community near Fort Worth, Texas. He attended Huston-Tillotson College, a historically black college in Austin, Texas. In his junior year, Secretary of the Interior Stewart Udall offered him a seasonal ranger position at Grand Teton National Park as part of a program designed to recruit minorities to the parks. Stanton would later say that not all the black ranger recruits were welcome at their respective parks. However, at Grand Teton "the three African Americans, including myself, working at Grand Teton in '62 were warmly and truly welcomed to the workforce. It spoke volumes about the quality and the professional integrity of those who were there at Grand Teton in 1962."[9] Stanton was, of course, entranced by the scenery, but what moved him toward a career with the NPS was "the quality of the professional staff at Grand Teton." Stanton singled out Grand Teton Superintendent Harthon "Spud" Bill, Chief Ranger Jack Davis and Ranger Russ Dicksenson as men with a contagious passion for the job. By graduation he was offered an advantageous position as Assistant to the President of Huston-Tillotson College. He took it, but not for long. The memory of his days at Grand Teton and the people he met drew him back to Wyoming. In the years to follow he crafted a distinguished career in the NPS, but it was Grand Teton National Park and the staff which first provided an example of the path he would follow.[10]

Today the National Park Service has become a huge bureaucracy, managing almost 400 park units. It could be easy to lose your way and forget why you joined the agency. Some do. A number of the NPS staff have found employment elsewhere. However, at Grand Teton National Park it is hard to be a dispassionate pencil pusher. To live out-of-doors or even to look out the window is to be reminded just where you work and why your labor is important. Rangers that leave the park often return. Others who retire, frequently remain because of friendships made here, but also because they wish to live out their days in the shadow of these remarkable mountains.

Grand Teton is a spectacular park that is home to wildlife. We know that both the expansion of grizzly population and wolf reintroduction have come to pass. In the eyes of most observers, this has been an absolutely appropriate change for the park. Not all agree, and management of these magnificent species will represent an ongoing challenge. There will be other issues as yet unidentified.

Grand Teton is home to wildlife, but also a place for human inspiration. The park's mountains, rivers, wildlife, and high country make it a one-of-a-kind place. The fascinating story of human habitation adds to its allure. It is a story of human conflict, born of love of this land. Consequently, both the NPS and the pubic are watchful and protective. This speaks well for the future.

[1] Wallace Stegner, *The Sound of Mountain Water* (New York: Doubleday, 1969), 42.

[2] Comments of Jackie Skaggs to author, January 21, 2013.

[3] Interview of Ira Blitzblau, Deputy Chief Ranger, by author, January 30, 2013.

[4] John W. Henneberger, *Rangers*. See *http://www.nps.gov/history/history/online_books/npsg/nps65/sec8.htm*

[5] Edward O. Wilson, "Mission Statements," *The George Wright Forum*, Vol 21, Number 1 (2004), 5.

[6] Horace Albright, *The Birth of the National Park Service*, 310.

[7] The policies and principles for the NPS can be found in *Management Policies, 2006* (U. S. Department of the Interior, Washington D. C., 2006).

[8] Meeting with Scott, Consolo-Murphy, Gary Pollock, September 26, 2012. Interview with Victoria Mates by author, September 27, 2012.

9 "Oral History Interview with Robert G. Stanton," conducted by Janet A. McDonnell, three parts, 2004, (NPS: Department of the Interior, 2006), 9-10. Stanton lived with other seasonal rangers at the Buffalo Dorm, near the Moran entrance station.

10 Ibid.

Acknowledgments

THIS BOOK IS A COLLABORATION OF MANY MINDS that possess plenty of knowledge. It represents the accumulation of facts, ideas, and wisdom of numerous persons who love both Jackson Hole and Grand Teton National Park. In a sense I am merely a scribe who have put their many ideas into book form.

First and foremost, I must thank all the people in Grand Teton National Park who played a major part in this book. Former Superintendent Mary Gibson Scott encouraged a history of more recent events and policies even before it had entered my mind. She believes in the value of history and the idea that the past is prologue. I appreciate her encouragement and constant support and her willingness to set me free from the strictures of a formal administrative history. Throughout this process she and her staff have worked toward factual accuracy, but no one has questioned my right to express my opinions regarding people or policies. I also what to thank Jan Lynch, Director of the Grand Teton Association for her constant encouragement and effort to direct this project to a successful conclusion. Gary Pollock patiently answered many of my questions, often more than once. During the first year of this project park curator Alice Hart helped me find the files and reports that I needed. Katherine Wonson deserves a special thanks for finding so many reports and documents while continually keeping her sense of humor and helpful demeanor. There are so many Grand Teton folks who helped me with information and interviews, gracefully giving of their time (and occasional patience) that I will simply recognize them without their official titles but with my sincere thanks: Richard Sellers, Andy Fisher, Scott Guenther, Mallory Smith, Chip Collins, Mike Nicklas, Victoria Mates, Andrew Langford, Sherman (Shan) Burson, Linda Franklin, Vanessa Torres, Craig Struble, Jackie Skaggs, Roger Scott, Jack Davis, Michael Nash, Katie Miller, Laurie Lafrancois, Betsy Engle, Sue Consolo-Murphy, Karen Gordon Bergsma, Ira Blitzblau, Steve Cain, Deb Frauson, Karen Frauson, Leslie Mattson-Emerson, Kim Mills, and Bob Vogel.

Of course this is also the story of the people who live in Jackson Hole and strongly associate with the park. The following people agreed to interviews, providing me with information or points-of-view regarding the park and its management. I thank the following people for their honestly and willingness to make themselves available to my questions and to read and comment on parts of the manuscript: David Kathka, Charlie Craighead, Hank Harlow, Story Clark, Phil Hocker, Penny Maldonado, Tom Mangelsen, Lyle McReynolds, Sheila Bricher-Wade, Pete Jorgensen, Sara Adamson, Harrison Goodall, Ray Bishop, Ken and Betty Down, Dan and Marly Merrill, Jack Huyler, James Watt, Franz Camerzind, Barbara Pahl, John Turner, Bob Smith, and Sherry Smith.

Earlier in these acknowledgments I suggested that I was a mere scribe. However, that would absolve me from a number of controversial opinions which I have felt free to express. I am sure that many who read this work will find my positions not to their liking, but no one in the Park Service or locals have censured any of my occasional subjective opinions. This sort of freedom is important, for neither I nor the park want a whitewash of policy or an exclusively congratulatory work. I hope I have struck a tone of love for the park, yet with the obligation of critical appraisal.

As in the past, my wife and partner, Sherry Smith, has gently lead me toward an evenhanded manuscript, calling attention to my bias as she patiently listens and reads. She is also an unsurpassed editor who dispenses her wisdom with compassion for those with sensitive egos. Thanks Sherry.

Robert W. Righter
May, 2014

Index

White Grass Ranch, *12, 92,* 187, 188, 192–95, 196, 259

wilderness. *See* natural parks

Wilderness Act (1964), 21, 29, 32–33, 246

Wilderness Society, 29, 32, 139, 246

Wilderness Watch, 220

wildfires. *See* fires and fire management

wildlife, 130, 139, 144, 246–47, 264–65, 277

    See also Jackson Hole Wildlife Park; National Elk Refuge; individual animals

Wildlife Brigade, 156–57, 249

Wilkinson, Todd, 247

Williams, Al, 191, 193, 195

Wilson (town), 42, *89*

Wilson, Edward O., 123, 275

Wilson, Woodrow, 68

Winger, Richard "Dick," 18, 38, 40, 41, 142–43, 170–71

Wirth, Conrad, 15–16, 24–26, 28–31, 38, 41, 47, 81–82

Wisconsin volunteers, 187, 191, 248

Wister, Fannie Kemble, 259–60, 262

Wister, Owen, 179, 259

Wolff Ranch, 197

wolves, 149–50, 158–59, 277

Wonson, Katherine, 166, 188

World War II, 11, 87, 172, 180, 205, 236

Wort, John and Jess, *203,* 204

Wright, George, 122–23, 143, 151

Wyatt, Jim, 122–23

Wyoming, the Monument and the GTNP, viii, 4, 11, 13–19, 33, 222–23

See also, grazing, rights and privileges; elk herd; Jackson Hole airport

Wyoming congressional delegation, 11, 15, 16, 33, 211, 221, 223, 224, 261

Wyoming Continental Divide Snowmobile Trail Association, 222

Wyoming Game and Fish Commission, 16–18, 21, 124, 143, 147–50, 153, 159

Wyoming Honor Farm, 185

Wyoming State Historic Preservation Office (SHPO), 167, 175, 177, 183, 184, 185, 186, 191–92, 193–94

Yard, Robert Sterling, 10

Yeager, W. Ward, 169

Yellowstone Ecosystem Managers Subcommittee, 156

Yellowstone National Park

    creation, viii

    extension, 68, 145–46

    fires, 131, 137–39

    vs. GTNP, 167

    law officers, 110–11

    and the Rockefellers, 14, 170

    snowmobiles in, 221–23

    wildlife, 49, 140–42, 151–52, 154, 155–57

Yosemite National Park, 108–10, 110–11, 154, 171–72, 206, 256–57

Young, S.B.M., 111, 145–46

Young Stewards and Leaders program, 267

Yount, Harry, 110

Youth Conservation Program, 265

yurts, 59, 60

Zahniser, Howard, 28–29

About the Author

ROBERT RIGHTER is the author or editor of eight books. He earned his Ph.D. at the University of California, Santa Barbara. He enjoyed a successful teaching career at the University of Wyoming and the University of Texas at El Paso. He is now a Research Professor of History at the Southern Methodist University. Wind energy has been the focus of three of his books, but his first love is our national parks. He has written on Yosemite National Park, but he is most devoted to Grand Teton National Park. This is his second book on the Grand Teton, bringing the history of this incredible park to the present.

THIS BOOK WAS PUBLISHED BY GRAND TETON ASSOCIATION, a nonprofit organization founded in 1937 that has long been an important bridge between visitor and environment in the Greater Yellowstone Ecosystem.

The Mission of the Grand Teton Association is to increase public understanding, appreciation, and enjoyment of Grand Teton National Park and the surrounding public lands, through aid to the interpretive, educational and research programs of our partners.

We provide educational materials, fund learning programs, give research grants, host art events, and and provide financial support for the NPS in many other areas. Please consider shopping at our online store or becoming a member to help us carry out the essential work we do.

If you have photographs relevant to this book's subject matter, please share with us. We may be able to incorporate into the ebook version.

Grand Teton Association
Grand Teton National Park
PO Box 170
Moose, WY 83012
307-739-3606
gtre_assoc@partner.nps.gov
www.grandtetonpark.org